Hugh Mehan is Professor of Sociology and Director of the Teacher Education Program at the University of California, San Diego. He has studied the construction of identities such as the "competent student," the "learning disabled student," and the "mentally ill patient." He is co-author of *The Reality of Ethnomethodology* (1975) and *Handicapping the Handicapped* (1986) and author of *Learning Lessons* (1979).

Gerald M. Platt is Professor of Sociology at the University of Massachusetts, Amherst. He has published four books and several articles. His interests are in theory, history and social change.

Theodore R. Sarbin is Emeritus Professor of Psychology and Criminology, University of California, Santa Cruz. He is co-author of *Hypnotism: The Social Psychology of Influence Communication* (1972), *Schizophrenia: Medical Diagnosis or Moral Verdict?* (1980), and editor of *Narrative Psychology: The Storied Nature of Human Conduct* (1986). He is currently working on a narrative approach to the study of emotions.

Karl E. Scheibe is Professor of Psychology at Wesleyan University and Visiting Professor at the Center for Alcohol Studies, Rutgers University. His publications include *Beliefs and Values* (1970) and *Mirrors, Masks, Lies and Secrets* (1979). Forthcoming are *Self Studies* and *The Drama of Everyday Life*. His research interests include the study of alcohol and drug dependencies.

Kim Lane Scheppele is Arthur F. Thurnau Associate Professor of Political Science and Public Policy and Adjunct Associate Professor of Law at the University of Michigan. She is the author of *Legal Secrets* (1988), co-author of *Crime and Punishment: Changing Attitudes in America* (1980), and is currently working on a book, *Nothing but the Truth: Fact, Fiction and Narrative in the Law*.

Morton Wiener is Emeritus Professor of Psychology at Clark University and a practicing clinical psychologist. In addition to his current interest in re-conceptualizing "psychopathologies" within a social constructionist framework, he has written about verbal and nonverbal communication, conceptual analyses of reading difficulties, subliminal perception, and more recently, the phenomenon of stereotyping.

Preface

The plan for this book matured over several years. It had its origin in a series of seminars taught jointly by the two editors. The seminars brought together two faculty members from different disciplines, Psychology (TRS) and Sociology (JIK), reflecting the spirit of interdisciplinary explorations that has been encouraged and practiced since the founding of the Santa Cruz campus of the University of California. Both had been influenced by the insights of George Herbert Mead and other scholars who pursued the theme of symbolic interaction. The seminars brought together graduate students and advanced undergraduates from the two departments, occasionally augmented by graduate students in literature and dramatic arts. The seminars provided the participants with opportunities for looking at phenomena from more than one disciplinary perspective.

We concentrated on the development of the social constructionist movement in psychology and sociology. The scope of the seminars was exceedingly broad. A few of the topics covered give the flavor of the academic enterprise: the social construction of emotions, a social constructionist analysis of rates of missing children; a constructionist analysis of social identity; how social problems are constructed, negotiated, and communicated; constructions of family; the social construction of incest; the social construction of narrative; constructions of gender; the social construction of homosexuality; contributions of metaphor to constructionist analysis; social constructionist approaches to deviance.

A word about terminology. The guardians of our literature, editors and publishers, apparently have no preference whether "constructionist" or "constructivist" is the appropriate descriptor. We have chosen "constructionism" and "constructionist" as the more apt terms. "Constructivist" has been pre-empted for other communication contexts. We are not being "constructive" in the sense in which the word is commonly used, as in "constructive criticism." Constructionists focus on how ordinary members (and sometimes professionals) create and employ constructions, on observing how others interact with those constructions, and on interpreting and sometimes proposing alternate constructions.

Preview

The various chapters in this book are exemplars of claims-making. It is apparent that the pursuit of science is characterized by claims and counterclaims. What is usually regarded as psychological or sociological theory is the announcement of claims and the organization of such claims into a coherent story. For example, Andersen (Chapter 7) begins from the observation that Galton and his followers made the claim that some entity, force, or power within the individual was responsible for intelligent behavior. Reviewing the history of the use of the IQ, Andersen introduces a counterclaim – that the IQ is a moral judgment and is constituted of judgments issued by professionals.

The 12 contributions provide a cross-section of how contemporary scholars go about the task of *doing* social constructionist analysis. The sortings of the contributions are somewhat arbitrary and overlapping. All the chapters deal with the complexities of examining claims made by recognized authorities. The categories we have chosen for the sortings illustrate the kinds of issues that appeal to social scientists with a social constructionism bent.

The three chapters in the first group have in common the use of publicly available documents as sources. Mary Gergen (Chapter 2), in analyzing the contents of popular autobiographies, concludes that the authors make use of narrative plots that are contingent on gender. Her analysis makes clear that men's autobiographies follow different story lines from women's. Carol Brooks Gardner (Chapter 3), centering on Victorian advice manuals, brings to light the way in which pregnancy was constructed both by doctors and laypersons. The advice manuals reflect the use of a rhetoric of endangerment. Stephen Lilley and Gerald Platt (Chapter 4), in order to investigate images of leadership, read and sorted the contents of letters sent to Martin Luther King, Jr. The images of the leader are by no means uniform, reflecting some identifiable variations in what constitutes leadership.

The four chapters in the second group reflect sociopolitical factors as context for various social constructions. Kim Lane Scheppele (Chapter 5), focusing on victims' stories of sexual abuse, shows that in courtroom settings the interpretation of the victims' stories has been guided by a practice that privileges initial stories over reconstructed narratives, a practice which is augmented by a masculinist bias. She shows that in some cases the bias is neutralized by courts accepting revised stories in which sociopolitical factors are included in the reconstructed narrative. Mary Boyle (Chapter 6) examines the writings of experts to identify the sociopolitical factors influencing the construction of what is and what is not a "sexual dysfunction." Her analysis, like Scheppele's, points to a subtle masculinist bias in the experts' constructions. In a similar vein, Milton Andersen (Chapter 7) examines the concept of intelligence and its supposed marker, IQ. He traces the history of the hereditarian construction of intelligence and claims that the concept was created by followers of a political creed. Andersen makes a strong argument that identifying a sequence of conduct as intelligent or stupid is basically a moral (social) and not a scientific judgment. Richard Hallam (Chapter 8) interprets the meanings that have been assigned to "anxiety," a notion central to many theories of psychology. Unlike the traditional analyst of such conceptions, he takes pains to distinguish between scientific and lay discourses, and, at the same time, shows how the scientific models implicitly sustain a sociopolitical view of what constitutes "human nature."

The five chapters in the third group relate to the deconstruction of popular conceptions. In each case, the authors offer counterclaims to the claims made in the conventional literature. A moral impetus appears to be a factor in deconstructing stereotyped stories and in making, sometimes implicitly, counterclaims. Tia DeNora and Hugh Mehan (Chapter 9) examine the concept of genius. Reconstructing historical and biographical information about the life and times of Beethoven, the authors make a convincing case for the social definition of what constitutes genius. This is in contrast to the stereotype of genius as the expression of some internal gift. Christopher Bodily (Chapter 10) makes use of survey data to deconstruct the stereotypic construction of age. His analysis and conclusions make clear that his respondents correlated ageing and lack of competence. Karl Scheibe (Chapter 11) examines cocaine careers. In the United States, the concept of cocaine careers has been constructed from the perspective of law enforcement. This perspective has supported the notion of a causal connection between "use" and addiction. Scheibe provides data and argument to support a counterclaim: that cocaine careers are of many kinds; not all "users" become "addicts." The counterclaim has implications for social policy. The final two chapters reflect a characteristic common to most social constructions. The criteria for a class become dulled and flattened as the metaphoric quality of its descriptive label recedes into the background. As a result, the construction allows for polymorphous instances to be included in the class. Morton Wiener and David Marcus (Chapter 12) probe deeply into the meanings assigned to "depression." Employing a semiotic approach, they show that the concept as employed in professional settings embraces a heterogeneous set of actions. Moreover, these actions are not happenings produced by internal disharmonies, rather they are enacted by agents in the form of social transactions. James Holstein and Jaber Gubrium (Chapter 13) offer a constructionist approach to "family." They make use of conversations in which the concept of family is used. The conclusion to their analysis is that "family" is a construction employed in dialogues to convey a set of attributes that reflect a heterogeneous array of living arrangements.

Acknowledgments

The editors take this opportunity of thanking the contributors to this volume for their painstaking work. They all responded with grace and verve to the editors' suggestions and emendations.

Theodore R. Sarbin
John I. Kitsuse

Adlai E. Stevenson College
University of California, Santa Cruz

1

A Prologue to *Constructing the Social*

Theodore R. Sarbin and John I. Kitsuse

Conceptual Issues

In the spirit of "playfulness" that commentators have noted to be a feature of postmodern analysis, we tell a little story to open a discourse on the papers collected in this volume. Three baseball umpires are reflecting on their professional practice of calling balls and strikes. The first, a self-confident realist, says, "I call 'em the way they are," to which the second who leans toward phenomenological analysis says, "I call 'em as I see 'em," and the third closes the discussion with "They ain't nothin' until I call 'em."

The man in the street (possibly the woman as well) might get a chuckle out of this anecdote, and very probably their amusement would be related to their appreciation of the truth of the constructionist umpire's statement. In baseball it is certainly the case that "it ain't nothin' " until (even unless) the umpire makes his call.

What the umpire story also highlights is the "it's-a-matter-of-interpretation" character of the matter at issue. The constructionist umpire when challenged makes this almost but not quite explicit – he is saying that it doesn't exist unless he calls it, and in calling it, assigns meaning to it. In social constructionism, the analyst's self-referral as the agent who sees what he or she sees, conceives it within a given social frame, and asserts its meaning, is often not explicitly stated. It may be that the analyst, unlike the constructionist umpire, does not have the confidence of his/her official position in "the game."

Constructionist analysts are not as secure as the constructionist umpire if challenged as to the "validity" of their calls. The umpire, if challenged, can invoke his position (in the game) and say "because I say so," but what can the analyst say? What is the "game" the analyst can invoke? He or she can say, "that's the way it appears to me" and when pressed as to the grounds for warrant, might finally claim the perspective to be one of many, perhaps an infinite number of perspectives.

In everyday life, ordinary folk generally do not intuitively appreciate the claims of the constructionist perspective. It may be that the practice in baseball does not have an obvious analogue in social life even though we accept many constructions on the basis of legitimate authority. We accept some "calls" and not others, a fact that underlines the role of the umpire in baseball, that is, his authority, an authority defined by the rules of the game. In everyday life, we accept pronouncements that have the weight of authority, such as the "calls" of courtroom judges whose constructions of specifically delimited cases convey the assertion of reality.[1]

The logic of the papers in our collection that offer critiques of the established theories and formulations of various "phenomena" (anxiety, depression, genius, family, etc.) are responses to readings of the standard literature. These readings form the grounds for the presentation of alternative interpretations of the phenomena under review. In proposing these alternative interpretations, what grounds might the constructionist invoke to respond to challenges as to the "validity" of his or her constructions? In order to engage conventional positivist theorists in dialogue, it would be necessary to solicit their serious consideration of the presuppositions of constructionism ("the rules of the game") which would include issues of epistemology and ontology. In the case of the umpire, it is "the game" that gives weight (and consequence) to his calls. Likewise, it is the constructionist "game" that finally sanctions the analyst's assertions.

Antecedents to Contemporary Constructionism

Central to constructionism is the premise that human beings are agents rather than passive organisms or disembodied intellects that process information. It is undeniable that human actors process information, but the processing is carried out in the context of cultural practices and purposes, not to mention beliefs and sacred stories. Those scientists who are guided by the traditions of positivism choose research methods that are consistent with the construction of human beings as passive organisms. From this perspective, human behavior is in principle predictable from knowledge of the person and the situation. However, as we all know from experience, the power to predict behavior is reduced when persons perform as *agents* with their own purposes and intentions rather than as vehicles for stimulus–response connections (Scheibe, 1979; Mixon, 1989).

The choice of methods of study is related to how the objects of study are perceived. Because sociology and psychology are so "method-oriented" the question is often raised: How does one *do* psychology or sociology from the social constructionism perspective? This question was the impetus for the present book. We enlisted the collaboration of psychologists and sociologists who were committed to the social constructionist epistemology. Our selection was not random. From a preliminary list of topics, we chose not to include those that had already been the object of social constructionist analysis, such as social problems, schizophrenia, gender, homosexuality. We chose to concentrate on social phenomena that had not heretofore been subject to social constructionist analysis.

The perspective known as social constructionism is well-established in sociology, having been stimulated by such standard works as Schutz (1967), Berger and Luckman (1967) and Mannheim (1936), among others, in which the idea was developed that social objects are not given "in the world" but constructed, negotiated, reformed, fashioned, and organized by human beings in their efforts to make sense of happenings in the world. The social interactionism of the "Chicago School" of Wirth, Faris, Park, Burgess, and Thomas was articulated with the phenomenological perspective on the social world to lay the foundations for the development of various strains of social constructionist thought. The most widely practiced application of the constructionist perspective was generated by symbolic interactionists who have produced a substantial body of empirical research, particularly in the sociology of social problems (Schneider, 1985).

Influenced by the founders of the Chicago School of sociology, a large number of contemporary sociologists have devoted their energies to demonstrating that the phenomena of daily life are socially constructed. The widespread dissemination of the works of the late Erving Goffman provided visibility to the burgeoning social constructionist movement. Goffman's *Presentation of Self in Everyday Life* (1959) and *Stigma* (1963), among other works, activated theoretical and empirical work by young sociologists in the 1960s. More recently, social constructionism has been critically examined by sociologists of ethnomethodological, feminist, postmodernist and deconstructionist persuasions (Holstein and Miller, 1993).

Within a relatively brief period of approximately 20 years, social constructionism has acquired a substantial presence and influence in sociology, particularly in the sociology of social problems, and in science and feminist studies. It is notable that this achievement has taken place without stirring the animus of the established positivism in the discipline. The tolerance of development of the constructionist perspective has been due in part to the historical importance of the aforementioned Chicago School with its particular mix of qualitative research in field settings, earning its adherents the dubious status in sociology as practitioners of "soft methods." Qualitative sociologists have in common a shared insistence on the central theoretical issue of *meaning* as a product of everyday social interaction. The receptivity, and even sponsorship, of diverse qualitative research and writing by the "secondary" sociological journals (*Social Problems, Symbolic*

Interaction, Urban Life, Theoretical Perspectives on Social Problems) have been of strategic significance in establishing social constructionism as an important and viable alternative to the dominant sociological literature.

The theoretical work of Harold Garfinkel's formulations in the 1960s provided major impetus to the development of social constructionism in sociology. Reflecting the influence of the writings of Alfred Schutz (1967), Garfinkel coined the term "ethnomethodology" to refer to the systematic study of conceptions, understandings, and social practices by which "common sense actors" constitute their social world. Issued as a radical challenge to the prevailing structural functional theory, Garfinkel energized a new generation of sociologists, notably in studies of deviance and more generally in studies of social organization. Known during its inception as the "West Coast School," research emphasized detailed observation in natural settings to document social interaction in everyday life from the perspective of "ordinary members."

More recently constructionism in sociology has been stimulated by infusions of the lively postmodern, poststructural and deconstructionist debates from literary criticism. Perhaps as a consequence, the work of social constructionists in sociology has been engaged less in challenging established theories and methods in the discipline than it has in laying the foundations for an alternative theoretical perspective for the study of social problems, science claims, educational testing practices, the institution of psychiatric categories, and so on.

In contrast, the discipline of psychology has been slow in adopting the social constructionist perspective. The great men and women of psychology provided no context for contemporaries to build theories that centered on *meanings* rather than faculties, powers, traits, instincts and other conceptions that supplied a vocabulary for making claims about the purported internal causes of behavior. It is noteworthy that academic psychology regards its progenitor as Wilhelm Wundt, the founder of the first laboratory of psychology at Leipzig in 1879. The laboratory emphasis moved psychology more and more toward adopting models, methods, and metaphors that had proven useful in the development of the natural sciences. It is ironic that Wundt's seminal work, *Völkerpsychologie*, consistent with modern formulations of social constructionism, was relegated to the dusty archives of a few European libraries (Kroger and Scheibe, 1990).

It is not that influential psychologists have completely ignored the importance of *meaning* in human action. As early as 1932, Bartlett proposed a theory of remembering as reconstruction, a theory that was contrary to the traditional claim that remembering was the report of internal pictures located in the mind or brain. Bartlett demonstrated that rememberings were constructed and reconstructed under the impetus of social and linguistic factors. It is significant that Bartlett's work, after being dormant for many years, has been revived by students of learning and memory as more useful than theories advanced under the guidance of positivist, mechanistic frameworks.

An opening in the positivist, realist framework was created when George Kelly published *The Psychology of Personal Constructs* (1955), a constructionist theory of personality in which a person's constructs guided his or her commerce with the world of occurrences. The underlying metaphor, man as scientist, was instrumental in getting across the idea that human beings behave like the ideal scientist, construing the world from the mix of stimulus inputs and previously acquired constructs. In keeping with the older traditions of psychology, Kelly and his followers focused on cognition. Had Kelly broadened his program to include action, he would have had to replace the "scientist" metaphor with an alternative metaphor, "actor." Such a change in metaphors would have put him close to the insights of the symbolic interactionists. In recent years, some personal construct psychologists have reconstructed their underlying metaphors under the influence of the social constructionist movement and also the constructionist orientations emerging from studies of memory and attention (Mancuso and Adams-Webber, 1982). Although Kelly's followers have formed an international organization and published a journal, his views have not been widely adopted by mainstream personality and social psychology. The prevailing mechanistic worldview has favored the competing perspectives – psychoanalysis and learning theory.

Perhaps the most important influence that brought psychologists around to considering the constructionist perspective was the penetration of the insights of George Herbert Mead into social psychological theorizing (Sarbin, 1943, 1954; Cameron, 1948; Newcomb, 1951). The Berger and Luckman (1967) book, *The Social Construction of Reality*, and Goffman's numerous writings have had considerable influence beyond the boundaries of sociology. Beginning in the 1970s, interest in social constructionism increased. Certainly, Kenneth Gergen's frequently-cited paper, "Social psychology as history" (1973), has had great influence as a counterclaim to the realist, mechanist way of construing the world.

The rise of interest in social constructionism is coterminous with the recognition of a malaise, noted by Elms (1975) as a "crisis" in social psychology, a condition brought about by the reliance on laboratory experiments in which the phenomena under investigation were decontextualized. To recover from this malaise, some psychologists cast about for a framework that would be more satisfying than the traditional realist and mechanistic metaphysic. The search for *meaning* had not been a central feature of traditional psychology. This condition is changing rapidly. With increased interest in the study of discourse processes, hermeneutics and narrative, *meaning* is displacing internal determinants as the privileged topic of interest. Books and papers by Gergen, Shotter, Harré, Morawski, Bruner, and others, have been instrumental in the perception of constructionism as a preferred alternative to traditional psychological approaches to understanding human conduct.

The papers in this volume offer not only a range of exemplars of the constructionist perspective, but also a representation of the varied phenomena to which the perspective may be applied. The chapters also pose, implicitly or explicitly, an array of theoretical and methodological issues for examination. The constructionist literature in psychology reflects a commitment to the rhetoric of criticism in which constructionists have examined and deconstructed the dominant positivist epistemological assumptions and methodologies. Gergen has outlined the main features of the social constructionist orientation:

> The mounting criticism of the positivist-empiricist conception of knowledge has severely damaged the traditional view that scientific theory serves to reflect or map reality in any direct or decontextualized manner. . . . How can theoretical categories be induced or derived from observation, it is asked, if the process of identifying observational attributes itself relies on one's possessing categories? How can theoretical categories map or reflect the world if each definition used to link category and observation itself requires a definition? How can words map reality when the major constraints over word usage are furnished by linguistic context? (1985: 266–7).

Narrative Structure in Constructionist Accounts

In reviewing the contributions to this volume, it becomes apparent that the underlying structure of constructionist accounts is the narrative. Although written in conventional academic style with attention to the rhetoric of objective science, the discourses each tell a story. For example, in Chapter 10, Bodily tells a story about ageing nurses who uncritically use the unexamined category "age" as the reason for not participating in professional activities. In Chapter 4, Lilley and Platt tell a story about the heterogeneous images of a charismatic leader. In Chapter 9, DeNora and Mehan construct a narrative account of the life and times of Beethoven to illustrate the claim that "genius" is socially constructed. In Chapter 2, Mary Gergen gives an account of the gendered nature of popular autobiographies, a narrative that directs the reader of her chapter to recognize the subtle social processes operating in the autobiographers' adoption of traditional plot lines.

Some of the chapters present historical narratives. Andersen (Chapter 7) goes back to the nineteenth century eugenics movement and traces the development of the notion of intelligence and its popular index, the IQ. Gardner (Chapter 3) paints a portrait of Victorian life in her constructionist account of women's and doctors' beliefs about pregnancy, while in Chapter 8, Hallam consults historical sources to tell a story of the origins and development of the social constructions of "anxiety." Boyle (Chapter 6) constructs a narrative in which ancient religious beliefs are shown to influence (unwittingly) contemporary experts' constructions of sexual dysfunction.

It is not that the authors of these chapters avoid the rhetoric of science. Some, in fact, make use of quantitative methods (for example, Lilley and Platt, Bodily, Scheibe, and Wiener and Marcus). In these cases, the rhetoric of science is employed to reinforce the narrative structure. Scheibe's telling the story of cocaine addiction, for example, makes use of derived data to establish a quantitative warrant for his constructions formed from members' accounts of their introduction to and use of cocaine. Espousing a view that there is more than one kind of constructionism (see below on the distinction between "contextual" and "strict" constructionism), we see no contradiction in employing a method that traditionally is the sine qua non of positivist, mechanist research, that is, numbers, charts, tables, statistical wizardry, etc., if we recognize that these are aids in the telling of a particular story by the professional investigator. At the same time, we do not ignore the observation that the use of such quantitative devices serves rhetorical functions. Numbers, charts, and other quantitative communication devices are emblems of a rhetoric of objective science and are employed to reinforce the claims of the analyst as a scientific story teller.

Like all good stories, each chapter has a dramatic impact. In most instances the drama is a version of the David and Goliath plot, the drama of the truth-seeking champion challenging an apparently invincible tradition. It is pertinent here to recall Jerome Bruner's (1986) distinction between two modes of doing science: the paradigmatic and the narrative. The paradigmatic mode has its home in positivism and is characterized by hypothesis testing, the search for invariance, the decontextualization of the phenomena of interest, the construction of law-like statements, and an epistemology of correspondence with some objective "reality." The narrative mode is employed by historians, biographers, and other practitioners of human sciences. The objective is to tell a story about phenomena in their natural contexts. The criteria for acceptance or non-acceptance of a particular story is coherence – how well it hangs together. The users of the narrative mode, ready to incorporate into their stories the influence of multiple contexts on their constructions, are necessarily committed to the ontology of contextualism.

The practices of constructionists are like those of the narrativists in that their work is grounded in the contextualist ontology. It would be appropriate to look upon social constructionism as an epistemology and contextualism as the coordinate ontology (Pepper, 1942; Rosnow and Georgoudi, 1986; Sarbin, 1977, 1986). Contextualism recognizes change, novelty and contingency as fundamental categories. The mechanistic worldview, by contrast, supports the search for invariance as exemplified in positivist doctrine. Pepper (1942) forcefully argued that the root metaphor of contextualism is the historical act. In deconstructing this root metaphor, Sarbin has shown that historical acts are communicated and remembered as narratives (1986, 1993). One might say that the narrative is the most suitable form for reporting the work of constructionist/contextualist analysts.

Members of a collectivity (ordinary people) convey their constructions of the social world through narrative to fellow members, to professional analysts, and even to self. Even though ordinary folk are more likely to be realists, having reified the constructions acquired through experience or authority, they nonetheless report their constructions of the world through the use of stories. What they report are their social experiences the making of which follow well-established narrative plots (Carr, 1986). Members' stories are the raw materials for constructionist research. Following Hallam's suggestion, these are "p" stories – narratives told by persons, the folk – uninhibited by the constraints imposed on "P" stories, narratives told by professional analysts for specialized audiences. Thus, the analyst constructs his or her narrative from the narrative accounts rendered by members. The chapters in this book for the most part reflect analysts' narratives. In some cases, a third kind of narrative is constructed – a narrative that attempts to look simultaneously at both the folk construction and the analyst's construction. Hallam's chapter is an exemplar of the latter narrative, making sense of both folk and professional constructions of "anxiety."

The Moral Impetus

Narratives are, of course, shaped by and reflect the perspectives of the narrators who produce them, and constructionism explicitly acknowledges and sanctions the differential perspectives in the observation and interpretation of social phenomena. The logic of constructionism fosters the introduction of multiple perspectives to counter the positivist presupposition of a uniform and objective social reality. The response to this sanctioning of the relativism of multiple realities has generated some markedly political constructionist research agendas. Asserting that mainline psychological and sociological studies have been biased and shaped by positivist theory and methodology, constructionists have been activated to propose alternative (sometimes stated as "more complete") narratives that give voice to members of politically, economically, and culturally disenfranchised groups. Scheppele's essay (Chapter 5), for example, documents the ways in which legal practices assign greater credibility to a woman's first account of sexual abuse in contrast to a later, more reflective narrative of "what actually happened."

If there is an underlying moral impetus here, it might be viewed as neutrally directed toward providing "correctives" for institutionally sponsored and legitimated positivist research in psychology and sociology. In a strict sense, the logic of constructionism impels a challenge to the "scientific" bases of the practices and policies in that scientific constructions and the values that shape them are not privileged over others. However, the rhetoric in some constructionist work may escalate beyond the boundaries of dispassionate academic discourse, reflecting in various degrees the research analysts' ideological commitments to ameliorating the life circumstances of the aged, combating racism and sexism, protecting the environment, etc. Thus, reports of constructionist research often present arguments that are infused with various moral perspectives. In the present collection, Boyle's essay, for example, demonstrates that a masculinist bias pervades diagnostic systems proposed by institutionally-recognized experts on sexual dysfunction. Bodily's moral concerns are expressed when he notes the devaluation of professional competence in the communications of inactive nurses who attribute their devalued self-image to "being old." The moral concern in Andersen's chapter is quite explicit in his discourse on the IQ as a tool to implement discrimination in educational settings.

In engaging in claimsmaking conduct, the energy for the contributors' work comes from the recognition that the claims they are countering support unevenly distributed fairness or injustice. One can detect an implicit moral message in the claims of Holstein and Gubrium (Chapter 13) that "family" may represent a large number of social arrangements – many of which are not the mainstream arrangement espoused by some politicians in their call for a return to "family values."

These more or less explicit expressions of moral concern in constructionist work are grounded in analyses of various "inequities" of existing social and institutional arrangements. For example, Wiener and Marcus's essay on "depression" examines how clinical interpretations of "symptoms of depression" produce diagnostic and medication practices directed to people to whom the official diagnostic label has been assigned. The authors analyze the "symptoms" as well as the classification system that identifies "depression" as a medical condition. They conclude that the "symptoms" and the diagnosis are social constructions of the psychiatric profession and that they are demonstrably inadequate for dealing with social conduct. The authors offer a "more complete" interpretation of the conduct in question, first, by demonstrating the polymorphous character of conduct officially labeled "depression," then demonstrating the transactional nature of the various social actions subsumed under the medical diagnosis of depression.

Reflexivity

The issue of the "moral concerns" that direct the researchers' stance toward subjects' constructions of their everyday world introduces questions about whether and in what ways those concerns influence their observations of the phenomena under investigation. Thus a fundamental issue that constructionism poses for the practice of social science is the researcher/analysts' awareness of and reflection on how they are "situated" with regard to their subjects' everyday world. As members in common (however minimally) of the subjects' life worlds, researcher/analysts are involved in an activity in which the data they produce are shaped by the researchers' tacit understanding of the subjects' daily practices. In their reports of those daily practices, researchers import observations and interpretations reflecting their biographically-conditioned perspectives.

This problem of reflexivity in social science, indeed any scientific activity, is central to the practice of constructionism. It ramifies into a number of theoretical issues which leads ultimately to the question as to whether science, especially human science, is possible at all. The radical relativism implicit in the logic of social constructionism has led to assertions that the researcher/analysts' constructions are no more privileged with respect to "objectivity" or "truth" than those of ordinary members. They are to be viewed and treated as narratives implicitly shaped and expressing the social, moral, political, philo-sophical and other concerns of the narrator. Specifically, the question relates to the process by which social data are produced – what goes into the researcher's practices of observing, participating, and recording the activities of everyday people in the contexts in which they occur? This is the point of the methodological issue of what we have identified in the papers of some of the psychologists as the "P" and "p" issue ("P" = psychologist's or other professional's constructions; "p" = person's or member's constructions. See Hallam, Chapter 9). More generally, discourses on the issue of reflexivity engage the sociologists, particularly exemplified in Bodily's chapter. This concern about the data-producing (constructing) process goes beyond the distinction between "P" and "p". Reflexivity introduces the additional perspective of analysts' critically examining the grounds of the researcher's own constructions of "P" and "p." If we read closely the papers on anxiety, depression, sexual dysfunction, etc., it is evident that the authors implicitly impute the meanings that "P"'s have built into their constructions.

These papers can properly be viewed as studies in the sociology of knowledge (particularly exemplified by the research on IQ), the institution of academic psychology being the site of those studies. In contrast, the sociologists' papers are focused on the description and analysis of the constructions of everyday members (in Gardner's paper those members are primarily professionals of one kind or another which is similar to the psychologists' data). This difference between the psychologists' and sociologists' contributions to our volume is also reflected in the note of critique in the former's papers. Offered as an "alternative" theory or perspective, the authors are engaged in what is currently called a "deconstruction" of the "P" formulations of "anxiety," "depression," etc. As we discussed in previous paragraphs, a moral impetus appears to drive constructionist analysis. The normative element is frequently just below the surface if not right on top. The issue of "public policy" and how it implicitly or explicitly is the target (consumer) of research inevitably reflects a normative dimension in the data as well as the analyses.

Sometimes the normative element takes a realist form as expressed by one of our students, "After all, there is an ultimate truth." Insofar as that position expresses a departure from relativism it does "privilege" one perspective over all the others. At the very least, it seems to express a yearning for an absolute which is one of the intellectual resistances to the unyielding relativism of the constructionist program. It is this yearning that appears to influence the resistance to the counterintuitive feature of constructionist assertions in psychology. In sociology it has become framed in the questions about the "usefulness" of constructionist studies that are focused strictly on the social constructions of members without regard to the antecedent and concurrent conditions that give rise to those constructions.

Constructionist analysis may press the relativism more radically by challenging the ontological status of various institutionally-recognized and sanctioned phenomena to ask: what is the basis of the claim that the phenomena exist at all? The counterintuitive character of questioning the objective existence of the phenomenal world may generate an ambivalence and tension even among the advocates of constructionism. For constructionist analysts, no less than for ordinary members of a collectivity, it requires an act of imagination to suspend the realist's belief that "after all, there is a world out there" and that the claims that people make are not constructed out of "nothing." The task of suspending belief is not unlike the obverse task of suspending disbelief when reading fairy tales, science fiction, and other contrafactual stories.

The research analyst departs from constructionism when he or she adopts the realist's perspective, effectively sharing with the positivist a privileged status that accords his or her descriptions and accounts of "reality" greater objectivity and credibility than those of ordinary folk. That is, if there is an objectively verifiable world "out there," trained and disciplined professional researchers may claim that their descriptions of the world are more accurate, complete, and credible than those of ordinary members who are untrained and undisciplined. Acceptance of this privileged perspective may express the commonsensical assumption of an objective verifiable world in which all reality is objectively grounded, an assumption that the analyst shares with ordinary members.

Among sociological theorists, this intellectual resistance to the counterintuitive feature of constructionism is the subject of lively debate. The "strict" constructionist holds that all conceptions, assertions, and accounts of ordinary members express their understandings of their everyday world and must be entertained without regard to their "validity." On this argument, the creationist construction of life would be as credible and viable among some segments of the society as the modern evolutionary construction. This view has been criticized as unwarranted and without reason, if not playfully frivolous. Such criticisms contend that ordinary members *after all* organize their activities in response to "something" that objectively exists in the social context in which they live. To deny the relevance of examining the empirical basis of members' constructions is to subscribe to a form of solipsism that can only lead to a privatized hall of mirrors. On this view the research task is to examine the bases of social constructions in the social contexts and assess their accuracy as expressions of the "social structural features" of those contexts. In this regard the contextualist project becomes focused on problems in the sociology of knowledge – that is, what are the social bases of social constructions?

In short, the "contextual"[2] view argues for a commonsensical view of "reality" that rejects a solipsistic construction of the world. Joel Best (1993), a critic of the "strict" constructionist position, titles his critique "But seriously folks: the limitations of the strict constructionist interpretation of social problems." His title rhetorically cautions his readers to avoid the frivolity contained in the solipsistic position. He makes the argument that the claims ordinary members make are about "something" – that is, a construction about some "social conditions" that are open to empirical verification as the basis for a more complete understanding of the construction.

DeNora and Mehan in Chapter 9 offer an instructive example of some issues that are raised by contextual analyses of "something:" the nineteenth-century Viennese construction of Beethoven's "genius." One position might focus on an objectively verifiable condition called "talent" that gave rise to the development of Beethoven's "genius." For DeNora and Mehan, however, the constructionist task is not one of examining the nature of Beethoven's "talent," but rather to document the social and cultural context which influenced Beethoven's being anointed a genius.

It may well be that in the case of music it would be difficult to create a genius in the absence of any musical talent whatever, but would it be impossible? The question presupposes a more or less culturally shared conception of musical talent such that any observer would recognize the case of "no musical talent whatever" thus excluding the possibility of "genius." Such a consensus may exist with reference to certain canons of music, but the issue becomes more problematic when we consider less conventional forms of music, such as rock, heavy metal, rap, and other forms. The last decades of the twentieth century have witnessed numerous examples of "genius" that underline the problematic relation between something designated "talent" and the organized press agentry that produces awesome "genius" for public adulation.

Returning to the distinction between the "strict" constructionist position and the "contextual" position, we argue that the distinction represents more than differences in research strategies. Schneider and Kitsuse, commenting on this distinction as it relates to the sociology of social problems, make the point:

> Rather than competing with members over what is true or real or accurate or reasonable, the strict constructionist seeks to pursue . . . [a] quite different project. It is a *theoretical* project that is contrasted with the members' *practical* projects that may include organizing protests, testifying before governmental bodies, holding news conferences, soliciting and recruiting expert advice, and even reviewing official reports and statistics to garner useful materials to increase the credibility and effectiveness of their claims. Strict constructionists *themselves* are interested in doing none of these things, nor do they choose to sit in judgment of how well or poorly members do them. Rather than seeking to build a professional sociological theory to supersede members' theories, the strict constructionist strives to describe members' theories and how they use them in their practical activities (emphasis in original). (1989: xiii)

What is at issue is a fundamental difference in theoretical orientation. The strict constructionist focuses on how members in everyday
life (the folk, Hallam's "p") rhetorically phrase claims about their
worlds in interaction with others, the morality conveyed in rhetorical
expressions, the responses of others to the claims so phrased, etc.
Moreover, the strict constructionist is interested in the narrative
production of members' claims about their moral concerns without
regard for their accuracy, veracity, adequacy or other analytic criteria.

Woolgar and Pawluch (1985) have analyzed the logical inconsistencies posed by constructionist theory that present formidable
methodological barriers to the conduct of research. They hold that
constructionist theory requires researchers to be devoid of social and
cultural presuppositions and thus have no interpretive frame in which
to record their observations. Metaphorically speaking, such a
researcher would be ontologically suspended in midair. In practice,
Woolgar and Pawluch contend, researchers *assume* a pre-existing
ontological reality to locate themselves perspectivally in order to
observe and record the social constructions of members' everyday
activities. They view the practice of what has been termed "bracketing"
social phenomena (Schutz, 1967) in the process of investigation to
constitute an avoidance of the strict methodological requirements of
constructionist theory. Woolgar and Pawluch coin the metaphor
"ontological gerrymandering," to connote the use of this research
strategy, that is, assuming an ontological reality while problematizing
the reality under investigation. They assert that the "bracketing" of
social phenomena requires a vantage point from which the bracketing
can be accomplished. This cognitive maneuver assumes the ontological status of the research analyst's standpoint as distinct from the
members' variable constructions of their worlds.

None of the chapters in this volume is an exemplar of strict
constructionism. All would meet the criteria for contextual constructionism. It is questionable whether researchers can sustain any
method that would be consistent with the requirements of strict
contextualism. The very act of obtaining information from an
informant influences the form and content of the response. Investigators and analysts in spite of themselves cannot help but import their
interests, if not their professional agendas, into their interactions with
their informants.

In an effort to clarify the epistemological basis of constructionism,
Ibarra and Kitsuse (1993) have proposed that members of a collectivity
are oriented to a world of action, analysts are oriented to an
investigation and interpretation of members' constructions of that
world. That members assume or assert the existence of "child abuse,"
"urban decay," "dysfunctional families," etc., or for what purposes
and how they utilize such constructions in claimsmaking is not for the

analyst to assess as to their logic, accuracy, or adequacy. Analysts direct their attention to the question: How are members' narrative forms produced in their constructions of claims about what they consider socially and morally important in their everyday lives?

The more general issue in Woolgar and Pawluch's critique is the implication of the methodological requirement that the researcher's standpoint be socially, culturally, and even *physically* uncontaminated by, and independent of, the site of the investigation. On the contrary it places the researcher "in the field" as participant as well as observer, imposing a constant burden of reflecting on how his or her presence shapes the narrative account of field work. A constructionist who offers such an account may be confronted by a positivist who asks for a certification as to the adequacy (that is, the factual character) of the account. The researcher's response to certify his or her initial story as adequate may prompt the positivist critic to ask for a certification of *that* account, leading to a statement of infinite regress. This observation reminds us of an informant's cosmology reported by Clifford Geertz, as noted by Scheppele in Chapter 5. For this informant, the world rests on the back of an elephant, which in turn stands on the back of a turtle. When the informant was asked what the turtle stands on, the answer was "Ah, Sahib, after that, it is turtles all the way down" (Geertz, 1973: 29). Scheppele goes on to say "This is not exactly a comforting answer if one wants to believe there is some stable bedrock somewhere. But (as with the elephant and its turtles) in stories, it is narrative all the way down."

Whatever one's philosophical preference, the ontological and epistemological issues have been shaped by the fundamental problem of "meaning" in the framing of social phenomena. The positivist formulation of social phenomena deals with the problem of meaning by implicitly importing the researcher's interpretations of actors making sense of their worlds. The researcher's data – at whatever level, for example, interpersonal, organizational, institutional – in the final analysis imputes meaning to the conduct of actors reflected in those data. That is to say, the positivist researcher, as a socialized member ("human" in the first instance, but beyond that culturally differentiated – male, female, American, Japanese, Muslim, whatever) is a "constructionist from the outside." The meaning of the social phenomena he or she describes, analyzes, and interprets is imported into the research.

There is a persistent confusion in this regard because both reader and practitioner, first of all, assume that members' constructions are based on some defined, objectively identifiable state of affairs that the constructionist must verify. The impetus to verify is usually an expression of the lingering positivism to which analyst and members alike subscribe. To deny the relevance of the empirical grounds of the members' constructions leads to charges of solipsism and/or radical relativism. Such charges miss the fact of the constructionist's suspension of commitment to a realist ontology even as he or she respects and attempts to document the reality that informs and organizes the actions of members in everyday life.

Constructionist criticism of this methodological strategy and its playful attitude of openness to expressions of multiple realities is what committed positivists/realists view as a mischievous relativism in their theory and practice. The constructionist's theoretical commitment to the conception of social phenomena as a multiplicity of actively constructed and emergent realities imposes the burden of a serious examination of the logical implications of their perspective. Does a posture of openness to multiple realities provide license to disclaim commitment to any reality or to social/political action that such a commitment might entail? Does such a disclaimer sponsor the denial of ethical responsibility for active intervention in order to facilitate the construction of claims that are likely to produce social policies that ameliorate poverty, sickness, and other defined social conditions? Are some constructions of realities more politically viable, more readily discredited and dismissed, more damaging to life and limb? Does constructionism give license to the playful exercise of sheer curiosity? In brief, does the constructionist have a socially responsible and legitimate project as researcher/analyst of social phenomena?

Notes

1. The now-retired television journalist and anchorman, Walter Cronkite, ended his nightly broadcasts with "and that's the way it is."
2. In the sociological literature, "contextual" constructionism is posited as a competing orientation to "strict" constructionism. The use of "contextual" in the present setting should not be confused with contextualism, the label used by Pepper (1942) to identify one of four world views or metaphysical systems. Clearly the meanings overlap.

References

Bartlett, F.C. (1932) *Remembering: A Study in Experimental and Social Psychology.* Cambridge: Cambridge University Press.

Berger, P.L., and Luckman, T. (1967) *The Social Construction of Reality: A Treatise on the Sociology of Knowledge.* Garden City, NY: Doubleday.

Best, J. (1993) But seriously folks: the limitations of the strict constructionist interpretations of social problems, in J.A. Holstein, and G. Miller (eds), *Reconsidering Social Constructionism: Debates in Social Problems Theory.* Hawthorne, NY: Aldine deGruyter.

Bruner, J. (1986) *Actual Minds, Possible Worlds.* Cambridge, MA: Harvard University Press.

Cameron, N. (1948) *The Psychology of Behavior Disorders.* Boston, MA: Houghton Mifflin.

Carr, D. (1986) *Time, Narrative, and History.* Bloomington, IN: Indiana University Press.

Elms, A.C. (1975) The crisis of confidence in social psychology, *American Psychologist* 30: 967–76.

Garfinkel, H. (1967) *Studies in Ethnomethodology.* Englewood Cliffs, NJ: Prentice-Hall.

Geertz, C. (1973) Thick description: toward an interpretive theory of culture, in C. Geertz (ed.), *The Interpretation of Cultures.* New York: Basic Books.

Gergen, K.J. (1985) The social constructionist movement in modern psychology, *American Psychologist,* 40: 266–75.

Gergen, K.J. (1973) Social psychology as history, *Journal of Personality and Social Psychology,* 26: 309–20.

Goffman, E. (1959) *The Presentation of Self in Everyday Life.* Garden City, NY: Doubleday.

Goffman, E. (1963) *Stigma: Notes on the Management of Spoiled Identities.* Englewood Cliffs, NJ: Prentice-Hall.

Holstein, J., and Miller, G. (eds) (1993) *Reconsidering Social Constructionism: Debates in Social Problems Theory.* Hawthorne, NY: Aldine deGruyter.

Ibarra, P., and Kitsuse, J.I. (1993) Vernacular constituents of moral discourse: an interactionist proposal for the study of social problems, in J.A. Holstein, and G. Miller (eds), *Reconsidering Social Constructionism: Debates in Social Problems Theory.* Hawthorne, NY: Aldine deGruyter.

Kelly, G. (1955) *The Psychology of Personal Constructs.* New York: Norton.

Kroger, R.O., and Scheibe, K.E. (1990) A reappraisal of Wundt's influence on social psychology, *Canadian Psychologist,* 31: 220–8.

Mancuso, J.C., and Adams-Webber, J.R. (eds) (1982) *The Construing Person.* New York: Praeger.

Mannheim, K. (1936) *Ideology and Utopia: An Introduction to the Sociology of Knowledge.* New York: Harcourt Brace and World.

Mixon, D. (1989) *Obedience and Civilization.* London: Pluto Press.

Newcomb, T.M. (1951) *Social Psychology.* New York: Holt Rinehart and Winston.

Pepper, S. (1942) *World Hypotheses.* Berkeley, CA: University of California Press.

Rosnow, R., and Georgoudi, M. (1986) *Contextualism and Understanding in Behavior Science.* New York: Praeger.

Sarbin, T.R. (1943) The concept of role-taking, *Sociometry,* 6: 273–84.

Sarbin, T.R. (1954) Role theory, in G. Lindzey (ed.), *Handbook of Social Psychology,* Cambridge, MA: Addison-Wesley. *Vol. I,* pp. 223–58.

Sarbin, T.R. (1977) Contextualism: a world view for modern psychology, in A. Landfield (ed.), *1976 Nebraska Symposium on Motivation.* Lincoln, NE: University of Nebraska Press.

Sarbin, T.R. (ed.) (1986) *Narrative Psychology: The Storied Nature of Human Conduct.* New York: Praeger.

Sarbin, T.R. (1993) The narrative as the root metaphor for contextualism, in S. Hayes, L.P. Hayes, H. Reese, and T.R. Sarbin (eds), *Varieties of Scientific Contextualism.* Reno, NV: Context Press.

Scheibe, K.E. (1979) *Mirrors, Masks, Lies, and Secrets.* New York: Praeger.

Schneider, J.W. (1985) Social problems theory: the constructionist view, *Annual Review of Sociology,* 11: 209–29.

Schneider, J.W., and Kitsuse, J.I. (1989) Preface, in J. Best (ed.), *Images of Issues: Typifying Contemporary Social Problems.* Chicago: Aldine.

Schutz, A. (1967) *Phenomenology of the social world* (translated by G. Walsh and F. Lehnert, with an introduction by G. Walsh). Evanston, IL: Northwestern University Press.

Woolgar, S., and Pawluch, D. (1985) Ontological gerrymandering: the anatomy of social problems explanations, *Social Problems*, 32: 214–27.

I
PUBLIC DOCUMENTS AS SOURCES OF SOCIAL CONSTRUCTIONS

2

The Social Construction of Personal Histories: Gendered Lives in Popular Autobiographies

Mary Gergen

What created humanity is narration.

Pierre Janet (1928: 42)

Personal History as Social Construction

It is through hearing stories . . . that children learn what the cast of characters may be in the drama into which they have been born and what the ways of the world are.

(MacIntyre, 1981: 201)

Scholars from expanding circles of discourse, in fields as diverse as organizational theory, history, sociology, Jungian analysis, communications, philosophy of science, and the classics, have recently become engrossed in the problem of how literary forms are used in the creation of their subject matters (see, Campbell, 1956; White, 1978; Simons, 1989; McCloskey, 1990; Quinn et al., 1991). The endeavor common to this range of scholars is the analysis of the literary forms – myths, archetypes, tropes, and metaphors – from which the texts within their domains are derived. Their conclusions focus on the power that literary forms have in controlling the "realities" of the discipline represented. Noted anthropologist James Clifford has described this approach to analyzing the texts of a discipline in the following remark, "What appears as 'real' in history, the social sciences, the arts, even in common sense, is always analyzable as a restrictive and expressive set of social codes and conventions" (1986: 10). What there is – the raw material of the field – becomes configured by formal characteristics of the applied literary forms.

Perhaps the most extensive formative power is exhibited by narrative form. The mark of its story is powerfully displayed in the explanatory forms a culture produces. This chapter will focus on narrative forms as the grounding literary means for creating significant lives. We will explore how what is taken to constitute the personal realities of individuals is endowed by narrative.

In psychology, the exploration of narratives occurs at the periphery of the field, but in increasing abundance (see, Runyan, 1982; Sarbin and Scheibe, 1983; McAdams, 1985; Mishler, 1986; Sarbin, 1986; Tappan and Packer, 1991; Harvey et al., 1992). Psychologists interested in social constructionism, in particular, are keenly aware of the potential of narratives as a means of creating reality (Gergen and Gergen, 1983, 1986, 1988; K. Gergen, 1985, in press; Bruner, 1986; M. Gergen, 1991, 1992). One "reality" of central concern is the individual's understanding of self – and most particularly his or her personal history. Instead of regarding self descriptions as reflections of the teller's actual experiences, narratologists view them as forms of social practice in which an individual appropriates from a cultural repertoire of stories certain forms that become synthesized as personal stories. In the sense that people derive their personal accounts from the cultural resources, they become constructed in the process of their tellings. Their accounts of how they have grown up, responded to difficulties, coped with set-backs, enjoyed prosperity, and developed every other aspect of their identities and relationships are possible because of their familiarity with their culture's narrative resources.

People are exposed to a wide range of biographical stories from social acquaintances, friends and family members, as well as from the media (MacIntyre, 1981). *People* magazine, gossip columns in newspapers, television news, movies, dramas, and books all provide narrative models for people's self-understanding. When people are asked to give accounts of their own lives, they must resort to the modes of telling with which they are familiar. They cannot merely "tell it like it is, or was," that is, to reconstruct their lives from day to day remembrances. No one can perform this mental feat, and no one would want to listen to someone who might try. The selection process that must occur in order to make sense to others relies heavily on cultural heuristics – that is, on the conventional or acceptable biographical forms of the culture.

Training in this process begins early in life, and continues throughout. An example of this process in early childhood is James Day's recorded conversation with a four-year-old boy who saved the life of another boy, who ran into the street after a ball. When asked why he broke his mother's rule not to run into the street, the boy responded, "I thought of The Incredible Hulk, who always saves people in trouble" (Day, 1992). The child made sense of his actions by referring to the storied life of his television hero. While we most frequently rely upon these cultural heuristics unawares, at times, we may be able to make connections between our past exposures to cultural forms, and our own biographies. In one survey, a group of college students described their favorite childhood story; later when asked to recall any influence of that story on how they understood their own lives, most reported that they saw aspects of their current lives paralleling these childhood stories (M. Gergen, 1991). This reliance on familiar cultural forms for understanding one's life is not restricted to ordinary people in normal circumstances; famous people also tell their life stories based on cultural norms. In so doing they reinforce these stories as useful models for others who might wish to emulate them. This observation – that cultural heroes provide models of life stories for others – is the basis upon which the material in this chapter was drawn for analysis and will be discussed in greater detail below.

Over the life course, people may develop greater sophistication in their potential for telling a variety of life stories. As they shift environments and social contacts they develop the capacity to reconstrue their lives in ways that enhance their present stations, relationships and needs. At any moment, people piece together their lives by synthesizing the variety of potential stories at their disposal. Michael Sprinker has described the result of this effort, "Every text is an articulation of the relations between texts, a product of inter-textuality, a weaving together of what has already been produced elsewhere in discontinuous form" (Sprinker, 1980: 325). One may begin a life story (not unlike Joan Rivers, as she writes her auto-biography) as a "poor little rich girl," shift to a Cinderella motif, and end with the Frog Prince, should it appear that a compelling self-definition results from these transitions. At the same time, with each new twist to the story, the teller enriches the cultural repertoire (Hyde, 1979). Once this Joan Rivers rendition is publicized, other "Joan Rivers" transformations can emerge.

While novelty is produced by new syntheses, people cannot select their life stories from any template they might wish. Personal stories are parts of larger interactional frameworks, embedded within a variety of relationships, and thus they are open to sanction by those within the dialogic frame of the author. There must be some agreement among the relevant parties as to what is a suitable life story. Couples cannot disagree openly about the story of their marriage, unless they are heading for a separation. Differences in their narratives must be resolved or buried, or they will continuously be in conflict. Ideally stories of related individuals, such as family members, should be complementary. While some allowances are made for divergent perspectives, it is assumed that the couple is acting within the same story plot. A grown up child's version of sexual abuse by parents does not support a parental story of care, respect, and love. Thus, the freedom to portray oneself within a particular storyline is not a purely individualistic act, but is something that must be negotiated with the supporting players.

The choice of which story to tell has consequences for the tellers. This is significant because conventional relations within the culture exist between one's story and other verbal and non-verbal actions. Thus, the medals on one's uniform and the loss of a limb confirm one's stories as a war hero. Story lines also have reflexive qualities. Story lines suggest forms of action that may coordinate with them. If we are influenced by the Incredible Hulk, we may engage in more heroic adventures than if we see ourselves as living like Winnie the Pooh. At the same time, not all daily events are included in storied accounts. The events that count for our biographical accounts are selected for their fit, not as a summary that encompasses all of our activities. The relationship between social interactions and narratives is partial, inconclusive and negotiable.

The emphasis on the non-reflective relationship between events and storied renditions is related to a social constructionist approach to knowledge; this perspective emphasizes the centrality of language in the creation of the world (K. Gergen, in press). From this standpoint, language is not a reflection of the experiences of people, not mirrors, maps, nor translations of events into words. Every wording is an engagement in the social networks of which those words are a part. Thus, narrative forms shape the sense of what it means to live, to know, and to feel.

The Autobiography as a Literary Form

> Autobiography is a Low Rent art.
>
> Albert Stone (1982: 1)

Although the autobiography has never been granted a high status among literary forms, there has been a long tradition of autobiography beginning with Augustine, continuing with Rousseau, and pro-liferating today in a variety of venues, both literary and popular. Traditionally western culture has valued the autobiography as a moral tale (Stone, 1982). Through reading of the lives of heroic figures one learns about the cultivation of the morally sound and socially valuable life. This principle behind the autobiography has strongly influenced the themes of life stories, the form of the telling, and the personages who have been considered worthy of writing autobiographies. Because the function of the autobiography has been to describe an exemplary life, they almost exclusively delineate the life of cultural heroes – those who have achieved greatness through their accomplishments (Jelinek,

1980; Olney, 1980). The silent side of this coin is that those who are not regarded as individualistically prominent are not memorialized in autobiographical form.

In terms of voice, the prototypical autobiography takes "The stance of the wise and fatherly elder addressing the reader as son or niece" (Eakin, 1985: 29). The principal model of the autobiographical relationship is expert to novice, master to apprentice and powerful to powerless. Autobiographers use rhetorical devices for assuring that their self-image is presented as they wish it to be, which may include rebuttal to hostile or critical voices (see, *As I See it* by J. Paul Getty; *Mayor* by Ed Koch). For the most part the autobiographer has been a man in the late stages of life, desirous of justifying his existence to others and of showing others the means to his success (see, Erikson, 1975).

The ideal protagonist of the conventional autobiography is the hero. The plot is formed by his struggle to attain success in terms of a valuable social goal. This formulation adheres to the classical lines of the "monomyth," a form that classicist Joseph Campbell (1956) has designated as the single basic story of western civilization. In its clearest form, this heroic myth centers on the theme of the triumph of spirit over flesh; of good over evil; of mind over matter. The central plot of the monomyth describes the hero's life, from being chosen as a heroic figure, embarking on a quest, struggling against various adversaries and temptations, to gaining a final victory and being recognized for his achievements. The form of the story is one of gathering momentum, with its climactic moment seen as that of highest attainment. The narrative is centered on a single plot, a static goal and unwavering progress toward it. There are no irrelevant tangents, alternative goals, or repetitions of stages. Each event leads forward to the next in simple causal regularity.

Given the "old fashioned" nature of this plot line, one may ask why the autobiography persists as a literary form in western countries, given that many other forms of morality tales have become all but extinct; for example, myths, allegories, legends, and fables primarily exist in children's literature or in folkloric libraries. This question has interested many literary theorists, who subscribe to the notion that the autobiography flourishes in locations where individuals can become prominent within their social group. Edward Sampson argues that the autobiography has become a prominent literary form in the United States because individuality is the most dominant personality conception of modern western man (Sampson, 1989). Others agree. "The fascination with individual specificity leads to deep intrigue with life stories" (Eakin, 1985: 204).

The Popular Autobiography as a Source of Personal Life Patterns

> We assume that life *produces* the autobiography as an act produces its consequence, but can we not suggest, with equal justice, that the autobiography project may itself produce and determine life?
>
> Paul de Man (1979: 920)

While the traditional autobiography was restricted to patrician subjects, a new genre of autobiography, in which the author is a well-known celebrity, has become very popular in the United States. This prominence is indicated by the prevalence of autobiographies on the best seller list of non-fiction books compiled each week by major newspapers (see, *New York Times*, 1990–91 booklists). These auto-biographies are often written in formula formats designed by publishing houses for the purpose of attracting large audiences. Frequently these books are co-authored by a professional writer, whose career is dependent upon this activity. The function of this writer is to take background materials and the personal narratives as recorded in notes and on audio tapes from the central figure, and produce from the contents a viable book.[1] The public is inducted into these narrative forms through the life stories of famous people. In this chapter these autobiographies will elucidate the conventional forms of life stories, especially for the rich and famous. While other forms – television documentaries and mini-series, films and magazine stories, among others – might have been selected for analysis, autobiographies serve as convenient and familiar repositories of a popular form of life story. One might suppose that the form of the narrative for famous people might be the familiar hero tale, mentioned above. Yet one might also suspect that this view is limited because the heroic tale is unisexed. The coherence of heroic plot is easily recognizable as appropriate for the successful male protagonist, but this formulation may be more problematic if the author is a woman. Although several women's roles are defined within the monomyth, none is heroic. These women's roles tend to be maternal, supernatural, either as ally or evil alien, or as fair maidens, to be wooed and won. Women tend to be objects or forces that aid or impede the hero in pursuit of his quest, or serve as his reward. As Mary Mason has described this issue:

> the self presented as the stage for a battle of opposing forces . . . where a climactic victory for one force – spirit defeating flesh – completes the drama of the self, simply does not accord with the deepest realities of women's experience and so is inappropriate as a model for women's life-writing. (1980: 210)

The aim of this chapter is to suggest how these stories may reflect cultural trends as well as shape the repertoire of life story possibilities for their readers. In particular, this endeavor is designed to focus on gender related differences in autobiographical forms. Do men and women have equal opportunity to tell the same life stories, or are they restricted to separate spheres? Additionally, if men and women do inscribe their lives differently, what might be the consequences of these differences for their own lives?

The Sample of Autobiographies

A sample of autobiographies of 18 men and women published in the United States – primarily by American citizens in the last seven years – serves as the basis for this discussion. These books were chosen to reflect the range of autobiographies available in the popular market. The effort to select a sample from contemporary American sources is designed to minimize historical and cultural variations in what is appropriate as a life story form. The selection includes famous people who have engaged in noteworthy activities, and excludes auto-biographies based on people who are otherwise unknown except for their association with famous people. None of the sample has a literary career, thus no books are experimental in form (e.g. Philip Roth's *The Facts*). The authors of this sample do vary in age, primarily because many of them, in particular the athletes and performers, have become famous in their youths, and have written about themselves in their thirties. This relative immaturity exaggerates the usual problem of the autobiography – that is, the story is not "completed" because the biographer is still alive. However, despite this potential limitation, each author maintains a story structure that has the formal property of ending, at which time the reader will have "achieved a state of equilibrium . . . all passion spent" (Scholes and Kellogg, 1966: 212). The authors also vary in their career paths; in particular, there are no women authors who have equivalent careers to former IBM President Thomas J. Watson, Jr or to entrepreneur T. Boone Pickens. The women's successes often have been made in performance areas such as music, communication, and sports. The collections of popular auto-biography available to the public parallels in several respects the gender divisions in the workplace.

The autobiographies discussed here include those of the following men: Ansel Adams (photographer); Richard Feynman (physicist); John Paul Getty (Getty Oil company founder); Lee Iacocca (Chrysler executive); Edward Koch (mayor of New York City); T. Boone Pickens (corporate "raider"); Ahmad Rashad (professional football player); Donald Trump, Jr (real estate entrepreneur); Thomas Watson, Jr (chair of IBM); and Chuck Yeager (test pilot). Autobiographies from the following women were selected: Joan Baez (folk singer);

Sydney Biddle Barrows (escort service founder); Nien Cheng (oil company executive, political prisoner); Linda Ellerbee (newscaster); Gelsey Kirkland (prima ballerina); Martina Navratilova (professional tennis player); Joan Rivers (television personality); and Beverly Sills (opera singer).

In my initial approach to this sample, I used quantitative methods of analysis, for example, counting the instances of achievement related passages in each book. However, I found the lengthy and tedious process of sorting samples of prose into categories of contents and form more destructive and uninformative than helpful in assessing the overall flow of the book's content and form. Thus, I have chosen to abandon these formalized techniques in favor of a qualitatively tuned method that attempts to encompass the narrative form in a more integrated manner. Each method gains and loses in some aspects. The precision and apparent reliability of the first method is lost, but the interpretive strength of the latter in maintaining the holistic integrity of the books is appealing. In this analysis I am interested in looking at the ways that men and women tell their life stories differently, and then in relating these differences to possible outcomes in terms of other social consequences. I have looked at differences in narrative form, in content of the life story, themes of individuality versus relatedness, and "self understanding."

Autobiographies and Gender Roles in the Culture

> The structure of . . . a story that is at once by and about the same individual echoes and reinforces a structure already implicit in our language.
>
> Elizabeth W. Bruss (1980: 301)

Because autobiographies represent clear cut versions of lives, as given by the well-known personalities in a culture, analysis of their contents and form can tell us much about the lives of people in that culture, at least as they understand themselves through biographical means. To look at these autobiographies for evidence of separate paths for men and women is to discover something about the ways in which men and women hold different expectations and values about their lives. To illustrate the various ways in which men differ from women in their narratives of self, it is useful to break down the narratives into various clusters. Oscillating between the manstory and the womanstory, we can see the differentiations between them on issues of achievement, attachment, and physicality. Each of the characteristics used to describe the narratives will be illustrated by quotations from the various books in the sample. The quotations are designed to represent the general tendencies found within the relevant sample of books included in the study.

Achievement and Career Themes

The characteristics we find in men's autobiographies are those of the heroic figure engaged in a quest. These men write about themselves as dominated by the goals of vocational success, the rewards of success – money, reputation, and power – and the joy of the chase. For John Paul Getty, for example, the quest was for creating an empire from his oil business; for Donald Trump, the making of the bigger and bigger deals against the competition of other bidders. The joy and satisfaction from achieving are everywhere apparent in these autobiographies. For example, in Lee Iacocca's terms, the struggle to keep Ford competitive and innovative was invigorating: "My years as general manager of the Ford Division were the happiest period of my life. For my colleagues and me, this was fire-in-the-belly time. We were high from smoking our own brand – a combination of hard work and big dreams" (1984: 65). Chuck Yeager also expressed pleasure over the feelings of self-confidence that come from testing oneself as a fighter pilot in battle:

> I don't recommend going to war as a way of testing character, but by the time our tour ended we felt damned good about ourselves and what we had accomplished. Whatever the future held, we knew our skills as pilots, our ability to handle stress and danger, and our reliability in tight spots. It was the difference between thinking you're pretty good, and proving it. (1985: 88)

Echoing Yeager's "cocky" attitude, Edward Koch had these comments about his opportunities for achievement:

> I am the Mayor of a city that has more Jews than live in Jerusalem, more Italians than live in Rome . . . and more Puerto Ricans than live in San Juan. . . . It is a tremendous responsibility, but there is no other job in the world that compares with it. . . . Every day has the possibility of accomplishing some major success. (1984: 359)

Heroic tales in modern America are also replete with competitive struggle – losing and (especially) winning. The special quality of certain episodes is that there is often a sense of pleasure when the heroes bring their rivals to their knees. When John Paul Getty drilled his first great oil well, he was overjoyed: "The sense of elation and triumph was-and-is always there. It stems from knowing that one has beaten nature's incalculable odds by finding and capturing a most elusive (and often a dangerous and malevolent) prey" (1986: 28). T. Boone Pickens managed to insert some humor into one of his more difficult business deals. On one particularly bad day, when the chips were getting pretty high for a take-over deal, Boone described the situation:

> We could force Fred to take on even more debt, and he was gagging now. But there was no guarantee we would win.
> My father summed up the situation when he said, "It looks like you've got them by *your* balls, son". (1987: 257)

Often in more or less subtle tones the heroic autobiography indicates situations in which the protagonist must willingly sacrifice personal preferences or moral principles in order to do one's duty. The goal or end to which one is dedicated seems to justify many questionable ends. Chuck Yeager commenting on following orders to shoot German civilians from their airplanes: "We were ordered to commit an atrocity, pure and simple, but the brass who approved this action probably felt justified" (1985: 80). Discussing it with a fellow pilot, Yeager reported, "If we're gonna do things like this, we sure as hell better make sure we're on the winning side. That's still my view" (1985: 80).

The unquestioned sense that one must continue regardless of costs is inherent in Iacocca's report of his first wife's death. Mary, to whom he had been married for over 25 years, was a diabetic. Her condition worsened over the years; after two heart attacks, one in 1978 and the other in 1980, she died at the age of 57 in 1983. According to Iacocca, each of her heart attacks followed a crisis period in his career. He concluded, "Above all, a person with diabetes has to avoid stress. Unfortunately, with the path I had chosen to follow, this was virtually impossible" (1984: 301). The statement in reverse, a woman writing about her husband or child, would sound quite monstrous. It is acceptable in a man's story.

Within heroic stories the need to prove oneself to significant others, especially father figures, is central. Every author compares himself to his father's success, and often to his brothers' failures. (Women of the family do not figure as relevant comparisons.) The issue of who is more powerful or successful is often at stake. No position appears to be comfortable for the male author. Thomas Watson, Jr, wrote of himself as in awe of his father's superiority. His life development required that he finally fill his father's giant shoes. He was captivated by his autocratic father, a relationship he suggests by the title of his autobiography, *Father, Son & Co.* (a parodic illusion to God, the father, Jesus the son, and IBM as the Holy Ghost). Watson, describing his self-accounting on the anniversary of his father's death, wrote:

> I would spend a quiet evening taking stock of what IBM had accomplished in his absence, and then say to Olive [his wife], "That's another year I've made it alone." By then IBM was two and a half times as big as when Dad left it – over two billion dollars a year in sales, . . . and the value of our stock had quintupled. . . . For those five years I hadn't let anybody share the spotlight with me. Inside and outside the company I wanted to establish that Tom Watson Jr. meant IBM, and I guarded my power carefully. (1990: 342)

For most men, the autobiography has been a forum for describing abstract and idealized lives dedicated to career goals. One of the outcomes of a focus on goal states is that materials tangential to these ends are pared away. Additionally, the story emphasizes the individuality of the hero. He is autonomous in the creation of his destiny, and his rewards are often gained from less able, less intelligent, or ruthless competitors. Women's autobiographies are similar in discussions of their rise to prominence, yet they are rarely focused on only one goal at a time. Rather than subvert all energies to the achievement mode, several disparate aims may oscillate in the story space. In terms of the achievement theme, women's stories are full of the pleasures of achieving; however, unlike men's stories, they are less likely to individuate the teller, to alienate her from others, or to illustrate that she would pay any cost to succeed. The hostility to the rival is much less evident, as is the sense of competition with family members. Satisfying parental figures is frequently discussed, with fathers often rewarded with career achievements and mothers with personal adjustment and familial success. For women authors, there is a strong sense that they participate in the attaining of others' goals, wishes, and rewards. One achieves and makes many people happy, including oneself. It is rare that women claim their own happiness, without regard for others, and especially if it is at the expense of others. This need to encompass others in one's own joy of success can be seen in Martina Navratilova's description of winning a tennis championship:

> For the first time I was a Wimbledon champion, fulfilling the dream of my father many years before. . . . I could feel Chris [Evert] patting me on the back, smiling and congratulating me. . . . Four days later, the Women's Tennis Association computer ranked me number 1 in the world, breaking Chris's four-year domination. I felt I was on top of the world. (1985: 190)

Beverly Sills's description of her greatest singing success is also one that encompasses the responsiveness of the audience. Without them, it would not have been her finest personal triumph:

> I think "se pieta" was the single most extraordinary piece of singing I ever did. I know I had never heard myself sing that way before . . . the curtain began coming down very slowly . . . and then a roar went through that house the likes of which I'd never heard. I was a little stunned by it: the audience wouldn't stop applauding. (1987: 172)

Sydney Biddle Barrows wrote of her enterprise as one that would be successful because it would please many clients: "I was determined to create a business that would appeal to . . . men, who constituted the high end of the market . . . I was sure we could turn our agency into one hell of an operation – successful, elegant, honest, and fun" (1986: 48–9).

Women aren't always perfect, however. Joan Rivers, who describes many deep hurts in her struggle to the top, refers to her jealousy of Barbra Streisand's success while she is still a nobody. Rivers admits, "I have never been truly close to women, never had great women friends – probably because we see each other as threats, competing for attention as sexual beings" (1986: 103). One recognizes in her book the fangs of envy that rarely surface in most women's autobiographies.

In sum, both men's and women's texts reveal descriptions of great achievements and their rewards. A dedication to the pursuit of excellence and joy at succeeding are similarly described by both genders. The difference seems to be primarily in terms of how totalizing the theme of achievement is in the person's life, how individualistically the striving and success are framed, and how much the achievement is valued because others have lost, while you have won.

Emotionality and Personal Relationships
One obvious question concerns differences in men's and women's autobiographies in the amount of detail used in descriptions of interpersonal relationships, particularly those that are not connected to career goals. Additionally, emotional expressions, particularly those related to weakness and dependency, are likely to be represented very differently among men and women. In general the analysis revealed strong differences in these areas. Extreme discomfort at emotional scenes is clear in the manner in which Nobel prize winner physicist Richard Feynman discusses the death of his wife. She was fatally ill with tuberculosis and had been moved to a sanatorium in Albuquerque so as to be fairly near him in Los Alamos, where he had gone to work on the development of the atomic bomb. The day she was dying he borrowed a car to go to her bedside: "When I got back (yet another tire went flat on the way), they asked me what happened. 'She's dead. And how's the program going?' They caught on right away that I didn't want to moon over it" (1986: 113).

Donald Trump's autobiography, *The Art of the Deal*, is scant with reference to personal ties, perhaps because his marriage with Ivana was at that time "on the rocks." His description of his parents and his wife is based on one metaphor: people are rocks.

> I have a father who has always been a rock. . . . And I'm as much of a rock as my father. . . . My mother is as much of a rock as my father. . . . When I finally did get married, I married a very beautiful woman, but a woman who also happens to be a rock. (1987: 96–7)

In Thomas Watson's autobiography there are hints of grave emotional problems throughout the book. His asides reveal more detail about his instability than one normally finds in men's stories, but considerably less than if he had been born a woman: "I did not understand how to change pace when I left the office. . . . When I saw I could not bend my wife and children to my will, I'd feel totally thwarted and boxed in. Those were the blackest moments of my adult life" (1990: 315). When he was thwarted he frequently resorted to sudden outbursts of anger, which is an emotion that is "allowed" to men. At times when he was in deep despair he would lock himself in a large closet; his wife would then call his brother to come from a neighboring town to persuade him to come out of his refuge. After decades of marriage his wife walked out on him, much to his surprise. He refused to give her up, however, and marshaled considerable resources to get her back home. The details of why she left or returned are omitted from the text. The implied distress Watson and other men reveal over their inability to control family members may suggest why so many "heroes" prefer life at the office where they are unquestionably in charge.

And about our heroines? What do their stories tell about their personal relationships? Each woman autobiographer allows her deepest love affairs exposure to public scrutiny. Gelsey Kirkland describes herself: "There were two volatile passions shifting inside of me: my love for ballet and my love for Misha [Baryshnikov].... As if to act out the death wish of nineteenth-century Romanticism, I tried to destroy myself for love" (1986: 182).

And Joan Rivers:

> We were finished, and I have never again in my life endured such pain. I had lost the one man I had wholly loved; ... lost a living piece of a precious era of my childhood, lost the object of an intense physical attraction, lost my girlish illusion that when I met the man I loved, my life from that moment would automatically be a fabulous romance forever. I was left now with an endless, desolate emptiness. (1986: 310)

Joan Baez has many passionate relationships, both with people she knew well, and with those she adored in fantasy. Upon meeting Marlon Brando, a lifelong idol, she writes, "I told him that he'd been a big part of my life, and that I often dreamed about him . . . I thanked him for everything he'd been to me . . . . I was full of love" (1987: 303).

The necessity of relating to others in a womanstory is especially crucial in Nien Cheng's narrative about her imprisonment in solitary confinement. To avoid the bitter loneliness she adopted a small spider as a friend. She describes her concern for this spider:

> My small friend seemed rather weak. It stumbled and stopped every few steps. Could a spider get sick, or was it merely cold? . . . It made a tiny web . . . forming something rather like a cocoon . . . when I had to use the toilet, I carefully sat well to one side so that I did not disturb it. (1986: 155)

These minute details, which are intended to capture the relational character of her cell life, would be highly unlikely in a male author's story.

The evidence is overwhelming that for women, relationships are focal, not only in private life, but in the work setting. Unlike the men's stories, they are not presented as ancillary to career goals. In their spheres of work, male authors refer to partners and opponents, as the relationship affects goal oriented behaviors. Relationships are rarely if ever ends in themselves, in these stories. Occasionally, as with Chuck Yeager descriptions of carousing with other pilots, there are instances of what might be today called "male bonding." Mentors, coaches, and other father figures also receive tributes in men's autobiographies. Amad Rashad, for example, emphasizes his closeness with Viking coach Bud Grant:

> Right from the start, Bud and I had a special relationship. I think he first showed interest in me because I was a little different. . . . I think Bud came to look at me as somebody he could talk to, and even a stoical football coach needs that. (1988: 231)

In women's biographies, the line between the personal relationship as an end in itself and as instrumental to a career goal is extremely fuzzy.

Beverly Sills, whose professional achievements in opera have been outstanding said, "One of the things I always loved best about being an opera singer was the chance to make new friends every time I went into a new production" (1987: 229). After finishing a television special co-starring Carol Burnett, she wrote that they had cried when the show was over: "We knew we'd have nobody to play with the next day. After that we telephoned each other three times a day" (1987: 280). Their friendship continued long after their professional interdependencies were over. For most male authors, business relationships terminate or are curtailed when the work is over.

In contrast to men writers who usually frame their competitors as opponents, or even enemies, who either have you by the "balls" or vice versa, women writers open up other options. As Martina Navratilova described it: "I've never been able to treat my opponent as the enemy, particularly Pam Shriver, my doubles partner and one of my best friends" (1985: 167). Even though competition and winning must be a critical focus for professional athletes, she casts this into a relational frame as well: "You're totally out for yourself, to win a match, yet you're dependent on your opponent to some degree for the type of match it is and how well you play. You need the opponent; without her you do not exist" (1985: 162).

Within the women's texts, the relational appears significantly in even the most unlikely places. Sydney Biddle Barrows's book emphasizes her lady-like upbringing, sensitive manners and appreciation of the finer things of life. Her sensibilities were obviously threatened when she was arrested by the police and thrown in jail. On leaving a group of street-walking prostitutes with whom she has been held, she wrote:

> As I left the cell, everybody started shouting and cheering me on. 'Go get'em, girlfren!' I left with mixed emotions. These girls had been so nice to

me, and so open and interesting, that my brief experience in jail was far more positive than I could have imagined. (1986: 284)

The evidence is overwhelming that they are focal, not only in private life, but in the work setting. The extent of descriptions of emotional responses to life events, their loves and emotional involvements are woven into the fabric of every page in a woman's autobiography. The examples used above are chosen to represent the range of emotional ties, with particular note to the syntheses of relational concerns with all of life's episodes.

Physical Embodiment Within the Autobiography

In our society, discourses are gendered, and the split between mind and body – is a binary that identifies men with thought, intellect, and reason and women with body, emotion, and intuition.

(Judith Halberstam, 1991: 439)

While all humans are equally subjected to the biological conditions of their bodies, it is not clear the extent to which bodily states and circumstances are allowed a place in men's and women's auto-biographies. In terms of suffering and sensual pleasure, some examples may give the sense of a strong dichotomy in this regard. T. Boone Pickens describes how his mother used a form of corporal punishment to teach him not to disobey.

Once breaking the rules, I went hunting with my friend Gene Jones without telling my mother. It was a blustery fall day that . . . blew up into a sleet storm. The storm forced a lot of ducks to look for cover and we were knocking them down all over the place. Gradually I became aware of a car horn in the distance. It was my mother. She said very little, just made me tie the bike onto the front of the car and told me to hold it and sit on the fender while she drove the 7 miles home – through the storm! I could hardly straighten up when we got home. My mother was a no-nonsense person. (1987: 10–11)

In this case and in others found in men's stories, the suffering of the body is not regarded as a relevant topic to include, unless some greater good – such as a moral lesson – is involved.

The sensual appetites of the body also tend to be avoided by men; exceptions to this exclusion are descriptions of drunkenness, fighting, carousing, or engaging in pranks (for instance, Yeager writes of clipping off a treetop while "buzzing" a friend's house; Rashad, of football players fighting); rarely are these physical escapades pleasant, but, in fact, most often they are dangerous, painful or injurious to the body. Allusions to their sexual lives are kept almost totally within the realm of adventure, conquest or obligation, and are never explicitly detailed or sensual. The ultimate fig leaf remains in place within popular autobiographies written by men. Two examples may illustrate this puritanical side to the male authors' self-revelations.

Lee Iacocca related a humorous story of how a book designed to inspire him to greatness has other effects. In his only precise mention of sex in his autobiography, he said of *Appointment in Samarra*: "All I could remember about the book was that it got me interested in sex" (1984: 17). What he did with that interest received no further mention in his autobiography.

Physicist Feynman, whose professional world was male-dominated, was coached by a friend in how to avoid spending money on a woman who was not going to have sex with him at the end of the evening. He described his success in using his friend's technique on a date with a colleague's sister.

> We went into the bar and before I sat down, I said, "Listen, before I buy you a drink, I want to know one thing: Will you sleep with me tonight?"
> "Yes."
> So it worked even with an ordinary girl! (1986: 172)

In another interesting vignette Feynman describes turning down a job offer that had too large a salary, explaining that if he took it he would "get a wonderful mistress, put her up in an apartment, buy her nice things," but then he would get in arguments with her. Then, "I wouldn't be able to do physics well, and it would be a *big mess!*" (1986: 214). Feynman puts into words the general view of heroes that women get in the way of work, and it is one's work that counts, after all.

John Paul Getty, who was more forthcoming than most male writers concerning his involvement with the opposite sex, described his first sexual experience,

> Another classmate and I played truant . . . for a dalliance with two willing damsels we had met the previous week at a fiercely chaperoned dance. In my classmate's words, this initiatory experience was everything it was cracked up to be – and then some. I agreed wholeheartedly. (1986: 50)

Interestingly Getty's description closely parallels the monomyth itself, with the young daring heroes overcoming patriarchal discipline by skipping school and snatching these young ladies from the clutches of fierce (dragonic) chaperones; thus, they achieve their quests. Also of note, Getty puts the words into his partner-in-crime's mouth, thus avoiding the necessity of revealing his own particular experience of sexual intercourse.

Missing from women's stories are indications that parents or other authority figures strove to teach them moral lessons by physical deprivation or abuse. In some cases they tormented themselves through dieting, wearing uncomfortable clothing, or suffering for beauty or talent's sake. For example, Beverly Sills describes her horror at her rapidly enlarging breasts in junior high: "I didn't just become miserable, I became *hysterical*. I was so unhappy with the sheer size of me that my mother bought me a garter belt, which was about seven inches wide, and I wore it around my chest" (1987: 17). Women's revelations regarding their sexual lives are in strong contrast to men's. Martina Navratilova describes her first sexual experience, which was with a young man when she was seventeen: "When we got down to it, there were no bells, no stars, no flashing lights, no colors, and not a lot of affection or skill, either. I hadn't realized how painful it could be. I kept thinking: Who needs this? It hurts too much" (1985: 124).

Joan Baez, whose many sexual adventures, love affairs, and fantasies are delineated in her autobiography, described her first (and only) lesbian affair:

> One night we kissed, ever so lightly and briefly in the privacy of our little motel cottage. All my puritanical lineage loomed up in my face, wagging a finger of disapproval. I looked into Kim's eyes. . . . When Kimmie and I did finally make love, it was superb and utterly natural. It made me wonder what all the fuss was about. (1987: 78)

Her revelation concludes:

> I had an affair with a girl when I was twenty-two. It was wonderful. It happened . . . after an overdose of unhappiness at the end of an affair with a man, when I had a need for softness and understanding. I assume that the homosexuality within me . . . made itself felt at that time, and saved me from becoming cold and bitter toward everyone. (1987: 82)

Linda Ellerbee writes about having an illegal abortion:

> I'd been one of those women, young, unmarried, who'd gotten pregnant, then gotten the name of someone through a friend of a friend, paid six hundred dollars cash, and waited, terrified, at my apartment until midnight when a pimply-faced man showed up, exchanged code words with me and came in, bringing cutting tools, bandages and Sodium Pentothol – but no medical license I could see. I was lucky. I did not bleed uncontrollably. I did not die. (1986: 96)

In general women are more detailed in their descriptions of their sexual lives, and see their sexual behaviors as more closely tied to their personal identities than men do. Sexual development, love affairs, and even experimentation with unusual sexual practices are found in women's autobiographies, in much greater detail than would ever be found in men's stories.

For men, bodies are often written about as means of locomotion and goal attainment. They are not the "real" person, nor are they integrated with the core self. Professional athletes, for example, write about the instrumentality of their bodies at length, as well as the risk of injury. Ahmad Rashad includes this analysis of injuries:

> Football players laugh about injuries because they don't want to be intimidated by them. The worse the injury, the funnier it is to your teammates as long as you're not dead. A broken rib, a shot in the head that knocks you silly, a hit that knocks the wind out of you – those are all hilarious. When a knee goes, the laughter dies. (1988: 120)

The rhetoric that Rashad uses distances the injured part from the person who has been affected. "A broken rib, a shot in the head . . . a knee that goes," all sound like parts of a property, like a flat tire on a car; it is not my knee, or his knee, but *a* knee.

As a general surmise, the essence of a man's personhood is merely housed in his body. This body is an asset when it works well, and it is a liability when it fails the person; this situation of breakdown can be very frustrating. As Watson described it: "When you have a heart attack, you realize how fragile your body is. I felt that mine had let me down, damn near entirely, and for several months I had very volatile reactions to insignificant things" (1990: 394). Watson's comments underscore the relationship of man to body as one of master to servant. Like a bad employee, or a recalcitrant family member, his body had violated his expectations, even disobeyed him, and this made him angry and difficult to live with.

In sharp contrast, women refer to their bodies as integral aspects of their identities; they refer to their bodies, characteristics and processes, using "I," "me," "my," and "mine" rather than "it," as men do.

Gelsey Kirkland, one of the prima ballerinas of the century, writes from a position that is totally identified with her body; her personal and dance-related problems become funneled through bodily issues. "I clung irrationally to the idea that my body had been the cause of all my problems. I prayed for a perfect body." When she was miserable and overwhelmed by a problem, she described wanting to solve it by physically disappearing. "I wanted to make myself into a creature without substance. I wanted to lose my identity. . . . [At night,] I was able to dream my way into somebody else's body. I was no longer Gelsey" (1986: 205).

These obsessions were often unrelenting, and she described them in vivid detail:

> There were voices that told me I was not beautiful enough . . . to deserve the attention of men. . . . With the departure of my boyfriend, Jules, I had to prove that I was still attractive to the opposite sex. . . . I went through another round of cosmetic surgery. I had my earlobes snipped off. I had silicone injected into my ankles and lips. (1986: 126)

Joan Rivers also discussed her despair at her failed career and wretched personal life:

> That winter . . . suicide became one of my options; a way to strike back at all the people who did not appreciate me, a way to make them pay attention

and be sorry. . . . I wanted to do something terrible to myself, expend my powerless rage on my body, so I went into the bathroom and with a pair of scissors crudely chopped off my hair. (1986: 249)

While suicide seems like an end to personal involvements with others, an escape from connectedness, Rivers's text suggests that suicide itself is a part of a relational strategy. Perhaps it is because of this desire to continue in relationships she retreats from the ultimate act, and substitutes mutilation by cutting off her hair, for death. Rivers is not alone in her self-destructive behaviors. A frequent theme in women's biographies suggests that if women are rejected or humiliated they leave traces of their psychological experiences on their bodies. One might interpret these actions as ways of marking the outward self, or body, to indicate one's psychological state. Perhaps for men, who require freedom to advance their own goals, to reveal one's inward states would be a dangerous and foolish strategy that would minimize their options. To have one's physical state revealed is like exposing the cards in one's hand; the more information others have about you the more power they have as well.

Men's stories tend to neglect facts about the body that do not fit into the storyline. In some cases they discuss health concerns that have been assiduously avoided throughout the main body of the story. Tying up the loose ends, the hero confesses to a few seemingly "miscellaneous" bodily events that were possibly very traumatic and central at the time of their occurrence, but irrelevant to the storyline that is focused on career achievements. A good example of this delayed telling form is Ansel Adams's last chapter concerning his chronic and increasingly disabling physical problems: "As I cleared the decks for future projects, I found an ever-present complicating factor: Health. My mind is as active as ever, but my body was falling farther and farther behind" (1985: 365). (The reader may note that the "real" Adams is the mental form, and the body is a recalcitrant fellow-traveller who is lagging behind.) Adams described his heart surgery (a triple bypass and valve replacement): "Without surgery I was fast reaching an embarrassing state of inactivity; I could not walk a hundred feet without the crippling symptoms of chest pains and shortness of breath" (1985: 366). Adams's physical limitations had been increasingly stringent over many decades, but they are not mentioned at all in the earlier parts of his book. It is also interesting to note that Adams expresses a sense of shame at his infirmities, in part, perhaps, because they call attention to him, as an embodied self who has aged and become infirm.

The autobiographies of women tend to expose physical ailments in great detail as they arise. Nien Cheng's volume is replete with the physical consequences of her imprisonment. Beverly Sills discusses the struggle she has had with ovarian cancer, and her need to keep singing to prove she was still alive. Martina Navratilova and Gelsey Kirkland focus considerable attention on their ill health, and its consequences for their lives.

Consequences of Gendered Narrative Forms

Individuals construct themselves as subjects through language, but individual subjects – rather than being the source of their own self-generated and self-expressive meaning – adopt positions available within the language at a given moment.

Felicity Nussbaum (1988: 149)

In contemporary American popular literature, the narrative of the traditional hero is perpetuated within autobiographical texts. In addition, we have suggested the presence of an alternative form in which the once unworthy female tells her lifestory. Her story is one that embroiders heavily on the plain, linear line of the monomyth. Rather than concentrating solely on great achievements in a work sphere, she integrates into the storyline aspects of a rich interpersonal life as well. The man who writes describes himself in idealized, abstract and rational terms, as an entity in an arena of argument and force. He avoids his relational life, except for minor hints that he is an acceptable version of the "macho" man, who has aggressive impulses, the courage to do battle, and occasionally have "fun" (perhaps by making conquests of women).

The woman who writes incorporates her physical side, divulging her emotional, sensual and sexual experiences. She writes in terms of concrete events and objects, including herself as an embodied creature within her story, self-reflexively. This is in contrast to male authors who rarely "see" themselves as actors within a scene, but who look out from within at the unfolding scene. The form of a woman's writing is a pastiche, a confusing melange of heroic enterprises and tales of relatedness. Her tone is often ambiguous, rather than clear, as the male voice is. She is uncertain, self-reflexive, and aware of the difficulties in any choice she might make. This heroine tells a story oscillating between togetherness and separateness, desires of others and for oneself. In the end, her narrative form allows her to reflect on how well she has satisfied those whom she loves. Nien Cheng's book ends with sadness:

I felt guilty for being the one who was alive. I wished it were Meiping [her daughter who was killed in the Cultural Revolution] . . . going away to make a new life for herself. . . . Also I felt sad because I was leaving forever the country of my birth. . . . God knows how hard I tried to remain true to my country. But I failed utterly through no fault of my own. (1986: 535)

In the most satisfying stories women authors describe their successful relationships with others. Joan Rivers, for example, ends her book with an epilogue that states the dates of her marriage, her daughter's birth, and the month she "was named the first and only permanent guest host of *The Tonight Show Starring Johnny Carson*." Women authors often express a greater willingness to end their careers, to return to simpler pleasures and a quiet life. The pleasures and powers of fame and fortune and the need to maintain their highest level of accomplishment and control are not as compelling to them as to men.

For men, satisfaction depends upon the evaluation of the public world, and the knowledge that they have done their best and been respected; but, in addition, most still strive to keep a place in it. Trump, for example, ended by writing of his future, "I plan to make deals, big deals, and right around the clock" (1987: 367).

The naturalness with which these two sex-coded narrative forms pass without our awareness suggests that our expectations as a culture as to how great and famous people should live are also segregated by gender regulations. While famous high achievers, both men and women, are recognized for their exceptional abilities, men's standards are in different domains, their rewards are different and their conduct is regulated more stringently toward career goals. Women, regardless of how exalted their status in the public sphere, are expected to fulfill their dual roles of outstanding performers in their careers, as well as "relational caretakers." In these roles, they must constantly strive to satisfy both requirements, but they may also gain some freedom to resist expectations in either realm.

Autobiography and Everyday Life

> In altering the images and narrative structures through which we compose the stories of our lives, we may hope to alter the very experiences of those lives as well.
> Annette Kolodny (1980: 258)

Autobiographies give ordinary people templates for how successful lives are to be led. They give people a chance to compare themselves with those they admire. Men striving to excel are often the most avid readers of the success stories of the rich and famous, particularly men whom they wish to emulate. The chance of reaching the level of these heroes is minuscule, of course, and even when one does succeed in this hierarchical situation, the promise of staying at the top is not assured. Donald Trump, for example, may be bankrupt before this book is published. Certainly he is not the idol of the bankers today he was when his first book appeared. One might presume that considering the odds, and looking at the fragility of fame and fortune, as well as the costs in terms of personal relations, men might reject the template of the famous few. However, the brass ring of success seems to lure many despite the liabilities of pursuing this form of success.

Women, too, absorb a formulation of life from autobiographies. From men's stories they acquire another source of information that men's lives are dedicated to their career pursuits. A familiar message in the culture, it reifies what is obvious in other media and film sources. Women's autobiographies highlight for them the potential for intertwining relational goals on the one hand and personal goals of achievement on the other. Writ large there are the struggles that women have in daily life to meet often conflicting and ambiguous goals for enhancing the lives of others and for self-fulfillment.

While these forms seem to set men and women irrevocably apart, is this a matter of concern? What are the consequences in accepting the gendered narrative lines laid out for each group within the culture? For men, the cost may be in terms of psychological and physical disabilities. In terms of relationships, a career-driven man may follow a pattern that requires the sacrifice of family ties for professional gain. When he has achieved his goals, he may find that he has alienated those he assumed would be waiting for him. In addition, a lifetime of neglect of one's body can also have harmful effects. The goal-orientations that lead men to ignore signs of ill health can result in greater harm to the body than if the symptoms had been attended to earlier. Women's awareness of their bodies allows them to correct problems at an earlier stage. The great difference in life-spans between men and women might be seen as a consequence of differences in men's and women's personal narratives. Another implication for men of the heroic story line is that once life goals are achieved, there is nothing in life particularly interesting to live for. Thus, men die when their story ends.[2]

For women, following the narrative form means always having to maintain relational lives – the duties and commitments of having families and friendships despite heavy career demands. It also suggests that the highly talented and ambitious woman who wants to succeed in the "man's world" must adhere to their standards of career involvement, if she is to gain their approval. Most women find it problematic to reject a relational life, and in addition often regard the requirements of men's lives too narrow, restricting and unsatisfying, especially because of the single-minded focus on career goals. Yet to fail in this commitment is regarded by those in authority as a sign of weakness and failure to measure up. For women to achieve, a multitude of standards must be met.

Finally, one might consider the advantages to modifying or abandoning traditional narratives, and instead creating alternatives. These alternatives might prove to be liberating for both men and women, who might be able to de-genderize their choices to some extent, and find the proper balance for their own immediate situations. Perhaps certain work and family goals could be appropriate for one time of life, and others at other times, for both men and women. The integration of women's practices of blending personal and professional agendas into the work setting, as well as in personal life might be advantageous to men, as well; this synthesis of narrative forms might also help to lessen envy and defensiveness on both sides of the gender gap.

Many factors influence the tides of social life in a large and multifaceted country, such as ours. Narrative form within the genre of the popular autobiography coexists with many other artistic and literary forms that influence the ways in which people understand and communicate about their lives. This is an exercise in a possibility; it is not the last word.

Notes

1. It is commonplace for famous people to create their autobiographies with the assistance of a co-author, who is a professional writer. This is the case with the majority of the autobiographies included in this sample, as well as popular autobiographies in general. While it may seem that my interpretations are weakened by this pattern of authorship, further reflection suggests that the story forms for the autobiography of famous people are part of the cultural repertoire of stories, and thus, to a great extent, it does not matter who, precisely, is forming the telling. What becomes quite fascinating in this regard is that when professional writers are working with men they contribute to a story form suitable to the male subject, and when they work with women they use an entirely different approach. This cross-over became particularly clear to me when I analyzed the biographies of Lee Iacocca and Sydney Biddle Barrows, the "Mayflower Madam," which were both co-authored by William Novak. In similar fashion, Diedre Bair, prizewinning biographer of Samuel Beckett and Simone de Beauvoir, has made a self-reflexive statement of the tendency for biographers to tell two different stories, male and female. "I felt that it was important to discuss a woman's emotional life and a woman's physical life in a biography . . . every biography about a man . . . totally neglects the emotional life, and by this I mean both the relationships and the details" – her own works were included in this criticism. (Walton, *Philadelphia Inquirer*, September 9, 1990: 33).

2. This notion is supported by Ted Turner, *Time* Magazines's Man of the Year, who stated that his father's suicide in middle age was the result of his having achieved all of his life's goals; Turner plans to avoid this fate by taking on goals that outlive him, those that concern the fate of the planet (*Time*, January 6, 1992: 39).

Primary Autobiographical References

Adams, Ansel with Mary Street Alinder (1985) *Ansel Adams: An Autobiography*. Boston, MA: Little Brown.
Baez, Joan (1987) *And a Voice to Sing with: A Memoir*. New York: New American Library. Plume book.

Barrows, Sydney Biddle with William Novak (1986) *Mayflower Madam*. New York: Arbor House; London: MacDonald.

Cheng, Nien (1986) *Life and Death in Shanghai*. New York: Penguin.

Ellerbee, Linda (1986) *And so it Goes: Adventures in Television*. New York: Berkley Books.

Feynman, Richard P. (1986) *"Surely you're joking, Mr. Feynman!"*. New York: Bantam Books. (Originally published in 1985.)

Getty, J. Paul (1986) *As I See it: An Autobiography of J. Paul Getty*. New York: Berkley. (Originally published in 1976.)

Iacocca, Lee with William Novak (1984) *Iacocca: An Autobiography*. New York: Bantam Books.

Kirkland, Gelsey with Greg Lawrence (1986) *Dancing on my Grave*. New York: Doubleday.

Koch, Edward I. with William Rauch (1984) *Mayor*. New York: Warner.

Navratilova, Martina with George Vecsey (1985) *Martina*. New York: Fawcett Crest.

Pickens, Jr, T. Boone (1987) *Boone*. Boston, MA: Houghton Mifflin.

Rashad, Ahmad with Peter Bodo (1988) *Rashad*. New York: Penguin.

Rivers, Joan with Richard Meryman (1986) *Enter Talking*. New York: Delacorte Press.

Sills, Beverly and Lawrence Linderman (1987) *Beverly*. New York: Bantam Books.

Trump, Donald with Tony Schwartz (1987) *Trump: The Art of the Deal*. Warner Books.

Watson, Jr, Thomas (1990) *Father, Son and Company*. New York: Bantam.

Yeager, General Chuck and Leo James (1985) *Yeager: An Autobiography*. New York: Bantam Books.

References

Bruner, Jerome (1986) *Actual Minds, Possible Worlds*. Cambridge, MA: Harvard University Press.

Bruss, Elizabeth W. (1980) Eye for I: making and unmaking autobiography in film, in J. Olney (ed.), *Autobiography: Essays, Theoretical and Critical*. Princeton, NJ: Princeton University Press.

Campbell, Joseph (1956) *Hero with a Thousand Faces*. New York: Bollingen. (First published 1949.)

Clifford, James (1986) Introduction: partial truths, in J. Clifford and G. Marcus (eds), *Writing Culture*. Berkeley, CA: University of California Press.

Day, James M. (1992) The moral audience: on the narrative mediation of moral "judgment" and moral "action," in M. Tappan and M. Packer (eds), *Narrative and Storytelling: Implications for Understanding Moral Development*. San Francisco, CA: Jossey-Bass.

de Man, Paul (1979) Autobiography as de-facement, *Modern Language Notes*, 94: 920.

Eakin, Paul John (1985) *Fictions in Autobiography. Studies in the Art of Self-Invention*. Princeton, NJ: Princeton University Press.

Erikson, Erik (1975) *Life History and the Historical Moment*. New York: W.W. Norton.

Gergen, Kenneth J. (1985). The social constructionist movement in modern psychology, *American Psychologist* 40: 266–75.

Gergen, Kenneth J. (in press) *Construction, Critique, and Community*. Cambridge, MA: Harvard University Press.

Gergen, Kenneth J. and Gergen, Mary M. (1983) Narrative of the self, in T. Sarbin and K. Scheibe (eds), *Studies in Social Identity*. New York: Praeger.

Gergen, Kenneth J. and Gergen, Mary M. (1986) Narrative form and the construction of psychological science, in T. Sarbin (ed.), *Narrative Psychology: The Storied Nature of Human Conduct*. New York: Praeger.

Gergen, Kenneth J. and Gergen, Mary M. (1988) Narrative and the self as relationship, in L. Berkowitz (ed.), *Advances in Experimental Social Psychology, Vol. 21*. San Diego, CA: Academic Press.

Gergen, Mary M. (1992) Survey: impact of childhood fairy tales on adult lives. Penn State University, unpublished manuscript.

Gergen, Mary M. (in press) Life stories: pieces of a dream, in G. Rosenwald and R. Ochberg (eds), *Telling Lives*. New Haven, CT: Yale University Press.

Halberstam, Judith (1991) Automating gender: postmodern feminism in the age of the intelligent machine, *Feminist Studies*, 17: 439–60.

Harvey, John, Orbuch, T.L., and Weber, Ann L. (eds) (1992) *Attribution, Accounts and Close Relationships*. New York: Springer-Verlag.

Hyde, Louis (1979) *The Gift: Imagination and the Erotic Life of Property*. New York: Random House Vintage Books.

Janet, Pierre (1928) *L'évolution de la Mémoire et la Notion du Temps*. Paris: L. Alcan.

Jelinek, Estelle C. (1980) *Women's Autobiography: Essays in Criticism*. Bloomington, IN: Indiana University Press.

Kolodny, Annette (1980) The lady's not for spurning: Kate Millett and the critics, in E. Jelinek (ed.), *Women's Autobiography: Essays in Criticism*. Bloomington, IN: Indiana University Press.

McAdams, Dan P. (1985) *Power, Intimacy, and the Life Story: Personalogical Inquiries into Identity*. New York: Guilford Press.

McCloskey, Donald (1990) *If You're so Smart: The Narrative of Economic Expertise*. Chicago, IL: University of Chicago Press.

MacIntyre, Alasdair (1981). *After Virtue*. Notre Dame, IN: Notre Dame Press.

Mason, Mary G. (1980) Autobiographies of women writers, in J. Olney (ed.), *Autobiography: Essays, Theoretical and Critical*. Princeton, NJ: Princeton University Press.

Mishler, Elliot G. (1986) *Research Interviewing: Context and Narrative*. Cambridge, MA: Harvard University Press.

Nussbaum, Felicity (1988) Eighteenth century women's autobiographical commonplaces, in S. Benstock (ed.), *The Private Self*. London: Routledge.

Olney, James (1980) *Autobiography: Essays, Theoretical and Critical*. Princeton, NJ: Princeton University Press.

Quinn, Robert E., Spreitzer, Gretchen M., and Fletcher, Jerry (1991) The hero in the hierarchy: an analysis of managerial performance myths. Unpublished manuscript. School of Business Administration, University of Michigan.

Roth, Philip (1988) *The Facts: a Novelist's Autobiography*. New York: Farrar, Straus and Giroux.

Runyan, W. McKinley (1982) *Life Histories and Psychobiography: Explorations in Theory and Method*. New York: Oxford University Press.

Sampson, Edward E. (1989) The challenge of social change for psychology: globalization and psychology's theory of the person, *American Psychologist*, 44: 914–21.

Sarbin, Theodore (ed.) (1986) *Narrative Psychology: The Storied Nature of Human Conduct*. New York: Praeger.

Sarbin, Theodore and Scheibe, Karl (eds) (1983) *Studies in Social Identity*. New York: Praeger.

Scholes, Robert and Kellogg, Robert (1966) *The Nature of Narrative*. London: Oxford University Press.

Simons, Herbert W. (1989) *Rhetoric in the Human Sciences*. London: Sage.

Sprinker, Michael (1980) Fictions of the self: the end of autobiography, in J. Olney (ed.), *Autobiography: Essays, Theoretical and Critical*. Princeton, NJ: Princeton University Press.

Stone, Albert E. (1982) *Autobiographical Occasions and Original Acts: Versions of American Identity from Henry Adams to Nate Shaw*. Philadelphia, PA: University of Pennsylvania Press.

Tappan, Mark B. and Packer, Martin J. (eds) (1991) *Narrative and Storytelling: Implications for Understanding Moral Development*. San Francisco, CA: Jossey-Bass.

White, Hayden (1978) *The Tropics of Discourse*. Baltimore, PA: Johns Hopkins University Press.

3

The Social Construction of Pregnancy and Fetal Development: Notes on a Nineteenth-Century Rhetoric of Endangerment

Carol Brooks Gardner

SPILLED STRAWBERRIES An acquaintance, while riding out, saw some strawberries spilled by the side of the road, which she wanted very much; but her sister, who was driving, only laughed at her entreaties to stop, and [at her] apprehensions that the child might be marked, and drove on. The child was marked on the back of its neck, with a cluster of red spots, in shape resembling spilled strawberries.

O.S. Fowler, *Sexual Science* (1870)

The original insights of the social constructionism of Spector and Kitsuse (1977) have been supplemented by suggestions that those conditions deemed social problems can be further analyzed as moral discourses employing different types of rhetorics. The use of discourse and its associated vocabulary to describe the argumentation of social problems has thus far been mainly confined to present-day or to quite recent social problems (Ibarra and Kitsuse, 1990, 1991). However, this means of analysis can also be applied to earlier social problems; perhaps analysts eventually can link past and present patterns of discourse with regard to specific social conditions.[1]

Using literary sources mainly from advice manual and medical writing genres, I demonstrate that, in nineteenth-century America, the physical state and the social situation of pregnancy was used to explain physical and mental traits considered undesirable in children. Now we would often label these traits disabilities; yet among such traits were also flaws of character and temperament and minor physical events like birthmarks, the shape of head or hands, or personal attractiveness, signifying the many requirements that a "perfect" child was expected to have. Ibarra and Kitsuse (1990, 1991) use the term *condition-category* to refer to what claimsmakers perceive a social problem is "about." The condition-category of interest here was benign or endangering behavior during pregnancy.

Different articulations of the rhetoric of fetal endangerment portrayed different possibilities or different relevant actors in this condition-category. Newly professionalized physicians and writers of popular advice books claimed that women's problematic, often "unwomanly" conduct endangered a fetus; champions of women's rights and the marginal medical men with whom they were often allied (Rosenberg, 1976) saw men's abuse of women as at fault. I suggest that claimsmaking possibilities for both groups were characterized by a rhetoric of endangerment of fetal development, though each group featured a different articulation of that rhetoric: in the first case, the rhetoric of fetal endangerment was articulated to foreground the errors of the pregnant woman's ways that had marked her unborn child and also accentuated the harm rather than the good one might do to the fetus; in the second case, the rhetoric of fetal endangerment was articulated to emphasize the man's treatment of his pregnant wife as responsible for fetal problems and also emphasized the good that both parents might do the child. Always at risk in this moral discourse was the malleable embryo or fetus within the body of a pregnant woman; it was most often her emotional state, eating habits, thoughts, and activities that directly endangered the embryo or fetus, soon to be the child. In addition, both articulations affirm the idea that pregnancy can be managed and directed interactionally (in contrast, for example, to a genetics-dependent idea that pregnancy outcomes are largely foreordained by chromosomal makeup). In this, they elevate face-to-face interaction to a potent force that itself creates future interactants – and indeed creates the interactants it deserves. Women are the key interactants in this creative process. Thus, though each articulation represents antithetical conceptions of women's nature and needs, the similarity of the articulations is cemented by the fact that they both ultimately argued women were responsible for the children they produced.

Having problematized certain physical and mental traits or conditions apparent in children, claimsmakers used this rhetoric to evaluate and judge both prospective parents and unborn child. Through the exercise of this rhetoric, a parent's thoughts, feelings, and actions were deemed acceptable or unacceptable because of their alleged effect on the fetus. In addition, the rhetorical idiom implicitly judged a child's physical and mental disability, as well as a child's undesirable personality traits and physical appearance. This rhetoric of fetal endangerment therefore participated in the expansion and refinement of distinctions between disabilities and in the medicalization of disabilities that occurred in the nineteenth century (Haj, 1970; Blaxter, 1976; Liachowitz, 1988). The "successful" outcome of a pregnancy was not merely a live birth. Rather, all women were presumed capable of conceiving and delivering a "perfect" child;

therefore, children with shortcomings, large or small, could be read as evidence of moral failure during pregnancy.[2]

Rhetorics of endangerment characterize moral discourses associated with particular types of social problems. These rhetorics can be easily applied to perceived problems "that can be expressed as threats to the health and safety of the human body" (Ibarra and Kitsuse, 1991: 13). Thus, rhetorics of endangerment presume that individuals have a right to good health and safety; that the less endangered have a duty to protect the more vulnerable; that good health and safety are reasonable grounds on which to evaluate individuals; and that ill health and mental disability are at one extreme of a continuum that features small "marks" and "flaws" at the midpoint of the continuum and an apparently attainable bodily and mental perfection at the opposite extreme; and that all causal dangers can in fact be avoided by human effort and perfection thus attained. Rhetorics of endangerment are often distinguished because they target the effect of a condition or practice on others (and not the immorality of the condition or practice itself); but this is not quite so in the case of the prospective parents condemned in the nineteenth-century literature. Rather, there is a sense that (for example) the pregnant woman who disliked her husband and consequently bore a retarded child has been condemned for a feeling she should not have had in the first place. Thus, among other functions, this rhetoric of endangerment reinforced and elaborated nineteenth-century gender norms.

Moral discourse associated with the rhetoric of endangerment ergo crystalized beliefs about what constituted an undesirable disability and also formulated judgments about and enabled evaluation of physical attractiveness and personality. The literature of the day was a setting in which writers elaborated a moral discourse. Popular and scientific books, pamphlets, and articles appeared, with titles like "The wife's handbook: how a woman should order herself during pregnancy," *The Science of a New Life, Prenatal Culture,* and *The Radical Remedy in Social Science; Or, Borning Better Babies.*[3] In nineteenth-century America, the woman's conduct and feelings were labeled direct agents for the future child's physical well-being and mental stability, and this was extended to men's treatment of pregnant women by the end of the century. The clearest set of messages was that most directly relevant to acceptable gender behaviors for wives and husbands, and it is on this topic that I will concentrate.

Before characterizing the features of these two articulations of the rhetoric of fetal endangerment, I will discuss the sample of literary works I used, together with some of their possible advantages and drawbacks.

Methods

I used a sample of 52 primary sources from the nineteenth century which come principally from two genres: writing directed to and read mainly by women, including popular manuals concerning the role of the sexes in marriage, manuals concerning women's health, and writings by precursors of the First Wave of the women's movement; and writings directed to and read mainly by physicians, including journal articles, reprints of courses of lectures, and texts by both orthodox physicians and by medical "irregulars" – such as phrenologists and specialists in the use of electromagnetism – on the topic of pregnancy.

Of course, it is impossible to know if these works ever stimulated feelings or behavior in the individuals to whom they were directed – or, indeed, if they were ever read at all by the upper-middle-class white readership for whom they were intended (Aresty, 1970). Yet there are reasons for using these sources. First, they are the sole extant records of individuals' beliefs about pregnancy we have for this period in any number at all; and the medical literature – as well as the advice and women's rights literature – is available at specialized libraries. Many health and marriage manuals in particular were part of a burgeoning women's literature that included other genres – religious books, women's novels, women's "journals;" this literature elaborated upper-class white women's norms, emphasizing domesticity, fidelity, sub-missiveness to male authorities, and piety as virtues. Second, the written works for women may be one of the few ways these beliefs about pregnancy were recorded. As a keynote of the new "language of repression" for women, talk of pregnancy was forbidden even between mother and daughter, if either hoped to claim breeding and gentility (Gordon and Buhle, 1976). Thus, advice manuals and women's rights books may be more faithful records than oral interviews of the time would be.

Selfish Cravings and Dangerous Fears: One Articulation of the Rhetoric of Fetal Endangerment

I have discussed some general features of rhetorics of endangerment. In particular, the nineteenth-century rhetoric of endangerment in regard to pregnancy typically featured motifs of magnified effects and of disease. Endangerment often resulted from relatively small events in a parent's conduct subsequently writ large in fetal effects, and the fetus would grow to be a child in a nation "plagued" or "diseased" with others of its kind. This rhetoric also co-occurred with a highly melodramatic claimsmaking style (Ibarra and Kitsuse, 1991). It is the melodrama of this written claimsmaking style that has particularly changed during the ensuing decades.

This rhetoric of endangerment necessarily implied a good deal of control on the individual's part; simply, it was thought that the impression of events outside a woman's body or within her mind "marked" or "impressed" a fetus with physical or emotional harm. Thus, a pregnant woman might be told in an advice book of the nineteenth century to love and obey her husband, lest her child be born suffering from such diverse "maternal impressions" as mental retardation and character flaws; or a man with a pregnant wife might be advised in a tract on women's rights to treat her well, lest the child born be marked with some permanent evidence of his depravity such as stunted physical growth betokening the father's stunted moral development. This rhetoric lent itself to vivid cautionary tales of women who behaved inappropriately while pregnant or experienced inappropriate emotions and subsequently had children who were symbolically marked as reminders of unmet gender expectations. Claimsmakers carrying tales of this kind – appearing even in the medical journals and texts of the day – could suggest powerful negative sanctions for prospective parents, as well as for the male medical professionals who served them.

The price of disagreeing with this moral idiom would have been high. One would have to take a position against aiding the most helpless of children, those yet to be born. One would have to argue with the wisdom of thinking of the future good of the nation and indeed the world. One would have to stand up for one's right to put the satisfaction of what are often petty wants and desires against the physical and mental health of a child. Finally, one would have to do all this while knowingly contradicting those "expert" enough to write volumes relating the subtlety of the damage that could be done.

The adoption of a rhetoric of fetal endangerment, no matter how articulated, was facilitated and supported by folk beliefs and biological "knowledge" about women and pregnancy. In the nineteenth century pregnant women were believed to be capable of virtually any extremes. Pregnancy might cause women to become ecstatic or depressed, to steal or commit other crimes, to go insane, to become suddenly skilled at tasks they previously could not perform (Walker, 1839; Velpeau, 1852). As in ancient beliefs about hysteria, the womb was often held responsible for this astounding range of possibilities (Meigs, 1854: 18–20; and see Smith-Rosenberg and Rosenberg, 1973 and Smith-Rosenberg, 1985). Some physicians wrote of the pettishness of the pregnant uterus and the entire nervous system of the pregnant woman; others wrote of the "nervous excitability" and "hysterical symptoms" of pregnancy (Trousseau, 1868–1872: 365) or of the large nerves near women's reproductive organs as culprits for a pregnant woman's moods and behavior ("A Physician," 1874: 279).

Causes of Marking

Writers mentioned explicitly three principal causes as agents of harm to a fetus: first, imprudent or unnatural sexual intercourse or intercourse ("venery") that broke gender norms or expressed disregard for family relations; second, a "fright," that is, fear or surprise at seeing an unexpected (and presumably threatening) creature or person; and, third, a "craving," a desire either to consume food or drink or to commit an act that threatened to break family gender norms. Together, the imputed causes suggested that, were a woman to try and conscientiously take every instance of potential marking into account while pregnant, she would need to consider the impact of virtually every thought and deed. In effect, women were enjoined to have pregnancies that would leave them sequestered at home and robbed of many everyday pleasures.

Sexual Intercourse
Sexual intercourse – improperly practiced or too enthusiastically enjoyed – was a prime cause of marked children. Marking could result from improper behavior in either parent; and improper behavior might be: forcing a woman to have sex; masturbation; libertine life-style; intercourse during pregnancy; or intercourse for recreational, rather than procreational, purposes. When a couple engaged in "excessive coition" during the wife's pregnancy, they exerted a "profound influence upon the child" ("A Physician," 1874: 167). Resulting children might be idiotic, "deformed," "monstrosities," or of lascivious character.

Frights
However, the most common cause of marking, disability, or flaws of character were said to be frights or cravings during pregnancy. Telling anecdotes of frights and cravings were more melodramatically elaborated than were tales of "excessive venery" or "bestial intercourse" that were also believed to mark a child. Such an anecdote would contain a description of the child's deformity, often rendered in clinical detail that managed to suggest the supposed agent of the mark; next followed the mother's explanation of the crucial experience during pregnancy – rendered as a "fright" or "craving" – that might account for such a mark. These explanations were considered all the more convincing if given before a mother had seen her marked child, of course:

A woman gave birth to a child with a large cluster of globular tumors growing from the tongue, and preventing the closure of the mouth, in color, shape and size exactly resembling our common grapes; and with a red excrescence from the chest exactly resembling in figure and appearance a turkey's wattles. On being questioned before the child was shown to her, she answered that, while pregnant, she had seen some grapes, longed intensely for them, and constantly thought of them; and that she was also once attacked and much alarmed by a turkey cock. (Hammond, 1868: 7–8)

While a husband's imprudence was sometimes at fault when sex was the cause of marking, it was the pregnant woman's imprudence – in leaving the home and ergo being frightened, or in allowing her mind to dwell on some desired food – that led to virtually all cases of marking by frights and cravings in this articulation.

Sometimes it was noted that "emotion" was the marking agent in frights by animals; and in these cases writers sometimes pointed out that the woman was also indulging herself by leaving the home where she belonged to go on a frivolous errand, to a store, or "to a dance or ball." Some writers included every slight sign of indifference to married life as a "fear" that was injurious to a fetus. Even if a wife simply did not feel confident in her family life – if, for example, she disliked her mother-in-law – the results of these inappropriate emotions could be visited on the fetus (Newton, 1890: 9–11). Again, the woman's selfishness or weakness could injure an unborn child; the cause was her susceptibility to emotional "flooding out" at trivial events.

The substance of the writing on frights amounted to counseling a woman to adopt an agoraphobia of pregnancy. Advice manual and medical authors often prohibited the pregnant woman from venturing outside her house, since it was always possible that there she would see a fearsome creature like a dog, wolf, or "deformed" stranger. If she did, her child would surely be marked. Tales of women who foolishly went outside or, more foolishly still, worked outside the home or traveled were provided as cautions. This general proscription against going out of the house can be seen as a reinforcement of one characteristic of the growing "cult of true womanhood," namely, that a wife was to remain at home and cultivate her skills of decorative activity with relation to it (Gordon and Buhle, 1976).

Cravings

Cravings were also commonly featured within the rhetoric of endangerment as signals of selfishness on a woman's part: if a woman was to manage to protect the child within her, she must avoid losing control to such desires. Opinion varied as to whether a woman's food cravings should be satisfied or ignored: in general, the later nineteenth-century authors, especially physicians, claimed cravings were signs of a "diseased organism" and should be ignored lest a fetus be marked.

Feminist writers were exceptions, as when they mentioned a woman's altogether understandable "craving for freedom," which must be satisfied (Pendleton 1843, 1856; Hunt 1856; Lewis 1874).

Other writers besides feminists noted women's cravings for more than food, though they typically counseled a woman to avoid or refuse to indulge these cravings. A woman could be disappointed by her marriage or unimpressed by her husband or his occupation. She might long for more money, "better things," a different husband, or extramarital sex. Rather than attend to satisfying these cravings, women were reminded to spend their pregnant days in contentment with their husbands, and at home.

Physicians especially excoriated women who, they said, exploited cravings in order to secure some frivolous or luxurious item. One doctor wrote that the "indiscriminate" consumption of food could lead to abortion (Eberle, 1844: 4–5), and gave the case history of a foolish wife who imaginatively combined plum pie with "strong cheese" and therefore perished along with her unborn child (Eberle, 1844: 5–6). Others wrote of women who exploited their husbands far more. These women said they longed for – not just a fancy dessert – but an expensive clock, drawing lessons, or a horse and carriage. Such an opportunistic wife sent "her husband on a wild-goose chase to ease [her mind]", yet her craving "made the most baneful impressions on the physical, mental, and moral organization of the tender germ committed to [her] care" (Whitfield, 1862: 602).

In particular, physicians' cautionary tales of cravings often had something of the character of modern supermarket tabloid stories. Doctors also extended "craving" to "craving for excitement" and inferred disgust with husband and home. In a treatise on mental retardation, for example, a physician wrote of a woman who did not care whether she married or not and, once she became pregnant, "felt a strong antipathy for her husband [and] looked for all sorts of excitement, even of the most ferocious and brutal character; and would stare for hours at scenes once perfectly repulsive to her educated and normal tastes" (Seguin, 1865: 297). A child was born who was

> large, fleshy, healthy; but whose condition was exceptional, to say the least of it. At eleven . . . she had already menstruated. . . . Morally she is ready to be led astray by anyone, anywhere, without any idea of right or wrong, but by a natural propensity. . . . Mentally, she is extremely simple. (Seguin, 1865: 297–8)

By expanding the construction of craving to include a "craving" for other excitement outside of a wholesome family life, writers warned women against the mildest disloyalty or exploitation.

"Studying" for Pregnancy: An Expanded Timeline

One feature of the marking process was that a trivial transgression by a parent occasioned a large-scale event for a fetus. This hyperbole is one of this rhetorical idiom's salient traits, reaching an impressive elaboration by the last quarter of the century. Furthermore, claims-makers invoked an expanded retrospective timeline, sometimes cautioning prospective mothers to monitor their behavior for years in advance of actually becoming pregnant.

In addition, rhetoricians harked back to alternatively innocent or brutal times past (when, for example, pregnancy was either carefree or ended regularly in death), or warned of a flawed future for which the individual was directly responsible (when, for example, prospective parents were reminded of crowded cities peopled with the "dwarfish" results of irresponsible gestation, or simply reminded of a general lack of social "progress"). Though rustics of the past believed in innate depravity, progressive nineteenth-century Americans must understand that "children are made by their parents, not sent, with all their imperfections on their head, from heaven" (Evans, 1875: 83). Parents, especially mothers, should cease to hinder "the progress of the human race in so many ways" (Evans, 1875: 83). They were to devote themselves to preparing for the future – in fact, to devote themselves to preparing children who were themselves capable of preparing for the future (Evans, 1875: 108).

For women, an expanded timeline and melodramatic style would result, if put into practice, in pregnancy careers that could reach beyond the actual nine months of gestation. Indeed, nineteenth-century writers who articulated the rhetoric of endangerment to contain the potential for improvement sometimes suggested periods of two or three years of "preparation" and "study" for parents. Some wrote of a child marked by an event that happened before the actual pregnancy, but on which (for example) a woman unhealthily continued to "dwell" while pregnant. The best proofs of the significance of a woman's conduct before pregnancy were the children said to result from minor emotional turmoil and misbehavior: they remained, with such traits indelibly imprinted, to haunt their unhappy parents for a lifetime.

Claimsmakers did not always invoke effects that came so far after their putative causes. Particularly immoral activity by a woman could have speedy, symbolically fitting, and long-lasting reprisals, as might drinking alcohol. Thus, a fetus might "*also inherit the fatal tendency and feel a craving for the very beverages which have acted as poisons on their system from the commencement of their being*" (Lewis, 1874: 156; emphasis in the original). Even a woman who had ceased drinking could continue to give birth to feeble and sickly children, since her uterus might be permanently impressed with the effects of alcohol and her mind permanently impressed with immorality.

In contrast to orthodox physicians' and health advice book authors' articulation of women's guilt in marking, the rhetoric of fetal endangerment was rearticulated by feminists and marginal medical practitioners. Unlike the first articulation, feminists and medical "irregulars" dwelt on the good, not harm, that a pregnant woman could do her child; significantly, they drew the husband into the cast of characters, often as the true villain of the piece. Both articulations presumed that character and form could be shaped by parents during pregnancy.

Rearticulating the Rhetoric of Endangerment: Women's Freedom, Men's Abuse, and Parents' Powers

Writers on women's rights and medical irregulars, especially those who wrote in the last decades of the century, countered earlier character-izations of women as active, corrupt, and selfish agents of fetal harm by rearticulating the rhetoric of fetal endangerment to include the father's effect on his pregnant wife and to delineate the good that both mother and father might do. An early "philosopher of generation" wrote of the influence of both parents on the unborn child: "If we would have moral, healthy, intellectual, and good-humored children, it is in our power to effect; by putting ourselves in a proper state at the time of their conception . . . we can insure their being all we require" (Newman, 1849: 3). Similarly, feminists of the late nineteenth century, as well as "medical irregulars" like phrenologists and electromagnetic physi-cians, claimed that pregnant mothers might do their fetuses as much good as they had been accused of doing harm. In addition, they emphasized that husbands were obliged to control their conduct toward pregnant wives, invoking parental (not so much spousal) responsibility. Thus, appeals to a pregnant woman's sensitivity sometimes incidentally protected women themselves, along with their fetuses. Note that anyone who disagreed with this rearticulated rhetoric would be in the difficult position of defending men's right to enslave women and harm children.

Positive Impressions

"Positive markings" were valued qualities that prospective parents attempted to give unborn offspring. Writers had found more and more reason to argue with the articulation of the rhetoric of fetal en-dangerment of maternal markings. In rearticulating the rhetoric, writers often mentioned the "logical force" of positive impressions:

inasmuch as there could be bad influences, there could also be good. One author wrote as early as 1865 that it was parents' laziness that prevented the conception and gestation of spectacular children, since "If it was practical to produce a murderer, it may be practical to produce a saint" (Fernald, 1865: 55). Physicians in particular had sometimes objected to simple or pliable symbolisms, as when they noted that women proposed varied causes for a single mark. Physicians sometimes suspected mothers of easy hindsight, as the new mother who, seeing a blueberry-shaped mark on her infant, conveniently recalled having craved blueberries when pregnant (Flint, 1873: 391). Yet some physicians pointed out that mothers who feared markings were often vindicated by the birth of a child marked in just the way they had expected.

Positive marking featured both parents' roles. Though unfortunate combinations of traits sometimes produced children much worse than their parents, there were similar possibilities for good effects. One writer even proposed a "law": "This great law, briefly stated, is that *The active powers of body and mind in the parents previous to and at conception, and in the mother during gestation, will be the native strong powers of the child*" (Riddell, 1891: 17; emphasis in the original). Thus, one set of parents spent a happy day with friends, enjoyed a lecture, and the same day conceived a child who was a paragon (Riddell, 1891: 208–9). Writers continued to mention mothers' morality, as in the case of the prospective mother who read, managed her household carefully, was dutiful toward her family, did not become excited – and was rewarded with

a son, with a head ... with the reflecting and moral organs very conspicuous. A head, in short, on which nature had written in characters too legible to be misunderstood, strength, power, and capability, and of whom it is already said, "He is the youngest of his family, but will soon become its head." (Fernald, 1865: 130–1)

This rearticulation of the rhetoric of fetal endangerment often had, in fact, a motif of the child's leadership of the family, suggesting that the future of family life itself was ultimately at stake. A fetus – not even a child – could be father to the man.

Writers commonly proposed applications of the rearticulated rhetoric – practical action plans that the reader was sometimes invited to adopt. Often, the rearticulated rhetoric turned attention from the woman who harmed a child to the woman who created a child of genius; these literary settings were most elaborated after 1875. A writer sometimes presented steps that a pregnant woman could take to produce – not simply an acceptably healthy child of average intelligence – but a child of talent and/or intellect, bursting with health. Importantly, they suggested that talent and intellect could be readily and reliably channeled by an attentive prospective mother into specific foreordained avenues. Parents could produce at will a fetus with potential professional or musical talents, a future orator or artist, banker or great debator. Good intent and earnest effort by parents were generally all that were required, the manuals said significantly. Mothers sporting sows' ears could reliably be expected to gift their future children with silk purses of predictable cut and style.

Writers noted a woman's power to do good in pregnancy. Early feminists often reminded their audiences of the mother's general creative powers. As Nature could form a young plant, so would "the perfectly healthy mother do toward nourishing her unborn child [and] her higher human nature will also leave its holiest improve upon the young immortal" (Pendleton, 1843: 15–16). One early champion of women's rights informed her readers that "the mother's influence is almost unlimited, and it is, therefore, to the mother that one is inclined to apply all rules for the improvement of the race" (Evans, 1875: 101).

There are many anecdotes of erring parents who changed their ways. The general message of positive impressions was congruent with the doctrine of the self-made individual that began to be generally refined during the nineteenth century, though differently for women and for men (Brown, 1990; Gilbert, 1990). Claimsmakers required parents to better their lot by means of a lofty moral methodology. For example, a "misshapen" couple spent three years in assiduous study of the laws of inheritance and learned that "the day of miracles had not passed." Their study paid off with three ideal children (Lewis, 1874: 143–4). These, then, are stories of men and women who have changed not merely their fortune but their germ plasm, veritable Horatio Algers of pregnancy.

In the nineteenth century, the American philosophy was characterized by ameliorative progressivism – the assumption that the life of the nation, as well as of the individual, would continue to get better and better (Rosenberg, 1976). Luckily, those who had already produced inferior children could mend their ways and improve their future progeny, as did a husband who was "a wretched devotee of the quid and the pipe" and a wife who "just lived on tea." Their puny offspring alarmed them, so, after a study of three years, they succeeded in producing a daughter "altogether so much handsomer, brighter and happier, that it is difficult to believe they all belong to the same family" (Lewis, 1874: 143). These, then, were tales of relatively modest efforts – though characterized by hard work and determination – felt to be within an individual's control. Furthermore, persons lacking specific talents were informed that, should they choose to concentrate on these talents during gestation, the fetus would absorb the very talents its parents lacked.

Writers of marriage and health manuals in particular furnished, in cookbook fashion, considerable detail about specific abilities that might be imparted during the respective months of pregnancy. These directions abounded in the late nineteenth century. Even as early as 1851, a "doctor of electrical psychology" said positive impressions could be achieved by following a well-worked-out plan; since the fetus was malleable in particular ways during each month of its development, there were precise methods to secure desired effects (Dods, 1851: 233ff., 245ff.). Somewhat later, another medical irregular held that a pregnant woman should concentrate on physical capacities from the first month until the fourth, "but . . . the *mental* apparatus, and with it the *reasoning and moral* faculties form after the fifth month" (O.S. Fowler, 1870: 781–2; emphasis in the original). Many gave clear schedules for the purposeful transmission of positive characteristics. During one month a woman might be told to gaze at statues or pictures; during another, to do good works or attend sermons; during still another, to keep to her house and engage in housewifely duties.

It was not simply activities that a prospective mother (and sometimes father) must undertake. If they had misbehaved or erred in the past, they must repent, study, and practice new patterns of conduct. One author wrote of a woman determined to "put her house in order" and thereby give birth to an admirable child – specifically, an orator. Therefore she "gave herself up wholly to hearing orators, and reading poetry and classical works," attended church to hear pulpit speakers, and visited the legislature with the same goal. Her son was a "natural" orator (O.S. Fowler, 1870: 783). Among other contrasts, these pregnancy career schedules put to shame late twentieth-century claims of well-planned parenthood: earlier prospective parents were enjoined not only to plan family size but the future occupation of each child.

Men could exercise a powerful benign influence on the fetus, too. In the case of a repentant drunken father, "The father's life changed [and] he became the parent of far better children" (Houser, 1878: 8–9). But men's sexual conduct was often portrayed as their most crucial contribution, because of its alleged effect on wives and, through them, their unborn children. A fetus could be strongly affected by sexual intercourse that the wife did not desire. By waiting until a woman wanted to conceive a child, a man could also guarantee fine offspring. One feminist wrote of the mother as "an artist of immortal destinies" and told of the time when "One woman – begotten under the most abject conditions at which her mother could not but revel – said to me, 'I lived in sin nine months before I was born' " (Griffith, *c.* 1890: 6–7). In contrast, she wrote, was the enviable woman who conceived with a respectful partner:

> Imagine the newly-married pair reverently and lovingly conferring upon this matter [procreation]. Imagine their reaching some adequate conception of the import of generating a new immortal, and of the careful preparation of mind and body, and spirit and condition, which should precede an act so solemn and important; imagine the young husband solicitously inquiring whether his wife should be able to pass through such a crisis. (Griffith, *c.* 1890: 6)

Absent mutual concern and preparation, the sins of the fathers were literally still visited upon children: "Stultify, cramp, fetter, and bind woman, and you will see perpetuated what is now in our midst – dwarfish, puny physiques with ever active, nervous temperaments" (Hunt, 1856: 259–60).

The rearticulated rhetoric of fetal endangerment agreed that an identified problem existed in the form of children born with undesirable traits. However, men, not women, were the customary agents in the creation of children with physical and mental disabilities; further, it was men's repression of women's freedom and rights in particular that was to blame (see, for example, L. Fowler, 1900). In addition, writers rearticulating the rhetoric of fetal endangerment suggested that women were responsible for forming fetuses of great promise; interestingly, though work and determination were emphasized in the creation of a promising fetus, authors also emphasized that producing a model child was, in the end, "easy" (Pendleton, 1856) – perhaps echoing the ease with which rhetoricians of endangerment held that a fetus could be damaged. In the process of rearticulating the rhetoric of endangerment as "positive impressions," the pregnancy career for a woman began to be portrayed as an active, even enjoyable time.

Conclusion

Rhetorics of endangerment in general are suited to certain conditions more than others, as all rhetorics fit some conditions and categories more than others (Ibarra and Kitsuse, 1991). There are features of pregnancy that suit it in particular for the ills highlighted in a rhetoric of endangerment. First, as a status passage, pregnancy is a state that many cultures have found anxiety-provoking. Tensions of gender relations can be further exacerbated by a second factor, the physical reticence of the fetus. In addition to the privacy of fetal developments during pregnancy, there is a third factor, prolonged gestation. This makes pregnancy suited to a system of blame in which seemingly small misdeeds (eating a particular food or fleeting anger at one's husband) can have large effects – especially so if the pregnant woman is proscribed from committing a wide enough range of misdeeds or simply if she does not have total recall for nine months' time. Just the same conditions facilitate rearticulation of this rhetoric of fetal endangerment: a well-worked-out plan of action and argument for success would be welcome during a tense status passage, and the complex injunctions signal the importance of the parents' transition in status. The reticence of the fetus can make it equally easy to argue that much has gone right; and the extended period of gestation provides nine months' experience from which to choose in claiming that one has successfully "created" one's child.

I have centered my discussion on two articulations of a single rhetorical idiom. In general, it must be recalled that these idioms can be useful in helping individuals make sense of their own misfortunes. In particular, the rhetoric of fetal endangerment may have aided the relatively new class of medical professionals make sense of their patients' misfortunes.[4] In addition, the moral idioms used in writing about pregnancy are not a complete portrait of women's experience of pregnancy – or of medicalization. In fact, though the increasing medicalization of pregnancy and childbirth seem to have disadvantaged women in terms of the rhetoric of endangerment and certainly continued to rob women of control over women's medicine (Smith, 1976), there is some evidence that women welcomed the new technology and patterns of treatment that accompanied the rhetoric of endangerment (see Wertz and Wertz, 1979; Riessman, 1983).

The cast and actors invoked in nineteenth-century discussions of children's ill health, disability, or character varied in assigned responsibility. At some points and by some claimsmakers, women's misconduct alone was responsible for endangering, even ruining, the physical or mental health of fetus and hence of a child; at other times and according to other claimsmakers, it was men's misconduct toward their pregnant wives that was the less direct, but no less effective, mechanism for creating the same damaged children. For the authors of marriage manuals and advice books writing for a largely upper-class and white readership, the advice given and the claims made possible via the rhetoric of endangerment were consonant with the new nineteenth-century understanding of the upper-class white woman's place as relatively idle domestic and spiritual family guardian (Gordon and Buhle, 1976: 283–6). For emerging defenders of women's rights, arguments made according to the rhetoric of endangerment served as proof of wrongs against women; such wrongs could also damage children, whom presumably no reader wanted to see hurt. Regardless of who discussed women's pregnancy conduct, the particular advice given to prospective mothers presented authors as omniscient experts with regard to pregnancy outcomes, able to trace the smallest trait back to a telling prenatal event; thereby, authors of all these genres were added to the newly professionalized medical men as authorities over and interpreters of women's pregnancies. The melodramatic style featured in this rhetorical idiom may have also responded to the more dry, scientized event that pregnancy had become (Scholten, 1977: 444), restoring some of the drama.

In the nineteenth century, concern for the ability of the nation to survive physically and spiritually was sometimes clearly at stake when writers of advice manuals and medical articles voiced concerns about pregnancy. During the latter part of the century in particular, the eugenics movement flourished among upper-class whites, who saw themselves as "fit" and the lower classes and other races as "unfit" (Hofstadter, 1955: 163–4). Saving upper-class white racial stock was believed to be a way of ensuring the nation's future. Francis Galton, who coined the term "eugenics," proposed ways to produce superior offspring, among them conduct during pregnancy (Galton 1884). Part of the upper-class white woman's duty to propagate and so save the nation thus also became a duty to guarantee herself an easy, "successful" pregnancy. Depending on social class, women were thought to be differently subject to marking. Thus it was that the "unfurnished mind of the illiterate woman seizes on and retains the ugly or grotesque picture, which another rich in thought and experience would have dismissed at once" (Kirby, 1877: 21). Advice on pregnancy conduct thus reinforced class divisions.

Of course, conscious manipulation of the fetus is no less a subject of concern today than it was in the nineteenth century. At bottom we too often presume that, left alone, human beings are incapable of producing healthy, happy children and that fetuses are as malleable as the bear cub we once believed was licked into shape by its mother. Present advice also contains a mixture of cautions and rewards, though our rationales now feature cautions about nutrition and restraint from consumption of drugs and tobacco.

Finally, it is appropriate to note that the constructionist analysis of pregnancy and fetal development I have used goes beyond biological, physiological, psychological, and other sociological conceptions of pregnancy. To analyze the rhetoric of fetal endangerment in pregnancy is, first, to understand how some actors and some casts are chosen as relevant in blame-attribution – as were parents in the nineteenth century. It is also to understand that some casts and events relegated to the sidelines when fault is found – as were environmental conditions in the nineteenth century though not in the latter part of the twentieth century. Second, constructionist analysis levels "scientific" proofs and arguments with folk proofs and arguments, proposing that both are capable of being exploited by societal interest groups. Third, constructionism reveals that the same agents involved in social problems – here, women – can be differently conceptualized depending on how a rhetoric is articulated. In particular, I have revealed the operation of two different conceptions of pregnant women by two different sets of claimsmakers representing different interest groups and different agendas: to warn, on the one hand, and to exhort, on the other. Constructionism thus shows the power of each interest group to rearticulate a rhetoric that fingers its own villains and enshrines its own heroes.

Notes

I am grateful for the many suggestions of the editors and of William Gronfein, and for the research assistance of Wendy Hancock-Becher, Shari Hanesworth, and Karen Hurt. I also acknowledge financial support from the Faculty Development Office of Indiana University for part of the period in which I wrote this paper.

1. One problem with analyses of past social problem discourses is that sometimes they must rely on rhetorics evident in literature, and not necessarily observed in interaction – as is the case for this paper. In these cases, it is difficult to know if various literary genres faithfully repeat or report rhetorics actually used in everyday life. Thus, my usage of terms like "claimsmakers" or "claimsmaking activities" requires some license: though I imply the rhetoric I describe had a life beyond the printed page, in fact I can offer no evidence that this was so.

2. This rhetoric takes as given the desirability of a "healthy, normal" newborn free of various "anomalies" that, in other cultures or times, might have been received, accepted, and perhaps even sought after as auspicious portents or distinguishing traits. Thus, before the nineteenth century, non-human agencies were widely felt to intervene in fetal life. Sometimes God or Nature expressed a complicated message directed to an entire nation through the agency of a "marked" child or a child with a disability, as when such a birth was said to herald a change in monarchs or a victory or defeat in war (Thompsson, 1896: 8–10). In such births, what we would call a disability was interpreted as a vital communication.

Sometimes responsibility for a disability was assigned to the depraved moral tenor of the times. Alternatively, the disability could pertain to the most sign-worthy personage in the land, the ruler. There was also the practice of attributing children with disabilities to a demon that had had intercourse with a woman (Thompsson, 1896: 45). Beliefs of a range of other cultures – from Wishram to Kwoma to Indian – suggest that the fetus is sometimes believed to respond to tribe or nation more than to the conduct of the parents. See cross-cultural examples in Swain 1978, Sample and Mohr 1980, Sandhu 1980, Williamson 1983, as well as Schnucker's (1974) description of the English Puritans.

3. Recent book titles suggest that there is a similar literary setting available for today's parents, that the setting is also an amalgam of popular and scientific genres, and that these works too regard the reproductive process not as making do with the child with which one is presented, but rather as the creation of a satisfactory fetus (and thus implicitly affirming the idea that pregnancy can be directed). Recent titles have included *Caring for Your Unborn Child* and *The Genetic Connection: How to Protect Your Family Against Hereditary Disease*.

4. In this way, Sicherman finds a "language of restraint and injury" may have furnished early physicians with "a metaphor that helped physicians make sense of their own professional and personal experiences" (Sicherman, 1976: 899).

References

Among the references, I have listed all primary sources mentioned in this paper. I have not modified the publishing information of nineteenth-century sources.

"A Physician" [Nicholas Cooke] (1874) *Satan in Society*. Chicago, IL: E.W. Starr.

Aresty, Esther B. (1970) *The Best Behavior*. New York: Simon & Schuster.

Blaxter, Mildred (1976) *The Meaning of Disability*. London: Heinemann.

Brown, Gillian (1990) *Domestic Individualism: Imagining Self in Nineteenth Century America*. Berkeley, CA: University of California.

Dods, John Bovee (1851) *The Philosophy of Electrical Psychology*. New York: n.p.

Eberle, John (1844) *Notes of Lectures on the Theory and Practice of Medicine in the Jefferson Medical College, at Philadelphia*. Philadelphia, PA: Grigg & Elliot.

Evans, Elizabeth Edson (1875) *The Abuse of Maternity*. Philadelphia, PA: J.B. Lippincott.

Fernald, Woodbury (1865) *A View at the Foundations; Or, First Causes of Character, as Operative Before Birth, From Hereditary and Spiritual Sources*. Boston, MA: n.p.

Flint, Austin (1873) *A Treatise on the Principles and Practice of Medicine; designed for the use of Practitioners and Students of Medicine*. Philadelphia, PA: Henry C. Lea.

Fowler, Lorenzo N. (1900) *Should woman obey? A protest against improper matrimonial and prenatal conditions . . . Together with a special chapter by Prof. L.N. Fowler, entitled, Love, courtship, and marriage*. Chicago, IL: E. Loomis and Company. 142pp.

Fowler, O.S. (1870) *Sexual Science; including Manhood, Womanhood, and Their Sexual Interrelations*. Philadelphia, PA: National Publishing Company.

Galton, Francis (1884) *Hereditary Genius*. New York: D. Appleton and Company.

Gilbert, Alan (1990) *Democratic Individuality*. New York: Cambridge University Press.

Gordon, Ann D., and Buhle, Mari Jo (1976) Sex and class in colonial and nineteenth-century America, in Berenice A. Carroll (ed.), *Liberating Women's History*. Urbana, IL: University of Illinois Press.

Griffith, Mrs. M.L. (*c.* 1890) Ante-natal infanticide (pamphlet). Washington, DC: Association for Moral Education.

Haj, Fareed (1970) *Disability in Antiquity*. New York: Philosophical Library.

Hammond, William A. (1868) On the influence of the maternal mind over the offspring during pregnancy and lactation, *The Quarterly Journal of Psychological Medicine*, 2(1) (January): 1–28.

Hofstadter, Richard (1955) *Social Darwinism in American Thought*. Boston, MA: Beacon.

Houser, J.A., M.D. (1878) A glance behind the scene (pamphlet). Indianapolis: Indianapolis Journal Company.

Hunt, Harriot (1856) *Glances and Glimpses; Or, Fifty Years Social, Including Twenty Years Professional Life*. Boston: n.p. Reprinted 1970 by Source Book Press, New York.

Ibarra, Peter R., and Kitsuse, John I. (1990) Reconstructing the rhetoric of social problems discourse. Paper presented at Society for the Study of Social Problems.

Ibarra, Peter R., and Kitsuse, John I. (1991) Vernacular constituents of moral discourse: an interactionist proposal for the study of social problems. Manuscript.

Kirby, Georgiana (1877) *Transmissions; Or Variations of Character Through the Mother*. New York: S.R. Wells.

Lewis, Dio (1874) *Chastity, Or, Our Secret Sins*. Philadelphia, PA: George Maclea.

Liachowitz, Claire (1988) *Disability as a Social Construct*. Philadelphia, PA: University of Pennsylvania Press.

Meigs, Charles D. (1854) *Woman: Her Diseases and Remedies: A Series of Letters to His Class.* Philadelphia, PA: Blanchard and Lea.

Newman, J.B. (1849) *The Philosophy of Generation.* New York: n.p.

Newton, A.E. (1890) The better way: an appeal to men (pamphlet). New York: M.L. Holbrook.

Pendleton, Hester (1843) *Facts and Arguments on The Transmission of Intellectual and Moral Qualities, From Parents to Offspring.* New York: n.p.

Pendleton, Hester (1856) *Parents' Guide for the Transmission of Desired Qualities to Offspring, and Childbirth Made Easy.* New York: Fowler and Wells.

Riddell, Professor N.N. (1891) Private lectures to men: manhood: how obtained and retained – how lost and regained (pamphlet). Lincoln, NE: Hunter Printing House.

Riessman, Catherine Kohler (1983) Women and medicalization: a new perspective, *Social Policy*, 14: 3–18.

Rosenberg, Charles E. (1976) *No Other Gods: On Science and American Social Thought.* Baltimore, PA: Johns Hopkins University Press.

Sample, L.L., and Mohr, Albert (1980) Wishram birth and obstetrics, *Ethnology*, 19: 427–45.

Sandhu, R.S. (1980) Rites de passage of some scheduled castes: pregnancy and birth rites, *Eastern Anthropologist*, 33: 63–70.

Scholten, Catherine (1977) On the importance of the obstetrical art: changing customs of childbirth in America, 1760–1825, *William and Mary Quarterly*, 34: 426–45.

Schnucker, R.V. (1974) The English Puritans and pregnancy, delivery and breast feeding, *History of Childhood Quarterly*, 1: 637–58.

Seguin, Edward (1865) *Idiocy: And Its Treatment by the Physiological Method.* New York: William Wood.

Sicherman, Barbara (1976) The paradox of prudence: mental health in the gilded age, *Journal of American History*, 62: 890–912.

Smith, Hilda (1976) Gynecology and ideology in seventeenth-century England, in Berenice A. Carroll (ed.), *Liberating Women's History.* Urbana, IL: University of Illinois Press.

Smith-Rosenberg, Carroll (1985) The hysterical woman: sex roles and role conflict in nineteenth-century America, in *Disorderly Conduct: Visions of Gender in Victorian America.* New York: Knopf.

Smith-Rosenberg, Carroll, and Rosenberg, Charles (1973) The female animal: medical and biological views of woman and her role in nineteenth-century America, *Journal of American History*, 60: 332–55.

Spector, Malcolm, and Kitsuse, John I. (1977) *Constructing Social Problems.* New York: Aldine.

Swain, Saraswati (1978) Customs and beliefs associated with pregnancy and childbirth in rural Orissa, *Indian Journal of Social Work*, 39: 79–84.

Thompsson, C.J.S. (1896) *The Mystery and Lore of Monsters.* New York: Citadel.

Trousseau, A[rmand] (1868–1872) *Lectures on Clinical Medicine, Delivered at the Hotel-Dieu, Paris.* London: The Sydenham Society.

Velpeau, A[lfred] (1852) *A Complete Treatise on Midwifery: or, The Theory and Practice of Tokology: Including Diseases of Pregnancy, Labor, and the Puerperal State.* Translated by Wm. Byrd Page. Philadelphia: Lindsay and Blakiston.

Walker, Alexander (1839) *Intermarriage: Or, the Mode in Which, and the Causes Why, Beauty, Health, and Intellect, Result from Certain Unions, and Deformity, Disease and Insanity, from Others.* New York: J. & H.G. Langley.

Wertz, R.W., and Wertz, Dorothy (1979) *Lying in: A History of Childbirth in America.* New York: Free Press.

Whitfield, H. (1862) The hereditary transmission of mental and physical impressions: how and when produced, *British Medical Journal*, 1 (1862): 601–2.

Williamson, Margaret H. (1983) Sex relations and gender relations: understanding Kwoma conception, *Mankind*, 14: 13–23.

4
Correspondents' Images of Martin Luther King, Jr: An Interpretive Theory of Movement Leadership

Stephen J. Lilley and Gerald M. Platt

There were people who maybe didn't go to the mass meetings, who didn't do a lot of other things, but in some way, they contributed to what Dr. King was trying to do. When you sent a dollar, when you took your car and drove even to the next door neighbor's to keep them from riding the bus, you participated.

Mrs. Johnnie Carr, former Secretary of the Transportation Committee, Montgomery Improvement Association[1]

This is a study of the images imparted to Martin Luther King, Jr during the period 1956 to 1961. These portrayals of King are derived from correspondence sent from people who were more and less active in the movement. Although we focus upon the images these people accorded Dr King this is also a theoretical essay. We will use correspondents' perspectives to illustrate how participants construct their conceptions of leadership.[2]

We conceive of people in the Civil Rights Movement whether they were vigorously involved in the movement or merely sympathetic to it as engaged in making sense of the movement for themselves. Thus, we suggest that correspondents to King actively interpreted his leadership and the movement's doctrine shaping these to their interests, such as those they may find in their statuses, intentions, beliefs, and values.

Leaders and movement doctrine exhibit many dimensions of expression which the observers may interpretively fit to their interests. This interpretive process results in a diversity of types of portrayals of the leader and a variety of persons and groups committed to the movement. The evidence is overwhelming that movement adherents are objectively heterogeneous in their social attributes. We will illustrate that these participants also engage in constructing diverse images of movement leadership and more generally participants construct varying conceptions of the movement.

Conventional approaches to social movements such as resource mobilization or traditional collective behavior theory assume that persons who participate in social movements are more or less homogeneous in their objective characteristics and in their subjective consciousness; that is, they are similar in their class or other statuses, they are committed to the movement for similar reasons, and their conceptions of leadership and doctrine are alike (Morris, 1981; Killian, 1984; Oberschall, 1989).[3] Although social movements theory has addressed the issue of differences among participants, it has not taken this matter to its theoretical or empirical conclusion (Klandermans and Tarrow, 1988; Melucci, 1989). We will attempt to show that a close look at movement participants indicates that other approaches are too removed from the subjective experiences of movement participants. A critical problem facing social movement theory is the explanation of the objective and subjective heterogeneities found among participants in the same movement (Turner and Killian, 1972, 1987).[4] How do persons with different background characteristics, expressing varying conceptions of the movement come together to create collective actions?

Heterogeneous Movement Participants

The demography of social movements indicates they are populated with heterogeneous rather than homogeneous persons. Social movements exhibit a spectrum of types of participants from diverse social classes, races, ages, genders and so on (Traugott, 1985; Platt, 1987). Similarly evidence indicates that even ardent followers in movements display varying subjective conceptions of its leaders and its doctrine (Weinstein, 1980; Childers, 1990).

People in the Civil Rights Movement were exemplary for their objective diversity. At its outset movement adherents were working black women and men while their leaders were middle-class ministers (Morris, 1984). However, as the movement evolved, the Civil Rights participants were drawn from younger black and white men and women, more affluent and educated and from diverse class and cultural backgrounds. Black college youth spearheaded the Student Non-violent Coordinating Committee lunch counter sit-ins, voter registration and education projects in the early 1960s (Childs, 1989: 130–2) and affluent educated white youth from elite college campuses actively participated in the 1964 Freedom Summer (McAdam, 1988). By the mid-1960s the movement was populated with racially, economically, socially, geographically, culturally, and religiously heterogeneous persons.

How did these mixed populations construct the movement for themselves and how did they envision its leaders? These are perplexing questions which only those who were part of the movement can answer. We will concentrate our analysis upon participants' constructions of King's image as a leader.

Images of Martin Luther King

In 1974 James Hanigan published a paper summarizing the images attributed to King in the popular and scholarly literature. He provides a long list of King images:

> Most observers of King saw some religious significance in his words and work. A great variety of images taken from both of the Old and New Testaments, as well as from secular history, have been used to capture something of this significance: prophet, preacher, apostle; the black Moses, the American Gandhi, a modern-day St. Paul, a modern Job, a Socrates, even a Jesus. (1974: 77)

There has been little effort exerted to find out if these were the images of King held by movement participants. In no biography or sociology of King has his image been derived from the perceptions of him acquired from a broad spectrum of movement adherents. There were a very large number of participants, exhibiting a variety of degrees of involvement and activities in the Civil Rights Movement but only a small portion of those involved in the movement have been interviewed.[5] Almost all of these interviews were conducted with movement "elites" many years after their participation.[6]

The So-Called "Kind" Letters to Martin Luther King

It is possible to approximate a study of movement participants' images of King. During the Civil Rights Movement King's staff retained most of the correspondence to him. Included in the tidal wave of correspondence there were letters from participants in which they proffered their images of King's leadership. For the purpose of this essay movement participants are defined as those persons who wrote "kind" letters to Dr King between 1956 and 1961 and whose correspondence are held in the Boston or Atlanta archives. The content analyses in this essay are based on Stephen Lilley's research in the Boston archive (1989); these findings are supplemented by citing from oral histories and correspondence held in the Atlanta archive.

These archives contain thousands of letters, such as, speaking invitations to King, legal and business correspondence, letters from movement notables, hostile letters denouncing the movement and King, and so on. However, only letters from participants referred to by King's staff as "kind" letters were used in this study. The vast majority of these letters were disqualified because the description of King was too superficial, the letter was illegible, they lacked a date or an address, etc. Thus, the content analysis of participants' perspectives is based upon 621 "kind" letters to King held in the Boston archive.

The correspondents were active in the movement in varying degrees; some walked in the Montgomery Bus Boycott, others were members in the Southern Christian Leadership Conference, still others simply sent money and their support. For example, one woman wrote to Dr King, "May I add my small voice to the millions who offer you silent encouragement and moral support." However, another wrote, "I am a co-worker for the NAACP and I am working just as hard as you are." Another wrote to King with unqualified admiration for his leadership stating, "We see why 50,000 people were inspired to follow your leadership in an effort to improve their conditions. I am thoroughly convinced that no one can reach the people . . . and give them unshakable assurance as you can." Some letters were bold, offering advice and strategies, thus, one correspondent wrote in faltering English:

> You cannot never get full civil rights in the South if you are forever going to be entirely dependent on the ruling class white people in the South for a living, for a job. . . . I say colored people must now take a greater share in owning and controlling their own respective communities.

Whether it was through ardent praise, sympathy, advice, or friendly warnings the correspondents pressured King forward. Ultimately the great civil rights leader confided to his wife:

> People will expect me to perform miracles for the rest of my life. I don't want to be the kind of man who hits his peak at twenty-seven, with the rest of his life an anticlimax. Neither do I want to disappoint people by not being able to pull rabbits out of a hat. (Oates, 1982: 149–50)

Mrs Johnnie Carr's introductory remarks ring true for the correspondents: they all "contributed to what Dr. King was trying to do," they all participated in the movement.

Analyzing Correspondents' Images of King

In the social science literature and in popular media the people in the streets fighting for change are nameless and faceless; they are crowds obedient to leaders. By contrast the 621 correspondents to King are not anonymous – they left their names, their addresses, and considerably more about their experiences in the movement, such as their feelings and attitudes toward movement doctrine, their reasons for participating, and their perceptions of its leaders. We examine their correspondence to Dr King as an archeological proxy to Civil Rights Movement participants' constructions of King's leadership.

The 621 correspondents' letters to King have been analyzed for the writers' objective attributes and subjective attitudes.[7] Among the several objective characteristics that were ferreted out of the correspondence, we will focus upon the effects of race on perceptions of King because the sociological literature suggests race had forceful influences upon Civil Rights Movement participants' consciousness. We were able to discern the race of 391 (63 percent) correspondents of which 153 are black (39 percent) and 238 are white (61 percent). Using race to analyze its effects on shaping the images of King permits us to analyze expected projections derived from the status of race and those that vary from expectations drawn from race, the latter an important arena in which our constructive approach will be illustrated. It should be emphasized that all the correspondence are from adherents to the movement, thus, our findings are focused upon portrayals of Martin King's leadership from committed blacks and whites.

A Content Analysis of "Kind" Letters to Dr King

The contents of the 621 letters contain 21 separate descriptions of King's character and 27 depictions of his performance (Lilley, 1989: 80–1, 85–6, 92–3). The distinction between character and performance is based on correspondents' attributions to King as an individual in contrast to their explicitly expressed conceptions of what they thought King was attempting to achieve in his activities.

King's character was described by statements such as, a "prophet sent by God," a "true American determined to promote democracy," a "leader of the Negro race," and an "advocate of passive resistance." It was inappropriate to assume all the descriptions intended different meanings. By deriving analytic categories from the literature on leadership and inferring from the descriptions the intended meanings presented in the total contents of the letters, we reduced the portrayals of King's character to four impressions and his performances to five intended attributions. Further reduction would violate the intended meanings of the correspondents.

The four categories describing King's character are black leader (including such descriptions as "spokesman for blacks," "a modern-day Booker T. Washington," etc.), religious leader ("God's instrument," "Christ-like"), non-violent leader ("like Gandhi," "greatest teacher of non-violence today") and a leader for democracy ("upholder of democracy," "like Lincoln in your effort to expand democracy"). The five categories depicting his performance are, black goals ("uplifting our race," "bringing freedom to blacks"), religious goals ("helping to create heaven on earth," "spreading God's message of love"), non-violent goals ("teaching non-violence," "demonstrating passive resistance"), democratic goals ("perfecting this democracy," "fulfilling the Constitution") and other principled goals ("fight for justice," "work toward a brotherhood of men").

Even in these reduced forms of character and performance there is considerable perceived variation in the meanings King's leadership had for movement adherents. However, it is necessary to pursue further this analysis to discover the effects of race on correspondents' images of King.[8]

It has been suggested King was for whites a principled, moral, spiritual and religious leader, a leader who stressed Christian love and Gandhian non-violence. This has been contrasted with his meaning for African Americans for whom it has been suggested he played political and practical roles connected with their conditions of oppression and segregation (Meier, 1965; Hanigan, 1974; Marable, 1984).

There is in the correspondence to King an imperfect truth in this last formulation. Among the four characteristics attributed to King, black correspondents more frequently saw King as a "black leader" than did whites; however, only 41 percent of the blacks emphasized this theme (see Table 4.1). Fifty per cent of black correspondents stressed his capacity as "Christian leader," 7 percent as "non-violent leader," and 2 percent as a "democratic leader." While for white correspondents to King, 21 percent thought of him as a "leader of blacks," 56 percent as "Christian leader," 17 percent as a "non-violent leader" and 6 percent as "democratic leader."

If we follow the lead of previous commentators and assume "black leadership" depicts King in political and practical terms, while "Christian," "non-violent" and "democratic" are principled images of King we may collapse this analysis still further to uncover the degree to which blacks and whites viewed King as exhibiting practical or principled qualities. Table 4.2 indicates that most of his followers saw principled qualities in King although blacks stressed his practical side. Thus, there is some truth to perceptual expectations based upon race for black and white movement adherents. However, a closer look indicates that a majority of blacks and whites saw King's character in principled terms. Further, 62 black and 27 white correspondents or 38 percent did not subscribe to portrayals of King's leadership according to expectations derived from race; they "crossed-over" from expectations inferred from race.

More pronounced distributions by expectations are exhibited for blacks and whites regarding King's performance. Tables 4.3 and 4.4 indicate correspondents' conceptions of King's performance by race; a majority of black correspondents picture King's performance in terms of black goals and most whites view his leadership performance as expressions of principles. However, even in this distribution which conforms more closely to race-based expectations there are signs that show both black and white correspondents see King's leadership performance as practical and principled, thus holding mixed views of what they see King attempting to accomplish.

Table 4.1 *Impressions of King's character by race*

	Black	White	Total
Black leader	44 41%	27 21%	71 30%
Christian leader	53 50%	72 56%	125 53%
Non-violent leader	7 7%	22 17%	29 12%
Democratic leader	2 2%	8 6%	10 5%
Total	106 45%	129 55%	235* 100%

Chi square + 16.2, 3 *df*, *p* < .01

Table 4.2 *Impressions of King's character (collapsed) by race*

	Black	White	Total
Black leader	44 41%	27 21%	71 30%
Principles	62 59%	102 79%	164 70%
Total	106 45%	129 55%	235* 100%

Chi square = 11.6, 1 *df*, *p* < .01, Cross-over = 38%

*The number of respondents for each analysis varies with the available information in the letters.

Collapsing assumed practical and principled categories of performance indicates that 35 percent of the correspondents do not conform to expectations for perceived performance by race; 35 percent of both black and white authors of letters to King "crossed-over" from expectations derived from race-based interests (see Table 4.4). More specifically, 30 percent of the blacks described King's performance in principled terms and 38 percent of the white followers saw King's performance as directed to practical ends.

Excerpts from the letters contrast the differences between the writers who adhere to the expected racial pattern and those that do not. The excerpts are illustrative; images of King were determined through a scrutiny of the entire letter.

Table 4.3   *Impressions of King's performance by race*

	Black	White	Total
Black goals	95 70%	82 38%	177 51%
Christian goals	17 13%	40 19%	57 16%
Non-violence	7 5%	41 19%	48 14%
Democracy	1 1%	13 6%	14 4%
Other principles	15 11%	39 18%	54 15%
Total	135 39%	215 61%	350* 100%

Chi square = 37.7, 4 *df*, *p* < .01

Table 4.4   *Impressions of King's performance (collapsed) by race*

	Black	White	Total
Black goals	95 70%	82 38%	177 51%
Principles	40 30%	133 62%	173 49%
Total	135 39%	215 61%	350* 100%

Chi square = 34.6, 1 *df*, *p* < .01, Cross-over = 35%

*The number of respondents for each analysis varies with the available information in the letters.

Some black correspondents focused upon the inequalities they faced. They expressed desires for an end to segregation and for freedom and justice for African Americans. They saw King as the instrument to achieve these ends. Thus, a black man wrote:

> The Negroes of Montgomery needed a leader, so you came to lead them, and you did a great job. Now the Negroes of America are at a standstill for the lack of a great Negro leader.... You have all the qualities which make a great leader.... You organized the Negroes of Montgomery, why can't you organize the Negroes of America?

Another African American wrote similarly:

> I read with consternation the story of your possible resignation from the Dexter Avenue Baptist Church. . . . Freedom from second-class citizenship will not be handed to our race on a silver platter. Under your leadership Montgomery has become a pivotal point of attack. Your greater work remains yet to be done.

However, not all black correspondents emphasized King's indigenous campaign. Some writers viewed his work as transcending racial issues. A black woman wrote to King emphasizing the religious meaning of his leadership for her:

> God gave you many endowments of the spirit to be used in his service. . . . Don't let the devil fool you and keep you from the big things God has in store for you. It is ironic that we Colored people who are discriminated, despised, segregated and persecuted should be the ones who through the prompting of the Spirit should hold up to the world, the Lord Jesus Christ, and prove beyond a doubt that God is real.

Another black woman wrote in a similar fashion:

> I view your life and purpose as one sent of the Lord to stand on just such a pedestal for God. . . . When there is a job to be done and God needs a man, He has never lacked a witness. . . . What the world needs is Jesus, His ways, His attributes, His teachings and His life.

While another African American emphasized the principle of non-violence in his letter to King: "Your successful year of non-violent resistance was critical and a history-making movement for deprived people everywhere."

Some white correspondents emphasized aspects of King's work that transcend racial issues, such as, the importance of Christian faith in the creation of a more just and holy American community, a theme King frequently himself emphasized in his sermons, speeches and writings. A white woman wrote to King:

> America needs to be reminded forcefully of Christ's teaching of love to his fellow men! You endeavour to help America turn to Christ and His Word for a pattern of understanding and peace.

While a white man wrote:

> What you are doing is the only forcefully spiritual and Christian movement in the world today. As a northern American white I am truly proud of our American negroes. They have shown a spiritual faith and behavior that should make the world aware of our country's nobler qualities.

And still another white author wrote to stress the significance of non-violence in King's leadership:

> I applaud . . . the remarkable crusade you and your people carried on in Montgomery. This is not simply because it succeeded in doing away with an abominable discrimination but because it demonstrated the Gandhian

principle of non-violence. . . . It is a principle which we have to learn to use in international affairs or else the human race is doomed. You have lead the way in a great cause.

However, some white correspondents were concerned with practical matters facing the black community such as their oppression and their welfare. These white correspondents encouraged King to promote freedom and to achieve equal rights for African Americans. They perceived King's work in terms of the advancement of the black community rather than serving transcendent values.

A white man wrote succinctly, "Thanks from an old white man for your work to promote a better life for your people." And another wrote:

> As a leader and teacher of your people it is probably most assuring that your greatest victory is almost at hand. Montgomery is fortunate that you were on the scene. . . . It is unfortunate that most cities do not have Martin Luther Kings to intelligently lead the colored people successfully through the awkward and difficult days that lie ahead.

While another white woman wrote with a similar theme: "Your race is proud of you as well as your friends. I commend you for what you have done. . . . I believe there is nothing impossible where a people has a leader like you."

We focused upon the effects of race on correspondents' impressions of King because the literature suggests this structural variable influences movement participants' subjective experiences of it and its leadership. From this analysis we might conclude that this suggestion is at least partially correct because black correspondents did stress King's practical and political leadership. Therefore, we might also infer, as many others have, that black correspondents who perceived King as a practical and political leader were employing race-based interests to interpret King's leadership and his performances. However, not all black correspondents stressed the practical and political qualities of King's leadership; some blacks' images of King emphasized his principled qualities, such as religion, non-violence and democracy. Were these correspondents using structural bases other than their race to interpret King's meaning for themselves and if so what were they? Might we assume also that all white correspondents, whose structural circumstances are outside the experiences of black oppression, interpreted King's leadership solely by employing principles? Are the images of King they derived, whether practical or principled impressions, entirely determined by principles since their structural conditions appear irrelevant to their adherence to the movement?

Structural explanations of black and white correspondents' perceptions of King's leadership are too inconsistent. We will attempt to provide greater theoretical coherence to the findings.

Interpreting the findings

How do we interpret for social theory the correspondents' complex conceptions of King as leader? We could simplify the analysis, stressing the statistically significant findings, suppressing the details, underscoring King's essential images to the correspondents. The statistical analyses might suggest that blacks saw King as a leader who served their racial interests and whites perceived him as striving to achieve principles; blacks' perceptions were influenced by race-based interests and whites' images were derived from non-rational beliefs. But this formulation is not universally true; the chi-squares analyses shed no light on correspondents' perceptions of King's leadership that do not conform to expectations drawn from race.

Thus, the most interesting inference that one can draw from among these findings is that from 1956 to 1961 while King was an active and visible leader in the MIA and SCLC he bore several meanings simultaneously for both black and white participants in the movement. He was a diverse leader and accomplished different things for the correspondents. King may well have been what he wanted to be for himself but others committed to the movement found in him what they wanted to see for themselves. Correspondents saw in King and his efforts multiple conceptions of his leadership and performances (Gusfield, 1986).[9] King seemed aware of his multiple public meanings for he once confided, "I am conscious of two Martin Luther Kings. . . . The Martin Luther King that the people talk about seems to be somebody foreign to me" (Oates, 1982: 283).

Race may be a significant factor in shaping Civil Rights Movement adherents' impressions of King but it cannot be the only factor. We eschew, therefore, any attempt at simplifying the findings' complexities and their contradictions by focusing upon statistical significance. In a most important sense King's anomalous images according to race-based interests are decisive, for if taken seriously these perceptions of King recommend theoretical revision. We aspire for a more comprehensive theory; one that subsumes both the central tendencies consistent with expectations drawn from race and the anomalous images of King inconsistent with expectations derived from adherents' race.

An Interpretive Theory of Leadership: The Movement Constructed

Such a solution resides in reconceptualizing individuals' interpretive processes in relation to: (1) the structural positions they occupy such as, race, class, age, gender; (2) the rational calculations and the non-rational commitments derived from such positions; (3) the beliefs people hold and the emotions they experience resulting from their histories and their immediate circumstances (Platt, 1980). We insist that in describing social structural variables such as race, class, age, gender, etc., that their meaning to the individuals occupying them be paramount. Status holders can employ these structures in accord with the imputed cultural, political, and economic meanings embedded in them and thus these structures constrain volition by reproducing expected social meanings. However, these statuses can be interpreted alternately creating opportunities for varieties of meanings and for social change (Giddens, 1984: 83–6).

In both these circumstances, however, it is the status holders who are engaged in making sense of their social structural positions in relation to their past, present, and future activities, and in connection with their assessments of their immediate circumstances. Different statuses an individual occupies may be used as grounds for action also creating varying evaluative perspectives on the same qualities, statements, and performances expressed by leaders.

The result of this interpretive process is that individuals may devise myriad constructions of leadership by using unexpected bases for creating meaning. The important issue is that persons as active interpreters are continually engaged in fitting and modifying themselves and their social positions to the circumstances they face. They are engaged in constructing their conceptions of the social world and their place in it.

Adherents in social movements engage in these practices similar to persons in any social situation. These individuals can achieve diverse meanings within discourses of race-based interests, they may employ other statuses, or they may rely upon values, beliefs and the emotions they experience in relation to their historical experiences and the circumstances they face.

For movement adherents these are alternate ways of interpreting and thereby legitimating their stances against conditions of oppression and injustice. These are alternate ways of making claims for change and providing meaning and legitimacy to the activities in which they engage and in their strivings for freedom, justice and liberation for black Americans (Spector and Kitsuse, 1987: 73–96).[10] These interpretive processes permitted black and white Americans to fit themselves to the movement and to support their strivings for a just society although what a just society exactly meant was distinct for each correspondent. Analysts may reduce their meanings into coherent categories for presentation to professional audiences as we have done in this essay, but in truth, adherents' constructions of leadership are private and particular (Geertz, 1988: 8–20).

From the subjective perspective of particular adherents there were many different ways of making sense of a movement, of conceptualizing its leadership and justifying adherence. It is appropriate to assume that Civil Rights Movement participants confronted with abstract expressions such as freedom, justice, liberation, a just community, etc., provided unique subjective meanings to these terms which resulted in transcendent but unexamined commitments that bound them together in solidarity.

For movement activists cultural, political, and ideological doctrines are symbolic fabrics from which different threads may be woven into meaningful discourses of private interpretive stances to strive for liberation. Cultural, political, and ideological doctrines are open to interpretations; these are discourses rich with multiple meanings available for adherents' interpretation (Platt and Williams, 1988).

In social movements it is especially the case that leaders in their doctrinal expressions may be intentionally ambiguous in order to encourage people to see in the movement aspects of doctrine relevant to their interests whatever these may be (Williams, 1977: 39–40; Kertzer, 1988: 11). Leaders may employ rhetorical discourses in order to mobilize larger numbers of disparate persons to find meaning for themselves in the movement.

Thus, we suggest the movement correspondents existed within contexts of privately constructed social worlds to which a distinction can be made between the public appearance of a consensus and sub-rosa subjective differences. A movement event no matter how apparently unified cannot guarantee subjective homogeneity. David Kertzer has highlighted these conditions in political ritual. He notes that rituals and symbols can be ambiguous, therefore, "ritual action" can foster "solidarity without consensus" (1988: 69) and

> ritual can serve political organizations by producing bonds of solidarity without requiring uniformity of belief. This is of tremendous political value, since what often underlies people's political allegiances is their social identification with a group rather than their sharing of beliefs with other members. (1988: 67)

However, even when leaders attempt to be deliberately unambiguous their intentions can be alternately interpreted by adherents who listen to their discourse and observe their activities. Ralph Turner points out that the same role behavior can be assigned very different meanings. Turner notes, roles "that convey diametrically opposed evaluations and meanings are often expressed through behaviours that are objectively indistinguishable" (Turner, 1985: 30). This was the situation with King for as we noted during the period between 1956 and 1961 when King was actively leading the movement correspondents imputed multiple conceptions to his same performances; their portrayals of his leadership indicated he accomplished distinct things for the different correspondents. It is possible to infer from our findings as we have, that "King may well have been what he wanted to be for himself but others committed to the movement found in him what they wanted to see for themselves."

Thus, movement participants may use leaders' actions and doctrinal expressions combined with personal, political, and cultural commitments to provide meanings relevant to their own interests, such as those that grow out of their race, their beliefs, experiences, and emotions. The self-determined salient aspects of people's material and cultural interests are fitted to leadership's qualities and activities. The specifics of these interpretive processes can not be determined a priori and certainly not from theorists' preconceptions of what interests are embedded in people's statuses.

For movement participants the substance of these subjective constructions exist along a continuum from relatively coherent formulations about the movement to partial and fragmented notions highlighting dimensions of the movement particularly relevant to them. These privately constructed statements however, even when subjectively coherent, are not rational deductive portrayals of the movement. Rather they are simply constructed versions satisfying participants' needs to provide for themselves a meaningful place in the movement. Further, for each participant these constructions are unpredictable, because it is impossible to know in advance which factors will be intertwined into their private, complete or fragmented, constructed version of the movement.

This theory calls for an indeterminate interpretive process; it is up to persons in the movement to ascertain its meaning and their place in it for themselves. This is a theory in which volitional interpretive practices are centered thereby offering explanations consistent with the different images of King's leadership found in the correspondence to him.[11]

There is an analytic coherence to this theoretical formulation. This approach explains the complex constructions of King's leadership and the different attributed impressions of him from both black and white correspondents. It is consistent with the complex subjective experiences and the objective variations found among movement participants. This approach also implies that it is interpretive processes resulting in subjective diversity which influence the objective heterogeneity of movements. The consequence of interpretive processes is that objective and subjective heterogeneities are intertwined; the former in some degree the result of the latter. It is the interpretive processes which make our findings whole by explaining the objective and subjective heterogeneities in relation to the complex constructions of King's leadership.

Much of this approach to leadership is foreshadowed in Max Weber's theory of domination (1978: 212–16; 941–55). Weber well understood that leaders' capacity to command depended upon followers' subjective imputation of authority, whether this meant for followers power based upon normative legitimacy, expedient self-interest, habit of obedience, or emotional commitments. Weber theorized that there was no single basis for authority, rather that institutional forms of domination depended upon followers' situationally specific subjective imputations. The innovation we have appended to Weber's theorizing is that subjective bases for authority not only vary from situation to situation but vary *within* any particular situation depending upon the interpretive practices in which individuals engage in creating their conceptions of leadership and its bases for authority. We are attempting to add to Weber's formulation of subjective attribution additional degrees of volitional freedom while simultaneously suggesting that social organizations resulting from such personally achieved decisions about authority are more complex than can be inferred from assumptions about the structural aspects of persons (such as, race or class) or from the organizational appearances (for example, rational-legal authority) that their subjective decisions create.

Notes

This research was conducted in the King Special Collection, the Mugar Library, Boston University, and the Library and Archive of the Martin Luther King, Jr Center for Nonviolent Social Change, Atlanta. We are grateful to Dr Charles Gotlieb, Director, Mugar Library Collection, and Dr Broadus Butler, former Director of the Atlanta Archive, for their assistance. Permission to quote the correspondence to Dr King was granted by the King Center counsel; Dr Butler and Mrs Coretta Scott King made these arrangements possible. Diane Ware, the King Center Reference Archivist, was exceedingly helpful. Danny Bellinger was a thorough research assistant. This research was supported by The Albert Einstein Institution, Cambridge, Massachusetts and by Glen Gordon, the former Dean of Social and Behavioral Science, The University of Massachusetts. John Kitsuse, Fred Weinstein, Rhys Williams and Michael Fraser commented on early versions of this paper.

1. Mrs Johnnie M. Carr, Oral History Project, 1/27/1972, p. 34. King Library and Archive, Atlanta.

2. This approach is derived from Weinstein and Platt (1973), Weinstein (1980, 1990), Platt (1980, 1987, 1991) and Max Weber (1978).

3. For rational-structural analyses of students in sit-ins see Morris (1981: 744–67) and Oberschall (1989: 31–53). For a spontaneous-heterogeneous conception of sit-ins see Lewis M. Killian (1984: 770–83).

4. Turner and Killian recognize the diversity of the participants in social movements. They write that people in collective actions, "are heterogeneous in

motivation despite the similarity of their behavior" (1972: 27). Further they state, "we reject the assumption that a social movement is composed of people who are homogeneous in their attitudes and values. Adherents and even the leaders and activists bring divergent conceptions of the situation, the grievance, and the movement goals" (1987: 237).

5. King has been depicted as a charismatic in the sociological literature. Jack Bloom writes of King, he motivated "blacks . . . enabling them to find inner strength to stand up and fight" (1987: 144). Aldon Morris depicted King as "able to instill in people a sense of mission and commitment to social change" (1984: 11). Recently Morris depicts King's leadership interactively stressing the input of the black community (1990).

6. Oral History Collections focused upon the Montgomery Bus Boycott and the Anne Romaine Collection of Oral Histories focused upon the Mississippi Freedom Democratic Party. The Anne Romaine Collection was acquired in 1966–67 after the events of the 1964 Democratic Convention. Interviews with Septima Clark (November 1971), John Lewis (June, 1970), Ella Baker (March, 1967), Fannie Lou Hamer (November, 1966), and others of such stature in the Civil Rights Movement although valuable and significant should be considered those of "elites" rather than followers. There are outstanding published oral history anthologies, for example, Howell Raines (1977) and William R. Beardslee (1977). However, these too focus upon movement "elites" interviewed years after the events recalled.

7. The objective characteristics of the 621 "kind" letter writers are noted in Table 4.5.

Table 4.5   *Objective characteristics of the "kind" letter correspondents*

Attributes	Usable cases	Value name	Frequency of usable cases	Percentage of usable cases
Race	391	Black	153	39
	(63%)	White	238	61
Region	562	South	104	19
	(90%)	NEast	204	36
		West	120	21
		Central	134	24
Gender	603	Female	236	39
	(97%)	Male	367	61
Year of	621	1956	108	17
letter	(100%)	1957	136	22
		1958	71	11
		1959	43	7
		1960	104	17
		1961	159	26
Degree of	279	Low	125	45
activism	(45%)	High	154	55

8. Correspondents' race was scored on the basis of two types of statements: (1) a clear-cut avowal of race; (2) a contrast or comparison between the writer's race and King's, for example, "I am delighted to know that you are trying to help our race in the lunch project."

9. Gusfield suggests temperance movement participants exhibited similar diversities, for example, "Temperance and Prohibition are also multivalent and

polysemous. They have meanings at different levels and different dimensions" (1986: 202).

10. Neither status nor discourse define the boundaries of interpretation. For example, during the Montgomery Bus Boycott not all the city's black ministers were behind the movement; three were recruited by the city's mayor to scuttle the boycott in midstream (Morris, 1984). Also, southern racists often remarked that King's non-violent philosophy intended quite the opposite; it was meant to provoke violence. The boundaries of interpretation hinge upon membership in terms of publicly expressed commitment to the movement's goals. It was impossible to be defined or to define oneself as a member of the Civil Rights Movement if one's interpretation of the movement did not include something about commitment to "liberation," "justice" and "freedom" for black Americans.

11. Gene Sharp made this point indicating that consent to authority was a volitional condition and could be withdrawn. He also noted people could develop indigenous bases of power for themselves, if they wished to do so (1973: 25–32; 1980: 309–78).

References

Beardslee, William R. (1977) *The Way Out Must Lead In: Life Histories in the Civil Rights Movement.* Atlanta, GA: Center for Research in Social Change, Emory University.

Bloom, Jack H. (1987) *Class, Race and the Civil Rights Movement.* Bloomington, IN: Indiana University Press.

Carr, Johnnie M. (January 27, 1972) The Martin Luther King Jr., Oral History Project, Martin Luther King Jr., Center for Nonviolent Social Change Library and Archive, Atlanta, Georgia.

Childers, Thomas (1990) The social language of politics in Germany: the sociology of political discourse in the Weimar Republic, *American Historical Review,* 95: 331–58.

Childs, John Brown (1989) *Leadership, Conflict, and Cooperation in Afro-American Social Thought.* Philadelphia, PA: Temple University Press.

Geertz, Clifford (1988) *Work and Lives: The Anthropologist as Author.* Stanford, CA: Stanford University Press.

Giddens, Anthony (1984) *The Constitution of Society: Outline of the Theory of Structuration.* Berkeley, CA: University of California Press.

Gusfield, Joseph R. (1986) *Symbolic Crusade: Status Politics and the American Temperance Movement,* second edition. Urbana and Chicago: University of Illinois Press.

Hanigan, James P. (1974) Martin Luther King, Jr.: the images of a man, *Journal of Religious Thought,* 31: 68–95.

Kertzer, David I. (1988) *Ritual, Politics, and Power.* New Haven, CT: Yale University Press.

Killian, Lewis M. (1984) Organization, rationality and spontaneity in the Civil Rights Movement, *American Sociological Review,* 49: 770–83.

Klandermans, Bert and Tarrow, Sidney (1988) Mobilization into social movements: synthesizing European and American approaches, in Bert Klandermans, Hanspeter Kriesi and Sidney Tarrow (eds), *International Social Movements Research,* 1: 1–38.

Lilley, Stephen, J. (1989) Kind letters and support for Dr. Martin Luther King, Jr., PhD dissertation, University of Massachusetts/Amherst.

McAdam, Doug (1988) *Freedom Summer.* New York: Oxford University Press.

Marable, Manning (1984) *Race, Reform, and Rebellion: The Second Reconstruction in Black America, 1945–1982.* Jackson, MS: University of Mississippi Press.

Meier, August (1965) On the role of Martin Luther King, *New Politics*, 4: 52–9.

Melucci, Alberto (1989) Towards a theory of collective action, in John Keane and Paul Mier (eds), *Nomads on the Present: Social Movements and Individual Needs in Contemporary Society*, Philadelphia, PA: Temple University Press.

Morris, Aldon D. (1981) Black Southern student sit-in movement: an analysis of internal organization, *American Sociological Review*, 86: 744–67.

Morris, Aldon D. (1984) *The Origins of the Civil Rights Movement: Black Communities Organizing for Change*. New York: Free Press.

Morris, Aldon D. (1990) A man prepared for the times; a sociological analysis of the leadership of Martin Luther King, Jr., in Peter J. Albert and Ronald Hoffman (eds), *We Shall Overcome: Martin Luther King, Jr. and the Black Freedom Struggle*. New York: Pantheon Books.

Oates, Stephen (1982) *Let the Trumpet Sound: The Life of Martin Luther King, Jr.* New York, Harper & Row.

Oberschall, Anthony (1989) The 1960 sit-ins: protest diffusion and movement take-off, *Research in Social Movements, Conflict and Change*, 11: 31–53.

Platt, Gerald M. (1980) Thoughts on theory of collective action, in Mel Albin (ed.), *New Directions in Psychohistory*. Lexington, MA: D.C. Heath.

Platt, Gerald M. (1987) The psychoanalytic sociology of collective behavior: material interests, cultural factors and emotional responses, in Jerome Rabow, Gerald Platt and Marion Goldman (eds), *Advances in Psychoanalytic Sociology*. Melbourne, FL: Krieger Publishing.

Platt, Gerald M. (1991) An essay on the history and epistemology of Weinstein's "History and theory after the fall", *The Psychohistory Review: Studies of Motivation in History and Culture*, 20: 3–20.

Platt, Gerald M. and Williams, Rhys H. (1988) Religion, ideology and electoral politics, *Society*, 25 (5): 38–45.

Raines, Howell (1977) *My Soul is Rested: Movement Days in the Deep South Remembered*. New York: Penguin Books.

Sharp, Gene (1973) *The Politics of Nonviolence*, Boston: Porter Sargent Publisher.

Sharp, Gene, 1980. *Social Power and Political Freedom*, Boston, MA: Porter Sargent Publishers.

Spector, Malcolm and Kitsuse, John I. (1987) *Constructing Social Problems*. New York: Aldine de Gruyter.

Traugott, Mark (1985) *Armies of the Poor: Determinants of Working Class Participation in the Parisian Insurrection of June, 1848*. Princeton, NJ: Princeton University Press.

Turner, Ralph H. (1985) Unanswered questions in the convergence between structuralist and interactionist role theories, in H. J. Helle and S. N. Eisenstadt (eds), *Micro-Sociological Theory: Perspective on Sociological Theory, Vol. 2*. London and Beverly Hills: Sage Studies in International Sociology.

Turner, Ralph, H. and Killian, Lewis M. (1972) *Collective Behavior*. Englewood Cliffs, NJ: Prentice-Hall.

Turner, Ralph, H. and Killian, Lewis M. (1987) *Collective Behavior*. Englewood Cliffs, NJ: Prentice-Hall.

Weber, Max (1978) *Economy and Society: An Outline of Interpretive Sociology*, Guenther Roth and Claus Wittich (eds). Berkeley and Los Angeles: University of California Press.

Weinstein, Fred (1980) *The Dynamics of Nazism: Leadership, Ideology and the Holocaust*. New York: Academic Press.

Weinstein, Fred (1990) *History and Theory After the Fall: An Essay on Interpretation*. Chicago, IL: University of Chicago Press.

Weinstein, Fred and Platt, Gerald M. (1973) *Psychoanalytic Sociology: An Essay on the Interpretation of Historical Data and the Phenomena of Collective Behavior.* Baltimore, MD: Johns Hopkins University Press.

Williams, Raymond (1977) *Marxism and Literature.* Oxford: Oxford University Press.

II
SOCIOPOLITICAL FACTORS IN THE CONSTRUCTION OF SOCIAL CATEGORIES

5
Practices of Truth-Finding in a Court of Law: The Case of Revised Stories

Kim Lane Scheppele

Silences, First Accounts and Revised Stories

Rape victims, battered women, victims of sexual harassment and incest survivors have a lot in common. They are all victims of sexualized violence and many have similar responses. Many women do not report the violence against them to authorities and many do not talk about the events with anyone at the time (Scheppele, 1987: 1096–7; Pollack, 1990; Mango, 1991). Those who do talk about it at the time often present first accounts that try to make things normal again and to smooth out social relations, by minimizing the harm of the abuse, by engaging in self-blame, by telling stories that offer alternative explanations of events so that the full consequences of the abuse do not have to be dealt with at the time and by disguising the horribleness of the abuse through descriptive distortions of events (Walker, 1979; Scheppele and Bart, 1983; Herman, 1992). Later, however, often through working in therapy, or becoming overtly feminist, or getting enough emotional distance on the events to begin to deal with them, the women revise their stories (Herman, 1992). Women who were silent begin to speak out for the first time. Women who denied at the time that anything abusive happened, or who took the blame themselves if they admitted that something had happened, begin to tell stories of injury and harm. These later *revised stories*, replacing either silence or an alternative version of events, present problems in the law. They present problems because one of the implicit rules juries and judges use for finding stories to be true is that the stories stay the same over time. Stories told at the time of the abuse are believed much more than revised stories told later.

Anita Hill v. Clarence Thomas

We can see the strength of this bias toward first versions in the highly publicized second round of confirmation hearings on the Supreme Court nomination of Clarence Thomas, in which Anita Hill presented evidence that Thomas had sexually harassed her. Though the members of the Senate Judiciary Committee holding the hearings repeatedly emphasized that the proceedings were not a trial, legalistic conceptions of "burden of proof" and "presumption of innocence" were used throughout the three days of marathon sessions. But there the legal formality ended. Evidence was introduced without witnesses to support it; insinuations were made about Anita Hill's motivation and credibility that had no basis in evidence at all; questioning was limited by the unwillingness of then-Judge Thomas to answer questions outside the scope that he deemed fit for inquiry; witnesses who had relevant evidence to introduce were kept dangling and ultimately not asked for the information they had as part of the hearings. Whatever the Senate hearings might have been designed to accomplish, they were not well-designed to work out what had happened and they proceeded at variance with the sorts of rules of evidence that would be used in a trial. But the hearings do reveal some popular biases in the evaluation of evidence, particularly where women are making claims that they have been the target of abuse.

Those defending Clarence Thomas repeatedly emphasized that Anita Hill had changed her story. And there were many versions of events presented during the course of the hearings. Once her allegations became public, Anita Hill had three opportunities to narrate what had happened: once to the FBI agents who arrived at her house one evening after work to interview her; once to the Senate Committee staffers who were trying to work out what she would say if called as a witness; once as the whole world watched her testimony live on television before the Senate Judiciary Committee. In each of these stories, new details emerged that had not been present in the earlier versions, though none of the new details conflicted with earlier more general versions. In addition to these versions, all of which were recorded in permanent form, four friends and colleagues of Hill's testified from memory to versions of the harassment story that Hill had told them either at the time that it occurred (witnesses Ellen Wells, Susan Hoerchner and John Carr) or when she was applying for jobs and had to explain why she had left the Equal Employment Opportunity Commission (EEOC) where she worked with Clarence Thomas (witness John Paul).

On the other side, Clarence Thomas denied Hill's allegation and substituted in part his own narrative of what had happened – that he had always treated his whole staff professionally, cordially and without the interjection of personal distractions. Witnesses supporting Thomas presented alternative narrative contexts for Anita Hill's charges of sexual harassment, ranging from Hill's alleged grandiosity and ambition (witness J.C. Alvarez) to her status as a "scorned woman" (witness Phyllis Berry) to her alleged flights of fantasy (witness John Doggett). Other witnesses for Thomas expressed incredulity that he could do the acts alleged (witnesses Nancy Fitch and Diane Holt). Three versions from Hill's own accounting, a blanket denial from Thomas and many other versions from various witnesses left the Senate Judiciary Committee with a lot to pick apart. And much of the strategy of those who won by getting Thomas through the confirmation process and onto the Supreme Court depended on presenting Anita Hill's story to the committee as a revised account. Clarence Thomas deployed this strategy as much as any of the Senators working to defend him. In response to a question, Thomas answered:

> The facts keep changing, Senator. When the FBI visited me, the statements to this committee and the questions were one thing. The FBI's subsequent questions were another thing, and the statements today as I received summaries of them were another thing. It is not my fault that the facts changed. What I have said to you is categorical; that any allegations that I engaged in any conduct involving sexual activity, pornographic movies, attempted to date her, any allegations, I deny. It is not true. So, the facts can change, but my denial does not. (Federal Informations Systems Corporation [FISC], October 11, 1991, LEXIS: 78)

Thomas clearly was trying to use the idea that statements that remain the same over time appear more reliable than statements that appear to change. He was asserting that his categorical denials were more true than Hill's "changing" facts precisely because his denials had never been subject to revision.

Senator Arlen Specter's cross-examination of Anita Hill spent much time on pointing out the differences between Hill's accounts to the FBI and her public testimony, in an attempt to discredit her credibility (FISC, October 11, 1991, LEXIS: 25–8). Later, Specter pressed Hill on why she did not keep contemporaneous notes, knowing that such records would be admissible in court as particularly strong evidence of her perceptions at the time of events (FISC, October 11, 1991, LEXIS: 45–6). The notes Hill had before her were written out in preparation for the hearings, Specter ascertained, clearly implying that such notes could have been fabricated for the event. Throughout Specter's cross-examination, Hill's public testimony was presented as a *revised* version of events – revised, and therefore unreliable.

The Hill–Thomas hearings were not a judicial forum. But the tactics used in an attempt to discredit Hill's testimony borrow both from the courtroom and from daily life. Stories that are revised over time – elaborated, altered in tone, emerging in public out of a silence that went before – are presented as suspect *precisely because* they are revised. Though closer examination of the statements that Hill made to the FBI, to the Senate Committee and to her friends revealed that they varied only in the specificity of their allegations and not in their basic shape, the specter that her story had been revised continued to haunt the hearings. And Clarence Thomas was confirmed.

Reed v. Shepard

When we look at actual courtroom proceedings, we can see how the alleged revision of stories is mobilized to discredit the later accounts. This strategy is particularly common in sexual harassment cases. In *Reed v. Shepard*, 939 F. 2d 484 (1991), JoAnn Reed worked as a "civilian jailer" in the Vandenburgh County (Indiana) Sheriff's Department, beginning in mid-1979. The civilian jailer program employed people to take care of prisoners – guarding, feeding, transporting and processing them – as less costly substitutes for the more expensive deputy sheriffs who had formerly performed those jobs. In 1984, Reed was fired, without a hearing, for alleged misconduct in her job. In response to a charge brought under Section 1983 of the US Code that she had been denied due process, the district court and the appeals court found that she was not entitled, as an at-will employee, to have a hearing before her employment was terminated and that the allegations of misconduct were serious enough to justify her termination in any event. But she had sued on multiple counts, and in the others, she charged that her employer had engaged in sexual discrimination and that she had been sexually harassed on the job in violation of Title VII of the Civil Rights Act. The story she told about sexual harassment was clearly a revised story.

According to the trial judge (quoted by the Court of Appeals):

> Plaintiff contends that she was handcuffed to the drunk tank and sally port doors, that she was subjected to suggestive remarks . . ., that conversations often centered around oral sex, that she was physically hit and punched in the kidneys, that her head was grabbed and forcefully placed in members' laps, and that she was the subject of lewd jokes and remarks. She testified that she had chairs pulled out from under her, a cattle prod with an electrical shock was placed between her legs, and that they frequently tickled her. She was placed in a laundry basket, handcuffed inside an elevator, handcuffed to the toilet and her face pushed into the water, and maced. Perhaps others. (Unpublished opinion of Judge Gene E. Brooks, dated May 25, 1990, quoted at 939 F. 2d 486).

"The record confirms these and a number of other bizarre activities in the jail office," the appeals court added. "By any objective standard, the behavior of the male deputies and jailers toward Reed revealed at trial was, to say the least, repulsive" (939 F. 2d 486).

Why, then, did the court go on to conclude that, however offensive the conduct of her male co-workers was, it was *not* sexual harassment? Because, the court found, the conduct was apparently not repulsive to Reed *at the time*:[1]

> Reed not only experienced this depravity with amazing resilience, but she also relished reciprocating in kind. At one point during her job tenure Reed was actually put on probation for her use of offensive language at the jail. At the same time, she was instructed to suspend the exhibitionistic habit she had of not wearing a bra on days she wore only a T-shirt to work. She also participated in suggestive gift-giving by presenting a softball warmer to a male co-worker designed to resemble a scrotum and by giving another a G-string. Reed enjoyed exhibiting to the male officers the abdominal scars she received from her hysterectomy which necessarily involved showing her private area. Many witnesses testified that Reed revelled in the sexual horseplay, instigated a lot of it, and had "one of the foulest mouths" in the department. In other words, the trial revealed that there was plenty of degrading humor and behavior to go around. (939 F. 2d 486–487)

The court emphasized that this reprehensible conduct did not happen to other women working in the jail, but only to Reed. Three women working there testified that they had not been further harassed after they asked the men to stop doing these sorts of things to them. But apparently, Reed never told the men to stop. Why? Reed testified at trial:

> Because it was real important to me to be accepted. It was important for me to be a police officer and if that was the only way that I could be accepted, I would just put up with it and kept [sic] my mouth shut. I had supervisors that would participate in this and you had a chain of command to go through in order to file a complaint. One thing you don't do as a police officer, you don't snitch out [sic] another police officer. You could get hurt. (Quoted at 939 F. 2d 492. [Sic]s in the original.)

Reed's case involves a complicated reconstruction. She was not presented as having narrated the events in question any particular way at all at the time that they happened. Her "initial story" was constructed from the observations of her co-workers, inferring from her actions what her story must have been. As a result, the story that she presented in court appeared to be a revised story against the backdrop of this inferred narrative. And the Seventh Circuit Court of Appeals found that she was complicit in her treatment, barring recovery for sexual harassment.

Quoting from the Supreme Court's decision in *Meritor Savings Bank v. Vinson* (477 U.S. 57 [1986]), the Seventh Circuit panel indicated that harassment must be so severe or pervasive as "to alter the conditions of [the victim's] employment and create an abusive working environment" (quoted at 939 F. 2d 491), if a claim is to succeed. But to show that this conduct was "in fact" harassing, the victim of such treatment had to indicate *at the time* that she did not welcome the behavior in question. In this instance, Reed's claim could not succeed because she had not indicated while these events were occurring that this treatment was unwelcome. In other words, contemporaneous evidence is required to establish any claim of sexual harassment, and this requirement is hard-wired into the doctrine. Judge Manion quoted the trial judge approvingly that the plaintiff had been treated this way "because of her personality rather than her sex" and that the "defendants cannot be held liable for conditions created by [Reed's] own action and conduct" (939 F. 2d 492). Her failure to object at the time to this behavior and her attempt to deal with it by trying to act like "one of the boys" not only defeated her ability to make a claim, but justified the conclusion that she had brought this treatment on herself and was therefore the person who was primarily responsible.

But the record sustains another story, one not narrated by her co-workers who were witnesses at the trial. The record documents that Reed was physically beaten, that she was punched in the kidneys, that she had an electric cattle prod shoved between her legs, that she was forceably restrained by being handcuffed on numerous occasions, that her head was shoved into a toilet, that she was repeatedly tickled and that she was maced. That was on top of the extensive and personalized verbal abuse to which she was subjected. The court could have concluded that this evidence supported another account, one that did not erase the violence against Reed by constructing her as a consenting woman, but one that did present her at a minimum as the coerced victim of physical abuse.[2] Although Reed did not explicitly object at the time, the violence to which her co-workers subjected her would be considered felonies anywhere other than in a "friendly" setting.

The court failed to see her claim, I believe, because her sexual harassment complaint was delayed. Her complaint did not emerge for the first time until after she had been fired. The story she told in court was inconsistent with her co-workers' interpretations presented as if those interpretations were contemporaneous accounts. And the court, believing her co-workers' account as an initial story, discounted Reed's story as revised, assuming she had enjoyed the abuse at the time as her co-workers testified. When stories appear to have been revised, judges and juries use that very fact as evidence that the later story is false even when the victim did not grasp the chance to tell the first story herself.

State v. Frost

But not all revised stories are discounted by courts. Sometimes a victim's story of sexualized abuse can survive the usual screening rules. In recent years, this has sometimes happened when testimony of expert witnesses has been used to demonstrate that the victims of sexualized violence suffer from a form of post-traumatic stress disorder and therefore have *first* reactions that are not to be trusted. The professional undermining of initial stories allows the revised stories to be believed. *State v. Frost*, 242 N.J. Super. 601 (1990) provides one example of a case where expert testimony was successful in getting a revised story believed by a jury, and later by judges on appeal.

Early one April morning in 1986, L.S. was still sleeping when her former boyfriend, Gregory Frost, tapped on her shoulder. He had broken into her house. As she started to wake up, he started to yell at her. He hit her. Their baby began to cry, so L.S. picked up the child and ran to the front door to escape. Before she was able to open the door, Frost caught up with her and cut her arm deeply with a razor-edged box cutter.

Knowing how out-of-control he could be, L.S. tried to talk with him, eventually suggesting that they have sex because "that would calm him down." After they had sex, they went to the place where L.S.'s mother worked to get her car keys to go to the hospital to have the wound treated. L.S. asked her mother not to call the police. At the hospital, L.S. said she had cut her arm on the refrigerator. Her arm needed four sutures underneath the skin and 11 stitches to close the skin. But the story she told at the time was that she had cut herself accidentally, that she was in good hands with Frost to take care of her, and that she was ok.

After L.S. was treated, she, Frost and the baby went to L.S.'s home to get money, then went to a park where they drank beer and talked together. Eventually they went back to L.S.'s home again. L.S. was supposed to pick her mother up at work, but never did so. When L.S.'s mother arrived angry at having to find another ride home, she and L.S. got into such a huge fight that neighbors called the police. When the police arrived, they saw Frost running from the apartment wearing no shoes, socks or shirt. They recognized him as the person against whom a restraining order had been issued and arrested him. They charged him with contempt of court (for violating the restraining order) as well as burglary (for breaking into the house), assault (for stabbing L.S.), and various weapons charges (for possession of the razor). Notably, he was not charged with rape. He was convicted on all counts.

At the trial, Frost had claimed that L.S. had consented to spend the day with him, which he thought should cast doubt on any claim that he had broken in and attacked her that morning. But the prosecution introduced evidence that indicated that the relationship between Frost and L.S. had been plagued by Frost's frequent outbursts of violence against L.S. She estimated that he had hit her at least once per month during the time they had been romantically involved, starting on the second day that they knew each other. Police testified that she had called them to the house at least nine times to stop his violence. After suffering through three and a half years of battering, L.S. had left Frost to go to live with her mother. She got a restraining order to keep Frost away from her and the baby. Eventually Frost was sent to prison for theft from another person. L.S. had been responsible for his arrest in that case and, on the day he broke into her house and cut her with the razor, he had just been let out of prison. His first act as a free man was coming to get her.

Prosecutors also introduced expert testimony to the effect that L.S. was suffering from Battered Woman's Syndrome, an identifiable medical condition that was characterized by the court as follows:

> The battered woman places herself in the role of a victim. She blames herself, thereby becoming even more vulnerable to the point where she almost expects it. She is reluctant to tell anybody about what occurs, usually for a variety of reasons. She may be embarrassed, the man might keep her isolated from others, she may hope the situation will change, or she may fear it will get worse if she reports anything. Most significantly, the battered woman cannot just walk away from the situation. She is emotionally dependent on her "man" and is often involved in a love–hate relationship. (242 N.J. Super. 611)

The effect of the historical and the expert testimony was to provide a context within which a jury could believe that all the things L.S. said on the day of the attack were motivated by fear and therefore could be considered unusually suspect. Such a fear-induced account could be overridden by a revised story later. Without this framing, however, a jury might reasonably conclude (as Frost tried to argue) that she was now trying to get Frost in trouble because they had had a falling out after a pleasant day. After all, L.S. presented repeated and consistent explanations on the day in question about how she was ok, how she had just cut herself on the refrigerator, how no one should call the police because she was fine. But the specific violent history of the relationship between Frost and L.S. as well as the use of expert testimony convinced the jury that Frost had committed these acts and that L.S. had not consented. On appeal, the admissibility of the expert testimony so crucial to the prosecution's case was upheld.

Expert testimony can be very helpful to women in situations like this. But it comes at a price. Such testimony is effective with a jury because it gives them an explanation for a victim's conduct at the time in question by saying she is suffering from a form of mental illness. The victim stayed with her batterer because she was suffering from stress and shock. The victim may have *thought* things were going to get better, she may have *thought* he loved her, she may have *thought* that she wanted to be with him, but she was wrong, deluded and not a good judge of these things. As a result, whatever she may have *thought* happened on the day in question is also to be judged suspiciously. But making revised stories credible is very hard to do without an expert.

In this case, L.S. apparently wanted Frost convicted for these crimes. But she also visited him 11 times while he was awaiting trial back in prison.

The Problem of Truth in Law

So, how do judges and juries know when they have found the truth? It is an astonishing accomplishment that courts as well as ordinary individuals manage to operate on a daily basis as if the bases of factual judgments were clear and solid. While the idea of truth has been a contested subject among philosophers for as long as philosophy has existed, the idea of truth in daily life seems to generate much less debate. When asked to find "the facts" of a case, judges and juries do not puzzle over the meaning of that instruction. Why? The simple answer is that judges and juries, spectators and litigants, ordinary folks in the dailiness of life and specialists in the creation of knowledge, know truth when they see it. Within our own system of truth-finding, some cases may be easier and other cases are harder, but the idea of truth itself is rarely in doubt. If the truth is unclear in a particular instance, default rules are employed to settle matters provisionally so that whatever needs to happen next can happen without delay. In law, for example, default rules about the "burden of proof" or rules requiring proof "beyond a reasonable doubt" resolve uncertain cases in definite ways.

The structure of American courts relies on the widespread facility of ordinary citizens in reasonably workable practices of truth-finding. The jury system is premised on the idea that citizens, selected to serve on juries, can listen to the presentation of evidence and work out "what happened" independent of any specialized knowledge of the law (Scheppele, 1990). Lawyers and trial judges generally receive no special training in the evaluation of evidence or in strategies for discerning truth and so they too much draw on socially situated, unremarkable methods for determining "what happened." It is generally assumed that anyone who is not connected with the parties to the case and who does not have a special interest in the outcome of the case can figure out what to believe from evidence presented in a trial without specialized instruction. This is done because in the business of the evaluation of evidence, almost everyone is enough of an expert to be entrusted with finding facts.

But as we have seen with the examples detailed above, truth-finding is a socially situated practice. We all have a set of interpretive conventions, practices of truth-finding, that tell us when a particular story seems more credible than another, when one witness appears to be telling the truth and another seems to be lying. Most of us engage in the evaluation and construction of truth on a routine basis, finding the activity generally non-problematic and straightforward. Never mind that we are often dead wrong in doing this, regardless of our experience and professional training (Bennett and Feldman, 1981; Ekman and O'Sullivan, 1991). Most of the time, we are successful enough (or blind enough to the consequences of our inaccuracies) not to re-evaluate our practices. Whenever our failures call attention to our inadequacies in this regard, we engage in a patch-up effort to work out what went wrong in the particular case but rarely re-evaluate our entire scheme for evaluating the evidence that daily life presents us. And when we have to deal with the law, whether as professionals who do this all the time, as jurors or litigants who are called upon to do this on rare occasions, or even as observers or scholars of the judicial process, we bring our interpretive conventions with us.

So, what do people operating in the legal process see when they are presented with evidence? What interpretive conventions do people invoke when called upon to figure out "the facts" of cases?

The attribution of truth by judges and juries depends on properties of the stories witnesses tell (Bennett and Feldman, 1981; Jackson, 1988; Papke, 1991). Judges and juries decide whether a witness is telling the truth by evaluating how the story is constructed rather than by judging what it says. Some of the properties that matter in this judgment include internal consistency, narrative coherence, the reliance on "hard" or physical evidence and perhaps most importantly as we have seen, the stability of tellings of the story over time.

Narratives All the Way Down

Clifford Geertz is one teller of a tale that reports a cosmology in which the world rests on the back of an elephant, which stands on the back of a turtle. When asked what the turtle stands on, an informant answered, "Ah, Sahib, after that, it is turtles all the way down" (Geertz, 1973: 29). This is not exactly a comforting answer if one wants to believe that there is some stable bedrock somewhere. But (as with the elephant and its turtles) in stories, it is narrative all the way down (Bruner, 1990, 1991; Sarbin, 1986; Carr, 1986). Narratives become their own best evidence.

Why is this? Judges and juries cannot do what a correspondence theory of language would have them do; they cannot hold up testimony against events in the world to see which versions "match" better. They cannot do this most obviously because events are long over before cases come to trial and the "reality" in question is not around to hold any descriptions up against. (The idea of holding descriptions "up against" the world is metaphorical, and could not be done literally anyway. Some procedures would have to be devised for working out when a description corresponded to reality. Those procedures, then, not the "matching," would be doing all the work.)

But even if the descriptions were being constructed simultaneously with events or the events in question were preserved somehow (as happened with the videotape in the trial of the Los Angeles police accused of beating Rodney King), judges and jurors could not work out which single description best "matched" the world. The whole idea of matching descriptions against the world is misleading because it assumes that there is only one perspective, only one point of view, only one ideology, no room for multiple readings, no potential for disagreement – in short, no problem with understanding how accounts as socially situated cultural products relate to evidence of the world. But particular "true" stories and particular descriptive statements are always selected from among a set of arguably accurate versions of reality – it is just that other descriptions in the set give very different impressions about what is going on. The vexing question is not just whether the descriptions are accurate in some way, though it is crucially important to screen out lies, but rather how it is that some particular description rather than some other comes to be forwarded as the authoritative version of events (Goodman, 1978). This raises questions of power and ideology, of the "situatedness" of the descriptions that pass for truth and the social agendas they support (Haraway, 1991).

In law, these questions are not explicitly raised as problems. Questions about multiple versions of reality are largely ignored in the subject of evidence, where what is of greatest concern are limits to the sorts of statements that might be taken as accurate. Rules of evidence screen out *types* of information that are thought to be misleading, merely prejudicial, non-probative, or just plain unreliable. But the rules of evidence themselves are at best probabilistic judgments about categories of information and their likelihood in being false or irrelevant. It is not clear that rules of evidence actually accomplish their purpose of aiding in truth-finding, especially in light of the fact that most of us frequently use legally excludable evidence in making judgments outside of courtroom settings without apparently being wrong much of the time. Rules of evidence proceed on the assumption that individual bits of information can be screened out as unreliable, misleading or untruthful and that any "reasonable" assemblage of what is left counts as truth.

Rules of evidence provide no guidance about what to do once particular bits of information are admitted as evidence. In practice, judges and juries do the best they can to evaluate evidence the only way they can – through assessing the way the stories hang together with what else they know about the world and through spotting key characteristics in the stories that they hear, characteristics they believe are signs of truth.

Given the dependence of legal conventions of truth-finding on ordinary conventions of truth-finding, it is worth asking just what these ordinary conventions are for several reasons. First, the outcomes of individual cases are highly dependent on what is found to be "the truth" in that instance, so the integrity and reliability of the judicial process depends on these factual determinations. How they are made and what conventions they invoke should be made explicit if law is to be justifiable to those who are subject to it (Macedo, 1991: 38–77). Second, interpretations of fact and interpretations of law are not easily separable activities in the process of legal reasoning (Scheppele, 1990), and so any theory of judging needs to include some account of the interpretive conventions used in the construction of facts to represent the process adequately (Scheppele, 1989). Third, law often pretends to be above politics, prejudice and partiality by virtue of the principled nature of its practices in judging. Insofar as a large part of that practice depends on unexamined and possibly prejudicial conventions for assessing the facts on which judicial judgment depends, the practice of judging can hardly be said to be above these "contaminating" influences. So, we should explore these influences before relying on the assumption that law manages to sanitize bias through its appeal to principle.

In addition to these worries about legal legitimacy in the abstract, there is a more immediate practical issue involved in working out *whose* conventions of truth-finding are to be invoked, where there is more than one set of conventions operating in the social settings that a given legal system embraces. If we have learned anything in recent years about the operation of social practices, it is that they are usually specific to time, place, social location and embodiment in the lives of particular people. Saying that "we" have a set of conventions for truth-finding is already to beg the questions of who is in the "we" and whether "we" share these practices at all (Scheppele, 1989: 2077–79). So, working out how information is constituted as fact (or, at the risk of creating an unwieldy neologism, how information is "en-facted") requires both looking at the way conventions of practice are historically, socially, culturally situated in the lives of particular people and asking whose truth is being found when jurors and judges find it. But when we look more closely, we see that the whole metaphor of "finding" rather than "constructing" the truth relies on the assumption that truth is "out there" to be located rather than constituted through the operation of social practices. This way of talking about truth shows how the "facticity" of a truth-claim must be presented as if it is compelled by the external-ness of its referent rather than compelled or allowed by the agreement on conventions of description.

Evaluating Revised Stories

With these theoretical considerations in mind, we can now return to the specific problem of revised stories. If people generally believe that the first versions of stories are true and that later versions must be suspect unless there is some special reason to distrust the earlier version, what must their picture of truth look like?

The image people must have is of a precarious and fragile truth that decays over time, or is subject to the continual risk of subsequent distortion. As a result, information gathered before these inevitable processes of decay and distortion erode too much truth is considered to be especially important in figuring out "what happened." If accounts seem to change over time, it must be because something other than the initial, accurate perception of reality is being incorporated into the story.

But the distinction people make between initial stories and revised stories obscures an important feature they both share. They are both narratives, and as such they both represent strategies for organizing and making sense of evidence (Carr, 1986; Sarbin, 1986; Bruner, 1990). Neither story represents "perception without conception." We should not fall into the trap of thinking that the first versions of stories are raw material, processed by the mind without interpretation, and that revised stories take this raw material and shape it through interpretive processes absent in the first construction. As Wittgenstein showed in the duck–rabbit demonstration, "seeing" is often "seeing as" (Wittgenstein, 1976: 194). We do not first see things "as they are" and then interpret them. We see with the interpretive frameworks we bring to events as much as we see with our eyes. The woman who sees her abusive husband as revealing his love through his violence is not seeing some deeper, uninterpreted truth that is *then* interpreted through consciousness-raising. She is interpreting her husband's actions as much as a feminist observer or her husband's defense lawyer would. The difference is that she uses an interpretive framework the others would not use. In distinguishing between initial stories and revised stories, we might be tempted to contrast pure and untainted perception with contaminated and altered accounts. But all narratives are constructions and all descriptions are socially situated, making use of concepts and categories that are made available through the cultural location one occupies.

Nevertheless, we learn to describe as *true* the impressions we have at first because they appear to involve no conscious alteration, even though there may be a physical basis for other reports of those perceptions. Nelson Goodman reports that most of us on viewing a round table from the side still describe it as round, even though our eyes are perceiving the shape as oval because of the angle of vision (Goodman, 1978). Clearly, there is a large element of construction, however rapid and implicit, even in the most apparently uncontroversial descriptions.

What this all amounts to is that first accounts appear to be *simply true* as if perception were somehow free of organizing concepts and categories that are themselves social products. First versions are the "obvious" way to describe what has happened, while revised versions seem to involve conscious hard work to "make sense" of what has happened and are therefore more obviously contestable. The accounts we take to be "simply true" feel as though they are "straight" read-outs of unbiased perception. The accounts we arrive at by revising our stories to "make sense" of things seem to pull away from those initial perceptions and are distrusted as a result.

This is a general problem in the believability of narratives and it looks like a neutral rule. But it falls particularly hard on women. We know from experience, social science research and observation of the legal process that women who are the victims of sexualized violence often need to take time to understand what has happened to them because women have learned both to put up with sexual violence as a feature of daily life and to blame themselves for it as a first-pass explanation (Scheppele and Bart, 1983; Scheppele, 1987). Courts' exclusion of revised stories works disproportionately against women because women are disproportionately the victims of a socialization that masks the immediate recognition of sexualized abuse *as* abuse. Overcoming the first reactions takes time – but it is precisely the delay such realization requires that courts generally suspect as evidence of lying. The first stories we tell are not constructed in the absence of frameworks that help us to make sense of what has happened; they are simply constructed with our most uncritical frameworks, frameworks that may or may not be the ones we would think best to invoke upon further reflection.

Women's initial reactions in sexually abusive situations may lead others, particularly the men with whom they interact and those who judge women's reactions in court, to conclude that women enjoy the abuse and are encouraging the conduct. In a study of rape victims in Chicago that I worked on a decade ago, I was surprised to find how many women reported that they attempted to fight off their attackers by crying, by telling the rapists their life stories and by apparently agreeing to sex in order to lower the violence level in the assault (Scheppele and Bart, 1983). Several of the women in our sample of nearly one hundred each said that she began to tell the rapist (often a stranger) intimate details of her life in the attempt to get him to see her as a human being. If he saw her as a person, she thought, then he could not do this to her. Many women reported crying and bargaining rather than punching and screaming. Talking, crying and bargaining very rarely worked, but women thought of these strategies as aggressive attempts to defend themselves while the rapists no doubt interpreted these reactions as a lack of meaningful resistance. In the absence of bruises and scratches that come with a physical struggle, these women often had great difficulty proving their non-consent in court. As a surprising number of first reactions revealed in this study of sexual assault victims, women are afraid to stop being polite, even when they are being attacked. This may be because women have been found to be concerned with maintaining relationships, keeping them from break-ing apart (Gilligan, 1982).

In cases of sexual harassment, what victims seem to want most is for the conduct to stop. They do not want to leave their jobs, file formal grievance or rip up their lives to avoid what was not their fault to begin with (Pollack, 1990). Women often do not report sexual harassment, hoping it will go away (Mango, 1991). By the time they decide to fight it, it is too late. The initial story that they were consenting, or at least not objecting, has already stuck.

If we have a legal system that uses rules of evidence and principles for judging truth that are hostile to revised stories, then women will continue to be victims in court. But the few revised stories that *are* currently accepted by courts are not an unqualified good thing in empowering women. The revised stories that courts currently accept are generally the versions urged by expert testimony, not just by the woman herself. The presence of experts may remove a woman's individuality and unique voice by substituting a politically correct average experience that all women are supposed to share for the detailed, potentially idiosyncratic experiences each of us has. What a woman gains in feminist insight as a result, she may lose in distinctiveness. The use of expert testimony allows a woman to win a case against a man by having a "qualified person" testify that she was suffering from trauma or delusion and so was not in her right mind when she blamed herself, acted like nothing had happened from numbness, tried to show her deluded love for the person who injured her or changed her story. What she *really* meant (only the expert can say) was something else.

Not all revised stories should be believed. Nor should all first drafts of accounts. Strategies of belief need to be more complicated than that to do justice to the variety of knowledges present in any given society. Understanding how the stories are socially constituted as believable in the first place is one important step in that process.

Notes

I would like to thank Jane Bennett, Jerome Bruner, Sally Burns, Fernando Coronil, Peggy Davis, Louisa Bertch Green, John Kitsuse, Rick Lempert, Jack Meiland, Ted Sarbin, David Scobey, Peter Seidman, Richard Sherwin, Julie Skurski and particularly Roger Rouse as well as seminar participants at New York Law School and New York University Law School for making more comments than I could possibly take into account in revising this paper. The first account of these ideas was presented at the annual meetings of the American Political Science Association in August 1991, and readers will have to judge for themselves whether to believe the revised version.

1. I should explain something important about this case to put discussion of this opinion in context. Reed had been charged with trafficking marijuana to some of the inmates in the prison and with encouraging two female inmates to assault and beat another inmate with whom they shared a cell. There was apparently substantial evidence to sustain these charges, including a confession, though the evidence does not appear in the appeals court report and the confession was later retracted. The court clearly seemed to believe that Reed was not a terribly sympathetic character in general, and this undoubtedly affected their treatment of her sexual harassment claims. But the principles of law the three-judge panel unanimously confirmed and the evidence they used to illustrate such principles have implications for the consideration of sexual harassment claims more generally. I focus on the court's treatment of the sexual harassment claims in isolation, then, because the reasoning presumably applies even to more sympathetic victims.

2. In *Meritor* itself, the Supreme Court found that the appearance of voluntary participation by the victim did not defeat a successful harassment claim. The behavior that Michele Vinson complained of in *Meritor* was so obviously harassment in the view of the unanimous Supreme Court that her failure to object directly to her boss (who had forced her into a sexual relationship with him) did not bar her subsequent claim.

References

Bennett, W.L. and Feldman, M. (1981) *Reconstructing Reality in the Courtroom*. New Brunswick, NJ: Rutgers University Press.

Bruner, J.B. (1990) *Acts of Meaning*. Cambridge, MA: Harvard University Press.

Bruner, J.B. (1991) The narrative construction of reality, *Critical Inquiry*, 18: 1–21.

Carr, D. (1986) *Time, Narrative and History*. Bloomington, IN: Indiana University Press.

Ekman, P. and O'Sullivan, M. (1991) Who can catch a liar?, *American Psychologist*, 46: 913–20.

Federal Information Systems Corporation (1991) Transcripts of the Hearings on the Nomination of Clarence Thomas. Available through LEXIS.

Geertz, C. (1973) Thick description: toward an interpretive theory of culture, in C. Geertz (ed.), *The Interpretation of Cultures*. New York: Basic Books.

Gilligan, C. (1982) *In a Different Voice*. Cambridge, MA: Harvard University Press.

Goodman, N. (1978) *Ways of Worldmaking*. Indianapolis: Hackett.

Haraway, D. (1991) Situated knowledges: the science question in feminism and the privilege of partial perspective, in D. Haraway, *Simians, Cyborgs and Women: The Reinvention of Nature*. New York: Routledge.

Herman, J.L. (1992) *Trauma and Recovery: The Aftermath of Violence – from Domestic Abuse to Political Terror*. New York: Basic Books.

Jackson, B.S. (1988) *Law, Fact and Narrative Coherence*. Liverpool, UK: Deborah Charles Publications.

Macedo, S. (1991) *Liberal Virtues: Citizenship, Virtue and Community in Liberal Constitutionalism*. Oxford: Oxford University Press.

Mango, K. (1991) Students v. professors: combatting sexual harassment under Title IX of the Education Amendments of 1982, *Connecticut Law Review*, 23: 355–407.

Papke, D.R. (1991) *Narrative and Legal Discourse: A Reader in Storytelling and the Law*. Liverpool, UK: Deborah Charles Publications.

Pollack, W. (1990) Sexual harassment: women's experiences vs. legal definitions, *Harvard Women's Law Journal*, 13: 35–75.

Sarbin, T.R. (1986) The narrative as a root metaphor for psychology, in T.R. Sarbin (ed.), *Narrative Psychology: The Storied Nature of Human Conduct*. New York: Praeger.

Scheppele, K.L. (1987) The re-vision of rape law, *Chicago Law Review*, 54: 1095–116.

Scheppele, K.L. (1989) Telling Stories. *Michigan Law Review*, 87: 2073–98.

Scheppele, K.L. (1990) Facing facts in legal interpretation, *Representations*, 30: 42–77.

Scheppele, K.L. and Bart, P.B. (1983) Through women's eyes: defining danger in the wake of sexual assault, *Journal of Social Issues*, 39: 63–80.

Walker, L. (1979) *The Battered Woman*. New York: Harper & Row.

Wittgenstein, L. (1976) *Philosophical Investigations*, third edition. Translated by G.E.M. Anscombe. New York: Macmillan.

6
Gender, Science and Sexual Dysfunction

Mary Boyle

People with sexual difficulties have always sought help, from folk healers, medical men, midwives or the clergy. Systematic professional interest in such problems is, however, a recent phenomenon. It is not that there was no official interest in previous times; in Europe, at least until the sixteenth or seventeenth centuries, the nomenclature of sexual problems and control over action in relation to them rested with the Catholic Church, although it delegated parts of its authority, particularly in the matter of investigation, to lay people. Both the theory of sexual problems and professional practices surrounding them were subject to a vigorous process of secularization during the nineteenth century, against a background of a marked increase in popular discourse on sexual behavior (Foucault, 1981).

The new experts on sexual disorder were medical men. In part, this reflected the growing medicalization of unwanted behavior. It may also have reflected the fact that, as Foucault has noted, sexual behavior became central to the operation of power during the nineteenth century. It was thus appropriate that the sexually pathological should be openly discussed and therefore to some extent controlled, within the confines of a profession whose links with acceptable forms of social control were already well established (Scull, 1979; Moscucci, 1990). The links between medicine and sexual behavior have since been strengthened by the regular publication of classification systems for what are known as sexual deviations and sexual dysfunctions, by the American Psychiatric Association and the World Health Organization. I shall be concerned here with sexual "dysfunctions," that is, with problems of "performance," rather than "deviations," or performance under socially unacceptable conditions.

The nineteenth and twentieth century literature on sexual problems is characterized by four major themes. The first is that of named sexual disorders as properties of individuals. Sexologists have, of course, recognized the possible social origins of sexual problems and the role of the couple in etiology and maintenance. Such ideas, however, have been secondary to the construction of detailed classification systems of individual disorders. Thus, the individual or, at most, the couple, becomes the focus of research and intervention. The second theme is that of "sex" as an energy system. As Weeks (1985) has pointed out, this "hydraulic" model of sexuality, as a force which demands release and is then temporarily quiescent, has for centuries permeated western writing; within the Judeo-Christian tradition, appropriate release meant male ejaculation during heterosexual intercourse. Transferred to sexual problems, this model has led to the idea of sexual "dysfunction" as a subjective absence of force (lack of interest); insufficient build-up of force in sexual situations (lack of excitement/ arousal) and lack of or ill-timed release (anorgasmia, premature ejaculation, retarded ejaculation) or inability to achieve appropriate release (lack of orgasm during intercourse). A third theme has been that of progress through science. Sexologists of both the nineteenth and twentieth centuries have placed considerable emphasis on their allegiance to scientific theories and method. Indeed, as Weeks (1985) has noted, sexologists have gained much of their authority from public acceptance of such claims. The sexual dysfunction literature has, finally, been characterized by a preoccupation with gender relations. It would, perhaps, be surprising if this were not so, given the extent to which this issue has permeated the more general area of sexuality and sexual behaviour (Vicinus, 1982; Caplan, 1989).

This chapter will examine the ways in which these themes have shaped twentieth-century constructions of sexual problems. My focus will be on professional or "expert" constructions. One of the central tenets of modern constructionist theory is that discourse both reflects the ways in which "objects" are perceived and actively constructs them (Parker, 1990). Professionals who claim allegiance to science are in a particularly powerful position to construct "objects" for lay people; in effect, to provide a language and categories with which to organize thought and to communicate. In this case, they also provide definitions of normal and abnormal, appropriate and inappropriate, sexual behavior. In turn, professional discourse may be more acceptable if it accords with existing lay theories. Although I will explore each of the four themes mentioned earlier, the emphasis will be on the ways in which beliefs about gender relations have influenced the professional construction of sexual problems. There are two reasons for this. First, the issue of gender relations was the most pervasive theme of early sexological writing. As Weeks (1985) has noted, sexology quickly came to mean both the study of the "sexual impulse" and of relations between the sexes because, ultimately, they were seen as one and the same. At first glance, modern writers do not adopt the same prescriptive approach but this may simply mean that their prescriptions are expressed more subtly. The second reason for this emphasis is that it may offer a serious challenge to the apparent scientific neutrality of the professional literature. The rhetoric of modern science may impress us more than that of, say, Freud and Havelock Ellis. But it may obscure the influence of unarticulated values and make more important the task of deconstruction. The chapter will be divided into three historical phases: the early twentieth century, which marks the beginnings of modern sexology; a middle period marked by the publication of Masters and Johnson's influential research and by theirs and Kaplan's (1974) treatment programs and, finally, a modern period characterized by the development of the American Psychiatric Association's detailed classification systems for sexual problems in their Diagnostic and Statistical Manuals (1980, 1987), known as *DSM III* and *DSM IIIR*. The major classification systems are shown in Table 6.1.

Table 6.1   *Classification systems for sexual dysfunction*

Male	Female
Masters and Johnson	
Impotence, primary and secondary	Primary orgasmic dysfunction

Premature ejaculation	Situational orgasmic dysfunction
	    masturbatory
	    coital
	    random

Retarded ejaculation	Low sexual tension
	Vaginismus
	Dyspareunia
Kaplan	
Erectile dysfunction	General sexual dysfunction

Orgasmic dysfunction
    premature ejaculation
    retarded ejaculation
	Orgasmic dysfunction

	Vaginismus
DSMIIIR	
Erectile disorder	Sexual arousal disorder
Inhibited orgasm	Inhibited orgasm
Premature ejaculation	Dyspareunia
	Vaginismus
Hypoactive sexual desire disorder	
Sexual aversion disorder	

The Beginnings of Modern Sexology: 1900–60

Before Masters and Johnson introduced their elaborate classification system in 1970, sexual problems were usually described by the terms impotence and frigidity. There were two major changes in the use of these terms early in this century. These mainly concerned the ways in which female sexual problems were construed and it is on female problems which this section will concentrate. First, in the older ecclesiastical systems, "impotence" and "frigidity" could each be applied to men and women. Professional sexologists of the early twentieth century, however, applied the term frigidity exclusively to women. The terms anesthesia and dyspareunia were also used, apparently interchangeably with frigidity. Both "impotence" and "frigidity" carried several meanings. As in the theological system, impotence meant difficulties in achieving or maintaining erection and in ejaculating within the vagina. But by the early part of this century – and this is the second change – frigidity implied not simply an inability to have intercourse but referred to a woman's lack of *enjoyment* of intercourse, to her aversion to it, or lack of orgasm during it. And, although the term was applied to women who derived no enjoyment from any form of sexual stimulation, sexologists, including Freud, pointed out that many "frigid" women did enjoy sexual activity, but not intercourse.

Modern accounts of these earlier conceptions of sexual problems often depict them as an important advance because they recognized women's capacity for and right to, sexual pleasure (for example, Robinson, 1976; Leiblum and Pervin, 1980; Davison and Neale, 1990). It is certainly true that ecclesiastical systems of sexual problems were not concerned with women's sexual pleasure, but only with her ability to "receive" an erect penis. And the nineteenth century had witnessed a de-emphasis of women's capacity for sexual pleasure to the point of denial of its existence (Russett, 1989). Jeffreys (1985), however, has argued that the development of ideas about frigidity – ostensibly granting women the right to sexual pleasure – can only be understood in its social context and particularly against a background of intense activity by the Women's Movement around the turn of the century. While the campaign for female suffrage has been well documented, far less attention has been paid to a campaign of equal or greater intensity against male sexual behavior and female "sex slavery." Women's criticism focused on the idea of the male sex drive as powerful and uncontrollable, and on its perceived consequences: the sexual double standard, the use and abuse of prostitutes and the sexual abuse of girls and children. What made this campaign potentially so threatening to male authority was that, for perhaps the first time in recent history, women could have been in a position to achieve at least some of their social and political aims. As Jeffreys points out, many suffragettes made it clear that when they obtained the vote, they intended to change men's sexual behavior from a new position of strength. And it was not simply suffragettes who were apparently gaining strength: women in pre- and post-war Europe and in the United States were increasingly taking advantage of new educational and work opportunities.

It was against this background that writers such as Bloch, Ellis, Freud, Gallichan and Stekel developed their ideas about female sexuality and sexual problems. Jeffreys has argued that, while sexologists early this century may have acknowledged women's capacity for sexual pleasure, they also emphasized a relationship between women's sexual pleasure and her subjugation. This is perhaps most apparent in the development of the theme of innate differences between males and females: among other attributes, males are dominant and females submissive. These traits were expressed during heterosexual intercourse. The male role, that of initiator and controller of intercourse, enabled the woman to attain true femininity by surrendering to her husband. It was not enough simply to assent to intercourse. The woman had to enjoy it and preferably experience orgasm during it. Stekel was explicit about this. Presumably speaking only of women, he asserted that: "To be roused by a man means acknowledging one's self as conquered" and continued, "A woman should say: 'Do what you want with me!' and then: 'Enough! I am at the end of my powers. I have had enough!' Then only she acknowledges herself defeated, subdued, in the game of love" (1926: 3). The frigid woman, then, did not submit to her husband's domination: "Women who always want to rule and step on the bridegroom's toes at the marriage ceremony . . . remain completely anaesthetic in their husband's sexual embrace" (1926: 15). Similarly, Gallichan claimed that: "Being devoid of passion they are cool headed and calculating . . . [they] regard men as over-grown, good-natured boys, who can be managed and exploited" (1927: 68). Frigid women were also seen as masculine: "The true congenital frigide . . . is plainly mannish in appearance . . . her activities are diverted from the erotic and the emotional sphere into professional industry, social work, politics, sports, study and so forth" (1927: 43). By contrast: "the true female woman is susceptible to all the tender emotions of love, able to reciprocate physically and urged by her desires to seek a well sexed male man. This is nature's rule universally and inexorably" (1927: 46). And lest any man should be tempted to marry such a "masculine" woman, Chesser (1941) warned them that mating with women of masculine qualities, "in mind or physique" was due to the mental disorder of masochism.

Havelock Ellis, strongly influenced by Darwinism, developed an elaborate theory of sexual dominance and submission based on his interpretation of animal courtship: the male pursued, the female resisted (but did not really mean it) and finally surrendered. Gallichan agreed with this account: "Throughout the whole animal kingdom, including mankind, we find that the rôle of the male in love is in part aggressive while the female who is wooed is, in a certain degree, passive or semi-resistant" (1927: 100). It was not simply that this was nature's way, but that women enjoyed it: "Normal aggressiveness in the male appeals to the female in the same measure as coyness and slight resistance appeal to her partner in the sex act" (1927: 101); and: "The normal woman likes to feel herself conquered. A masterly touch in her lover is invariably pleasing" (Chesser, 1941: 66).

Within the medical framework in which these ideas were developed, frigidity was construed as an individual pathology, amenable to treatment. Gallichan, for example, claimed that the sexphobist was "intellectually and emotionally diseased" (1927: 57) and that "The frigid woman . . . is to be regarded as the subject of a serious handicap, that can, in most cases, be removed by suitable remedial measures" (1927: 17). But frequent use of terms like "stubborn," "resistant," "obstinate," and "refusal" in relation to frigidity showed that it was also seen as a conscious choice and, perhaps as such, as having major social implications. Stekel saw it as an "important weapon in the sex struggle" (1926: 14) while Gallichan claimed that: "The cold natured woman is often an active supporter of reformative organisations, female emancipation crusades, purity campaigns and societies for the suppression of vice. She comes very ill-equipped, emotionally and intellectually, into the field of social reform" (1927: 12), and that: "As a teacher, the frigide wields considerable power over the unformed minds of her pupils. She rarely takes pains to examine the justice of her indictment of man. . . . Her prudery is often imitated by the girls she is able to influence" (1927: 13).

What was to be done about such a serious problem? As well as treatment for individual cases, education was widely suggested as a solution. It appeared that there was a lamentable degree of ignorance about how to do sex properly. It is not clear how men were to learn these skills, but women's education was firmly entrusted to their husbands:

> So much depends on the behaviour, the understanding and the skill of the husband that the importance of knowledge in the initiator can scarcely be overrated. (Gallichan, 1927: 117)

> With [the mastery of the technique of lovemaking] he can take the lead in all that relates to sexual union. That is as it should be. He can educate his wife, one step at a time, in the art of joyous mating. I have said that the man should take the lead. Women want him to do so. (Chesser, 1941: 14)

It is important to remember that this "education" was not necessarily to be on the joys of sexual stimulation; many women had already discovered these, if we judge by the tirades against female masturbation and lesbianism. What was required was education on the joys of marital intercourse. The idea that women needed special education to enjoy intercourse was based on two assumptions. The first was that women were slower to arouse than men, and second that they found sex more difficult to enjoy and therefore needed skilled husbands to help them. Ellis (1936) compared woman to a complicated lock, which only the right man, with the right key, could open. Gallichan liked the analogy with a sensitive violin, from which only a skilled player "can produce sweet music" (1927: 112). The second assumption, popularized by Freud, was that women had to transfer their main source of sexual gratification from the clitoris to the vagina, and that this could take years to learn. It was therefore expected that some, if not most women would be "sexually anaesthetic," at the beginning of their marriages. Gallichan suggested that: "it is only after the experiences of marital life that the vagina adapts itself to intercourse. This adaptation involves a very considerable alteration . . . of the feminine attitude to the physical expression of sex desire" (1927: 30).

The sexologists of the early twentieth century therefore disseminated four important messages. First, that men were naturally dominant and females submissive. Second, that in order to achieve true femininity and womanhood, women had to surrender their bodies and personalities to their husbands through enjoyment of intercourse. Conversely, truly masculine men wanted to dominate women and were prepared to take responsibility for teaching their wives about sexual pleasure. A third message was that women were rather a problem sexually and that they needed men to teach them mature sexual responsiveness. Finally, if women rejected this route to fulfillment, they would be denigrated as emotionally diseased, as objects of pity and scorn and as a danger to the next generation. What made these messages particularly powerful was that they were presented within a framework which appeared to unite science and nature in the same conclusions. Darwinism provided one means for this integration as, to a lesser extent, did the new "science" of psychoanalysis. It was thus easy to portray women who did not enjoy "natural" sex as pathological or, at least, as handicapped and in need of help. French (1985) has noted the frequency with which the removal of physical and legal constraints on behavior has been followed by the development of psychological and social controls. It may be that it was unnecessary to pathologize, or even to be concerned with, women's lack of enjoyment of intercourse – as distinct from their ability to engage in it – when adequate social controls existed over their behavior. Jacquart and Thomasset (1988), for example, point to the lack of official concern over female masturbation and homosexuality during the Middle Ages, when women could not easily evade the social and sexual controls of marriage. By the early twentieth century, however, such controls were loosening, and both masturbation and homosexuality were seen as major causes of frigidity in marriage. And, as Gallichan said, frigidity was "a matter of serious social importance" (1927: 20).

1960–80: Masters and Johnson, and Kaplan

A number of researchers prior to Masters and Johnson had made more or less systematic observations about physiological responses to sexual stimulation (for example, Dickinson, 1933; Kinsey et al., 1953). Masters and Johnson (1966) not only provided extensive and systematic data on physiological responses, they are credited with settling the issue of clitoral versus vaginal orgasm and with describing women's capacity for multiple orgasms. They later (1970a) presented an elaborate classification system of sexual dysfunction – probably the first new system since the Middle Ages – and described a program of intervention which concentrated on couple communication, rather than individual psyches. Their ideas were developed and their classification system amended by Kaplan (1974). This section will look first at the ways in which cultural perceptions of gender appear to have shaped both the classification systems and intervention programs of Masters and Johnson, and Kaplan. I will then explore some of the means by which such influences may have been obscured.

Masters and Johnson have been associated with the second twentieth-century wave of sexual liberalism. They have been credited with 'freeing' women's sexuality, with reinforcing their right to pleasure and with providing scientific justification for obtaining it through clitoral stimulation. Indeed, Masters and Johnson, and Kaplan, in contrast to earlier sexologists, placed considerable emphasis on the similarities between male and female sexual response. Masters and Johnson remarked that: "In a comparison of male and female sexual function, it should always be emphasised that in sexual response, it is the similarities of, not the differences between, the sexes that therapists find remarkable" (1970a: 199). It is therefore particularly interesting to examine the ways in which their classifications and interventions differ for males and females.

In neither Masters and Johnson's nor Kaplan's systems, for example, is there a female equivalent of their male dysfunction, premature ejaculation, although the phenomenon of women climaxing "too quickly" was recognized as early as the twelfth century in an Arabic text (Jacquart and Thomasset, 1988). If climaxing more quickly than they wish is a problem for women today, we know very little about it. The more interesting question, perhaps, is why it should be seen as such a problem for men. Masters and Johnson might reply that it often leads to impotence. This is true, but their case studies suggest that it is not a natural progression; rather it is the result of several years of male performance fears and female sexual frustration. Such conflicts, however, arise partly from the belief, apparently shared by Masters and Johnson, and their clients, that prolonged sexual intercourse is necessary for female sexual satisfaction. Indeed, Masters and Johnson made this explicit by defining premature ejaculation in terms of the male's ability to prolong intercourse, on at least 50 percent of occasions, until his partner climaxes. They claimed also that: "If the male ejaculates regularly during pre-mounting play or during attempts at mounting or even with the first few penile thrusts after intravaginal containment, there rarely is opportunity for effective female sexual expression" (1970a: 93). Kaplan rejected Masters and Johnson's definition of premature ejaculation based on ability to delay until the woman climaxes, and emphasized instead the absence of voluntary control over the ejaculatory reflex. She claimed that:

> A man's ability to control his ejaculation is crucial for proficiency in lovemaking and for his successful sexual adjustment. The effective lover must be able to continue to engage in sex play while he is in a highly aroused state in order to bring the woman, who is usually slower to respond, especially when she is young, to a high plateau of excitement and orgasm. (Kaplan, 1974: 291)

These stringent requirements for men are barely distinguishable from those in the sex advice literature of the 1920s and 1930s. Men were enjoined to keep control of their passion while they raised their slow and untutored young wives (who would later learn to be quicker) to heights of excitement. Only then could both lose themselves in mutual orgasm. Behind these beliefs and behind professional concern with the timing of male orgasm, lie the ideas that women are dependent on lengthy contact with penises for sexual satisfaction and that male orgasm marks the end of the sexual encounter.

A second important difference in the way in which Masters and Johnson described male and female problems, is in the lack of a female equivalent of impotence. It is very difficult to justify this omission within Masters and Johnson's biologically-based scheme, which stresses the identity of physiological processes underlying erection in males and vasocongestion and lubrication in females. Masters and Johnson also claimed that: "from diagnostic and therapeutic points of view, it is easier and more accurate to consider [ejaculatory incompetence] as a clinical entity entirely separate from the classical concepts of impotence" (1970a: 116). This point was repeated several times. A female category of "low sexual tension" was tentatively suggested, but it is clear from the one case described that this does not necessarily refer to pre-orgasmic responses, in the way that impotence clearly does. Kaplan's system does have a female category roughly equivalent to male impotence, but although she also stresses the identity of male and female responses, her female category was given the vague title of "general sexual dysfunction."

This lack of identity of behavioral description of male and female problems has at least two important consequences. The first is that through both omission and non-specific language, women's sexual response prior to orgasm is rendered invisible. So widespread is the lack of attention to female pre-orgasmic responses that Masters and Johnson apparently did not even ask about them in their detailed history taking (1970a: 35). And Comfort's *Joy of Sex* (1987) – which discusses almost every sexual practice imaginable – could be read without readers discovering that female vasocongestion exists. It is reasonable to conclude that, if those who construct classification systems either omit or use vague labels for some of the phenomena the systems are supposed to cover, then these phenomena are not seen as particularly important. That this is the case is also suggested by Comfort's claim that: "unlike [women's] [men's] sexuality depends on a positive performance – he has to be turned on to erection, and not turned off, in order to function: he can't be passively 'taken' in a neutral way" (1987: 34–6). It is, of course, true that women can more easily than men acquiesce to intercourse when they are relatively unaroused physically; indeed they are often encouraged to use artificial lubricants to simulate physiological changes. But to equate such behavior with "positive sexual functioning" is to assume that women's pre-orgasmic responses are less important than men's. The neglect of female pre-orgasmic responses leaves women without a clear language in which to describe some of their sexual responses and reflects the absence of a female-oriented sexual language in lay discourse (Spender, 1985). Women may thus be made more dependent on the non-specific language of feelings. This point will be taken up again in the section on *DSMIII*, but it is clearly related to the second consequence of adopting different classification systems for males and females. By describing male sexual functions in terms of specific actions and performance – erection and ejaculation – such systems allow male dysfunctions to be conceptualized as mechanical performance failures: "the essential pathology [of impotence] is the impairment of the erectile reflex. Specifically, the vascular reflex mechanism fails to pump sufficient blood into the cavernous sinuses of the penis to render it firm and erect" (Kaplan, 1974: 256).

By contrast, Kaplan describes the "analogous" female problem as "the general inhibition of arousal" (1974: 342). This performance/feeling dichotomy is apparent also in Comfort's (1987) sections on "impotence" and "frigidity": impotence is the inability to perform, because the penis is not erect; frigidity is a dissatisfaction with sex, a lack of enjoyment. This contrast may not only make it difficult for men to integrate sexual activity with feelings, it may encourage them to seek physical explanations and interventions for sexual problems in preference to examining interpersonal issues. The emphasis on female feeling may also create the impression that the lack of female response is a dispositional problem, a problem of the person, as distinct from the male's local difficulty. And by concentrating on male actions, rather than emotions, the myth (see Hite, 1982) can be maintained that men who do not have erections in sexual situations are actually still aroused, excited, are still sexual beings, but just can't do it: "Although the impotent man may feel aroused and excited in a sexual situation and want to make love, his penis does not become erect" (Kaplan, 1974: 256). The contrasting statement about women is worth quoting in detail:

> General sexual dysfunction (and frigidity) refer to conditions which are characterised by an inhibition of the general arousal aspect of the sex response. On a psychological level, there is a lack of erotic feelings: on a physiological level, such a patient suffers from an impairment of the vasocongestive component of the sexual response: she does not lubricate, her vagina does not expand and there is no formation of an orgasmic platform. . . . In other words, these women manifest a universal sexual inhibition which varies in intensity. (1974: 342).

Finally, in both Masters and Johnson's and Kaplan's classification systems, the inevitability of the male orgasm during sexual encounters is assumed: it is not absent or lacking, just premature or retarded.

Intervention programs

Masters and Johnson's and Kaplan's classification systems suggest a preoccupation with heterosexual intercourse which is reinforced by their intervention programs. The major goal of these is penis–vagina intercourse culminating in orgasm for both partners. Masters and Johnson achieve an impression of merely encouraging natural behavior not only by uncritically adopting intercourse as the ultimate goal of sex therapy, but by creating an identity between the biological and the psychological. They claim, for example, that the female's biological response to sexual stimulation is essentially "an invitation to mount" (1966: 69) and that: "Full penile erection is, for the male, obvious physiological evidence of a psychological *demand* for intromission. In exact parallel, full vaginal lubrication for the female is obvious physiological evidence of a psychological *invitation* for penetration" (1970a: 195; emphasis added). Not only are physiological changes endowed with volition and purpose, but these just happen to reproduce the dominance–submission relationship so persistent in sexological writings. Indeed, so pervasive is the idea of male dominance and female submission in sexual and reproductive processes, it has provided a recurring metaphor for the "behavior" of sperm and ova. Gallichan for example, claimed that: "This intensely mobile germ cell, armed with a whip-like tail, is a physical symbol of the psychic-sexual activity of the male sex" (1927: 130). By contrast, the "relative passivity" of the ovum was said to symbolize the "relative psychic sexual passivity" of women. Martin (1991) has provided a detailed analysis of the ways in which this metaphor has persisted in the literature in spite of evidence that the idea of the "active" sperm and "passive" ovum is a misleading account of biological events.

But as well as construing intercourse as natural, Masters and Johnson endowed a male-oriented view of it with unique psychological attributes. Not only was the proper male conduct of intercourse seen as defining "consummation" of a marriage; if this had been delayed because of "ejaculatory incompetence," its occurrence was a moment of "rare reward" for the wife, whose levels of sexual frustration were "beyond comprehension" (1970a: 132). Masters and Johnson used the term consummation as if it were scientific, rather than social and legal. Masters and Johnson's male-oriented definition of a consummated marriage is, in fact, no different from that of the medieval and pre-medieval ecclesiastics who dictated Canon Law: the male must erect, enter and emit (Darmon, 1985).

Masters and Johnson placed themselves in a potentially difficult position by putting so much emphasis on sexual satisfaction through intercourse while at the same time claiming that clitoral stimulation was the key to female orgasm. To resolve this paradox, they suggested that penile thrusting causes "significant" indirect stimulation of the clitoris. Hite (1981) has discussed the problems of this assumption, while Kaplan claimed that "coitus provides only relatively mild clitoral stimulation which is often insufficiently intense to trigger orgasm" (1974: 38). She described coital orgasm as "ideal," however, and went to considerable lengths to teach women to grow "progressively less reliant on clitoral stimulation and more dependent on the use of coital thrusts to facilitate her orgasm" (1974: 407).

It was mentioned earlier that both Masters and Johnson, and Kaplan stressed the similarities between male and female sexual responses. As with their classification systems, it is therefore of particular interest to look at the ways in which males and females are treated differently during intervention. In both programs, greater importance appears to have been attached to male pre-orgasmic and orgasmic responses, and to male "release," than to female. Indeed, so important is it for a man to maintain and use his erection, that Kaplan quotes with approval the suggestion that men with erectile problems "be advised to take advantage of [their] morning erections and commence rapidly with intercourse without trying to stimulate [their] sleepy [wives]" (1974: 272). Similarly, if during the treatment of "general sexual dysfunction" "genital teasing [of the woman] is too stimulating and frustrating for her husband, the patient is instructed to bring him to orgasm manually or orally" (1974: 367). No suggestion is made that the man should do the same for his female partner, during his treatment for erectile problems. It is suggested, however, that men being treated for premature ejaculation may bring their wives to orgasm manually or orally. But the woman may have to go unsatisfied, because her husband is given "permission to ignore his partner's need for release" (1974: 307) and couples are warned that this focus on the male is the "curative factor" in treatment. Masters and Johnson's male clients were asked about their "ideal ejaculatory frequency" and women with sexual problems were told that their husbands "must" be manipulated to orgasm during the treatment period in which intercourse was forbidden. No similar instruction seems to have been given to men with sexual problems; rather, it was assumed that, once the husband could have prolonged intercourse, his wife's sexual needs would be taken care of.

A second way in which males and females were treated differently in intervention programs was in the availability of surrogates. Masters and Johnson were aware that their couple program could discriminate against single people. It soon becomes clear, however, that the surrogates are only for men, because: "The specific function of the partner surrogate is to approximate insofar as possible the role of a supportive, interested, co-operative wife" (1970a: 150). Masters and Johnson saw that in offering this service only to men, they could be accused of operating a double standard. They therefore provided a long apologia for their practice, and justified it by postulating basic differences between men and women. While men "validly" and "realistically" placed a "primary valuation on [their] capacity for effective sexual functioning" and could thus "regard the contribution made by a partner surrogate as [they] would a prescription for other physical incapacities", women had no such values. Nor were they to be encouraged to develop them. Instead, they valued "security," "real warmth," and "mutual emotional responsivity." (1970a: 155–6). But if the man regards the contribution of a surrogate as he would a prescription for other physical incapacities, why must she have so many of the qualities of a wife? Why must "every effort" be made to match the two in age, personality, education and social background? And why must they establish "social exchange" by wining and dining together? It is difficult to construe these efforts as other than attempts to establish an emotional relationship between the two, far beyond that expected in dealing with physical incapacities.

It is clear that social and moral considerations were involved in the construction of both Masters and Johnson's and Kaplan's theories of sexual problems. A number of factors may have masked these influences. First, Masters and Johnson transferred the language of their laboratory studies of human physiological sexual response to an area – of sexual complaints – which had little to do with laboratory research. They repeatedly referred to themselves as "authority," as if their laboratory background had equipped them with facts from which to construct their classification system and intervention program. Similarly, they stressed their clients' sexual ignorance and presented themselves as the source of scientific knowledge. A second and closely related factor was Masters and Johnson's and, later, Kaplan's, emphasis on the physiological sexual response cycle, implicitly based on the hydraulic model of "sex" as a force seeking release. The idea of a response cycle was not new although it was usually expressed in terms of male responses. But Masters and Johnson's and Kaplan's explicit use of it to construct a system of sexual "dysfunction" for males and females may have helped to create the impression of a natural relationship between descriptions of what often happens to people's bodies in sexual situations and statements about what is sexually problematic and sexually appropriate. In practice, Masters and Johnson's emphasis on male pre-orgasmic responses, on heterosexual intercourse and on orgasm during intercourse for both partners, may owe more to their personal beliefs that it is valid for a man to place "primary valuation" on his capacity for erection and intercourse (1970a: 155) and that "the most rewarding parts her society assigns to females [are] those of wife and mother" (1970b: 11) than to objective laboratory research. Finally, the relationship between social beliefs and theories of sexual complaints may be masked by the construal of such complaints as individual, or, at most, couple, dysfunctions. Both Masters and Johnson, and Kaplan emphasize the role of couple interaction and cultural learning in creating sexual problems. These processes, however, are seen as creating internal "blocks" to natural sexual functioning, rather than as helping to determine what is construed as natural sexual functioning.

1980 – *DSMIII* and *DSMIIIR*

The third edition of the American Psychiatric Association's *Diagnostic and Statistical Manual of Mental Disorders* (1980, revised 1987) presented a classification system of sexual dysfunctions markedly different from those of Masters and Johnson, and Kaplan. It attempted, for example, to use similar categories and language to describe male and female sexual problems. It also tried to remove the implication of pathology from women who did not climax during intercourse. Nevertheless, the changes do not represent a fundamental shift from previous approaches to sexual problems. They do not represent a change from the depiction of "sexual dysfunctions" as a series of natural categories, of individual disorders, objectively described by researchers. On the contrary, this impression may be heightened by *DSMIII*'s claim that it classifies "mental disorders which individuals have" (APA, 1980: 6) and by its inclusion – in the manner of medical texts – of headings such as "Age at Onset," "Course," "Predisposing Factors," "Differential Diagnoses" and "Sex Ratio".

The 1980 edition of the *DSM* abandoned the terms impotence, erectile dysfunction and general sexual dysfunction in favour of the generic "Inhibited Sexual Excitement." For both males and females, this was described in purely physiological terms. And while the term excitement is scarcely more specific than Kaplan's "general sexual dysfunction" it was at least being applied to both men and women. By 1987, however, in *DSMIIIR*, the similarity in language had disappeared with the listing of two separate disorders: female sexual arousal disorder and male erectile disorder. In reinstating the term erectile to refer to a category of disorder, however, the devisers of *DSMIIIR* have created an interesting paradox. Both female sexual arousal disorder and male erectile disorder can be diagnosed using either of two criteria: problems with genital swelling/lubrication or lack of a subjective sense of excitement or pleasure. As Hite (1982) has shown, men can experience genital swelling during sexual activity without much subjective sense of pleasure. Thus, men could, in principle, be diagnosed as suffering from erectile disorder even when they usually have erections. It seems unlikely that this will happen in practice. Women, too, however, may experience genital swelling and lubrication with little subjective pleasure (Morokoff and Heiman, 1980). But, as the vague category label of sexual arousal disorder can encompass physiology and feeling, we may find that more women are said to have arousal disorder than men are said to have its equivalent, although their experiences may be similar.

The second major change in *DSMIII* was in its apparent acceptance of the normality of women not climaxing during intercourse. The way in which the idea is expressed, however, suggests that women are still being judged by male standards of sexual expression. There is, first, a clear acknowledgment of women's need for direct clitoral stimulation. But this is often expressed in terms of women's needing "additional stimulation" or "simultaneous clitoral stimulation" or not climaxing "in the absence of manual clitoral stimulation" (for example, Kaplan,

1974; Jehu, 1979; APA, 1987; Comfort, 1987). But additional to what? It is well documented that the most reliable way to reach orgasm is through stimulation of the glans penis for men and the clitoris for women. Intercourse is an extremely efficient way for males, but not females, to receive such stimulation. The use of words like "additional," "simultaneous" or even "in the absence of," suggests that females need "extra" stimulation in order to climax whereas men reach orgasm in a more straightforward way. Hite's (1981, 1982) research has shown how strongly this idea of women's need for "extra" stimulation has communicated itself to some women and men, and how it may contribute to women seeing themselves, and being seen by men, as sexually problematic:

> It's our fault if we can't be as natural as men are [i.e. climax during intercourse]. (female: 1981: 252)

> There would be a lot less problems if women all orgasmed easily through intercourse. (male: 1982: 656)

> I didn't feel good for [women] [when I heard of their need for clitoral stimulation separate from coitus], like a car with a defect that the dealer wouldn't fix. (male: 1982: 659)

Another way of expressing women's pattern of not climaxing regularly through intercourse has been to call it a "normal variation of the female response" (Kaplan, 1974; APA, 1980, 1987). But if this is a variation, what is the standard? Hite's (1981) research shows clearly that the standard is for women not to climax regularly through intercourse and that those who do usually ensure that they receive the kind of clitoral stimulation which would bring them to orgasm during masturbation. It is, of course, the male standard to climax during intercourse; for women, this is the "normal va tion." And in spite of the statistical normality of not cli axing during intercourse, some women are still to be given a psychiatric diagnosis and offered "treatment." Hite (1981) has pointed out that diagnosing and offering "treatment" to women who do not climax with intercourse leaves the impression that this is "sick" or "abnormal," or, to use *DSMIII*'s own phrase, a "dysfunction." And it continues to disadvantage women as long as there is no analogous disorder and treatment for the many men who do not climax with indirect or inefficient penile stimulation.

An Overview

The presentation of the professional literature on sexual problems involves the assumption – both explicitly and implicitly – that sexual "dysfunctions" are scientific rather than social constructions. To suggest that this is not the case does not mean that the literature is valueless. On the contrary, ideas about, for example, non-demand pleasuring and about improving communication between partners may be of great value in increasing sexual satisfaction. But in terms of its individualistic and pathologizing theoretical framework, the professional literature helps to remove sexual complaints from their wider cultural context; in terms of the content and language of its classification systems, and the conduct and goals of its interventions, the literature can be seen to reflect traditional views of appropriate sexual conduct and may serve as one means of reproducing traditional gender relationships.

References

American Psychiatric Association (1980) *The Diagnostic and Statistical Manual of Mental Disorders*, third edition. Washington, DC: American Psychiatric Association. (Third edition revised, 1987.)

Caplan, P. (ed.) (1989) *The Cultural Construction of Sexuality*. London: Routledge.

Chesser, E. (1941) *Love Without Fear*. London: Rich and Cowan Medical Publications.

Comfort, A. (ed.) (1987) *The Joy of Sex* (revised edition). London: Quartet Books.

Darmon, P. (1985) *Trial by Impotence*. London: Chatto and Windus.

Davison, G.C. and Neale, J.T. (1990) *A Textbook of Abnormal Psychology*, third edition. New York: Wiley.

Dickinson, R.L. (1933) *An Atlas of Human Sex Anatomy*. Baltimore, MD: Williams and Wilkins.

Ellis, H. (1936) *Studies in the Psychology of Sex. Vol. 1 Part 2. Analysis of the Sexual Impulse, Love and Pain, The Sexual Impulse in Women*. New York: Random House. (Originally published 1903.)

Foucault, M. (1981) *The History of Sexuality. Vol. 1: An Introduction*. Harmondsworth: Penguin.

French, M. (1985) *Beyond Power: On Women, Men and Morals*. London: Jonathon Cape.

Freud, S. (1953) *On Sexuality: Three Essays on the Theory of Sexuality and other Works*. London: Penguin Books.

Gallichan, W.M. (1927) *Sexual Apathy and Coldness in Women*. London: T. Werner Laurie.

Hite, S. (1981) *The Hite Report: A Nationwide Study of Female Sexuality*. New York: Dell.

Hite, S. (1982) *The Hite Report on Male Sexuality*. New York: Ballantine Books.

Jacquart, D. and Thomasset, C. (1988) *Sexuality and Medicine in the Middle Ages*. Cambridge: Polity Press.

Jeffreys, S. (1985) *The Spinster and her Enemies: Feminism and Sexuality 1880–1930*. London: Pandora Press.

Jehu, D. (1979) *Sexual Dysfunction: A Behavioural Approach to Causation, Assessment and Treatment*. Chichester: Wiley.

Kaplan, H.S. (1974) *The New Sex Therapy: Active Treatment of Sexual Dysfunctions*. London: Ballière Tindall.

Kinsey, A.C., Pomeroy, W.B., Martin, C.E., and Gebhard, P.H. (1953) *Sexual Behaviour in the Human Female*. Philadelphia, PA: W.B. Saunders.

Leiblum, S.R. and Pervin, L.A. (1980) *Principles and Practice of Sex Therapy*. New York: The Guilford Press.

Martin, E. (1991) The egg and the sperm: how science has constructed a romance based on stereotypical male-female roles, *Signs: Journal of Women in Culture and Society*, 16: 485–501.

Masters, W.H. and Johnson, V.E. (1966) *Human Sexual Response*. Boston: Little, Brown and Co.

Masters, W.H. and Johnson, V.E. (1970a) *Human Sexual Inadequacy*. London: J & A. Churchill.

Masters, W.H. and Johnson, V.E. (1970b) *The Pleasure Bond: A New Look at Sexuality and Commitment*. Boston: Little, Brown and Co.

Morokoff, P.J. and Heiman, J.R. (1980) Effects of erotic stimuli on sexually functional and dysfunctional women: multiple measures before and after sex, *Behaviour Research and Therapy*, 18: 127–37.

Moscucci, O. (1990) *The Science of Women: Gynaecology and Gender in England, 1800–1929*. Cambridge: Cambridge History of Medicine.

Parker, I. (1990) Discourse: definitions and contradictions, *Philosophical Psychology*, 3: 189–204.

Robinson, P. (1976) *The Modernisation of Sex*. New York: Harper & Row.

Russett, C.E. (1989) *The Victorian Construction of Womanhood*. Cambridge, MA: Harvard University Press.

Scull, A.T. (1979) *Museums of Madness: The Social Organisation of Insanity in Nineteenth Century England*. London: Allen Lane.

Spender, D. (1985) *Man Made Language*, second edition. London: Routledge & Kegan Paul.

Stekel, W. (1926) *Frigidity in Woman in Relation to her Love Life*. New York: Liveright.

Vicinus, M. (1982) Sexuality and power: a review of current work in the history of sexuality, *Feminist Studies*, 8: 133–56.

Weeks, J. (1985) *Sexuality and its Discontents: Meanings, Myths and Modern Sexuality*. London: Routledge & Kegan Paul.

7
The Many and Varied Social Constructions of Intelligence

Milton L. Andersen

If any concept in psychology needs the full force of social constructionist analysis, it is the concept of intelligence. Fortunately, this analysis has existed for some time, though it has usually been embedded within a different frame of reference. It may have escaped our notice because it has appeared many times over the last 125 years in the form of the "nature–nurture debate," the "environment–heredity" controversy. This debate has been not only about the relative roles of nature (heredity) and nurture (environment) but has involved many other issues. In this debate, those writers referred to as "environmentalists" have recognized that the concept of intelligence is a social construction, while the hereditarians generally take a crude realist stance, use an "operational" or a statistical definition of intelligence, assert that it has a biological reality or nature, assert that it can validly be "measured," and present their data in a complex statistical form. The hereditarian position is a social construction despite the claims that its advocates are engaged in an objective, positive science untainted by social–political or ideological content. A central task of this chapter will be to trace the social construction of the hereditarian position.

The hereditarians are often psychometricians as well. Beginning with Francis Galton, statistical and genetic approaches became tightly coupled. Finding a quantitative "measure" of intelligence became an obsession. With the transformation by American psychologists of Binet's scales into a single, quantitative measure of intelligence, and the acceptance of the circular dictum that "intelligence is what the tests test," the psychometric tradition became dominant, and psychometric procedures, data, theories, and definitions became privileged over all others. The idea that intelligence was a social construction was submerged by the more powerful psychometric definitions that had been hardened in the crucible of statistics.

The Central Role of IQ Tests in the History of Psychology in the United States

Tests are one of the major products of US psychology, if not *the* major product. That is, if we define testing in the broadest sense, to include all forms of testing, assessment, diagnosis, and evaluation, then testing is definitely a major part of the daily work of many psychologists. In the history of US psychology, tests have played a crucial role. One key scholar has described the development and use of IQ tests early in this century as "putting psychology on the map" (Samelson, 1979). The testing of nearly two million recruits in the US Army was a turning point in US psychology.

Before World War I psychology was being taught in many universities and colleges, and there were many psychology laboratories in operation. Psychology already was an established profession. However, there was still an academic, philosophical aura about psychology. What was needed was a transformation of psychology into: (1) a respected science; (2) an independent academic discipline; and (3) a profession that would provide socially recognized and useful products (Fancher, 1985; Sokal, 1987; Morawski, 1988; Danzinger, 1990). The massive IQ testing during World War I satisfied these requirements for psychology: to be seen as scientific, practical, and professional. The IQ test had the properties of being created by experts, administered by experts (or by personnel under their supervision), and could be interpreted only by experts, with experts in control of all the data and analyses. This made it a professional activity. The test responses generated enormous amounts of quantitative data which were submitted to complex statistical procedures, providing an aura of hard science. Furthermore, the uses of the tests for practical, social purposes, showed that psychology could do applied, useful work. These tests were "useful" or "practical" mainly for administrators, such as personnel officers, school superintendents, and other officials, serving as gatekeepers in bureaucratic and institutional structures.

Francis Galton began many of the practices that are still central to psychology. Every psychology student learns about correlation coefficients, and the psychometric tradition he began is still very much alive. It reflects the Platonist grip the Galtonian approach has had on much of psychology. It has, as Shweder (1990) remarked, led psychology on an eternal quest in search of the universal, deep, innate, and transcendent central processing mechanism from which our thinking, feeling, and action are said to derive.

The Transformation of Social Constructs (Social-Political Beliefs) into Pseudo-Biological Concepts

Social-political beliefs and theories of intelligence have been intertwined at least since the time of Plato in the European world. A common use of theories of intelligence has been to justify social-economic inequalities. It has always been those peoples at the "bottom" of society that have been said to lack something, or have something wrong with them. The poor have always been blamed for being poor by those who have wealth and power. One particular inferiority of poor people is said to be their innately inferior intelligence (Andersen, 1978).

The Confusion of Malthusian with the Darwinian Concept of "Fitness"

With Thomas Malthus in 1798, this doctrine of inferiority became a respectable scientific theory. Malthus stated that the human population would always exceed the food supply. There were just too many people. The people that there were too many of, were, of course, poor people. Malthus stated that poor people had neither the right to be born nor the right to live. Their poverty he regarded as decreed by the laws of Nature and the laws of God. He advocated that their wages should always be kept low, and that diseases and other death-producing causes be encouraged among the poor to increase their death rate. He wrote: "Instead of recommending cleanliness to the poor, we should encourage contrary habits. . . . We should . . . crowd more people into houses and court the return of the plague" (Malthus, 1803, quoted in Chase, 1977: 68). Herbert Spencer, the early nineteenth-century English social philosopher, was greatly influenced by the writings of Malthus. Spencer's views about the poor were similar to those of Malthus. Spencer regarded the poor as unfit, and said they should be eliminated. He wrote: "The whole effort of nature is to get rid of such, to clear the world of them, and make room for better" (Spencer, 1874, quoted in Hofstadter, 1955: 41). The views of Herbert Spencer should not be confused with the strict Darwinian approach to evolution. Spencer, not Darwin, coined the phrase, "survival of the fittest," which he published in 1852, seven years before Darwin published the *Origin of Species*. Darwin did, however, later come to use this well-known phrase, "survival of the fittest," but it is crucial that the Spencerian or Social Darwinian definition of "fitness" be distinguished from the strict Darwinian definition.

The strict Darwinian definition of "fitness" refers to the ability of organisms to survive and produce fertile offspring, which will in turn produce fertile offspring, etc. The fitness referred to here can be *for any reason*. Fitness can occur because of better camouflage, smells to keep predators away, better armor or quills to discourage predators, an effective social organization to raise the young, anything that increases the chances of survival of offspring into their breeding age.

Ironically, if we look at European societies in the last 200 years, the low-income and non-white groups have been said to be overproducing, or "outbreeding" the more affluent classes. If these "lower" groups do have, in fact, a higher reproductive rate, then *they, and not the wealthy* and powerful groups, *possess the greatest fitness* in the strict Darwinian sense. The Social Darwinists and eugenicists, from Francis Galton to the present day, have used the Malthusian–Spencerian concept of fitness, not the Darwinian concept. They simply assumed that those persons in existing society whom they regarded as monetarily successful, were naturally more "fit."

The hereditarian position *required* the Malthusian–Spencerian concept of fitness. It was necessary to their ideology that the affluent, professional middle class be assumed to be the most capable. To utilize a Darwinian sense of fitness, and conclude that poor people were the most fit, was, literally, unthinkable. The hereditarians, of course, did argue that the poor were "artificially" kept alive by welfare and relief measures. But this argument would ask us to believe that the health and nutritional levels of the poor were higher than the levels found in the more affluent classes of society.

"Measurement" and Concepts of "Racial" and Class Differences

What was needed next by the hereditarian position was some "measure" of innate abilities. In the late 1800s, in the absence of measures of intelligence, Francis Galton began a study of "eminence." He regarded "eminence" as a valid indicator of innate ability. He studied English men who were regarded as having sufficient eminence to be listed in biographical dictionaries. His study showed that eminence "runs in families." Galton was aware of the effect of the favorable environments for eminence in well-to-do families, such as a great deal of leisure time and a good education, but he concluded that these environmental effects were not very important (Fancher, 1985: 31–2).

Galton had been interested in developing a series of examinations (tests) which could measure innate abilities. He was able to have about 9,000 people tested on such variables as head size, reaction time, sensory acuity, keenness of sight and hearing, color sense, and judgments in bisecting a line (Fancher, 1985: 41–5). Galton's belief was that since innate, natural ability was biological, there must be measurable qualities of the brain and nervous system that would constitute an appropriate test of inherent ability. Galton was wrong. His various sensory-motor tests just did not correlate with measures of intellectual performance or achievement. Later, with the items developed by Alfred Binet in France, and their transformation in the United States into unidimensional scales of general intelligence by Goddard, Terman, and others, the Galtonians finally had their method of "measuring intelligence" (Fancher, 1985; Sokal, 1987; Mensh and Mensh, 1991).

Another example of a social-political belief transformed into a pseudo-biological concept are the different definitions of "race." The biological definition of race used in modern genetics is statistical: *"Races are simply populations of the same species which differ in the frequencies of some genes"* (Gill, 1978: 27; emphasis in original). This is a very strict definition, with sharply specified and limited uses, and differs greatly from the social-political definitions based on cultural stereotypes concerning visible human features such as skin color, facial features, hair type, etc. In the debates about racial differences in intelligence, there has been frequent mention of an average difference of 15 points on IQ tests between two identifiable racial groups, black and white (Jensen, 1969). But, the definition of "race" has been the cultural stereotype, not the strict biological definition of race. What we have then is the correlation of IQ test performance with the cultural definition of race, not the biological definition. This correlation could be interpreted as indicating the magnitude of the discriminatory effect of being classified as a member of one racial group rather than another. It seems, then, that *the very data* used by various theorists who utilize a cultural-stereotypic definition of race *threaten* the theories that they have erected upon those same data. The data show, in fact, the effects (on IQ test scores) of being categorized and treated differentially due to stereotypical racial classification. In simple terms, the 15-point difference in average IQ test scores results from people of African-American ancestry being categorized and treated as black rather than being treated as white. Thus, the famous 15-point difference is a measure of the degree of discrimination rather than the degree of inferiority.

A second example is not a simple one of a transformation of a social construct into a biological concept. It is, however, an example of rejecting a social-class explanation, in favor of a biological or genetic one. It is the well-known study begun in 1921 by Lewis Terman, *Genetic Studies of Genius*, published in seven volumes. This enormous work seems like a continuation of Galton's study of eminent men in the last century. Galton began with eminence, while Terman began with high IQ test scores. Terman located 1,528 students in California schools, born between 1903 and 1917, with IQ scores between 135 and 196. These high IQ students were tested about every seven years, and in the 1950s their children were also tested (Minton, 1987, 1988). Terman found that most of his "termites" were located in the top social classes, and they were superior in many ways compared to those with lower IQ scores. Terman's "geniuses" were intellectually eminent, and had high occupational status and professional success. Terman's conclusion was that high IQ is highly predictive of later intellectual, social, and occupational status and success. Ceci (1990: 58) said about this study: "More than any other study in psychology, this is the one that has been touted as the single best validator for the IQ = intelligence = real-world success argument."

However, Terman seems to have made the same crucial mistake that Galton made many years before. Terman, like Galton, did not properly weigh the many effects of social-economic status. Terman compared his "geniuses" with children representing *all* social class levels, rather than comparing them with children from *their own* social class level. When the "geniuses" are compared to a cohort from their own social class, "the IQ scores of these 'geniuses' appear to have added little to the prediction of their life outcomes over that gained simply from a consideration of their parental income, education, and occupational status" (Ceci, 1990: 59).

An interesting note Ceci added to his analysis, is that two men who were rejected in Terman's study, because of low IQ scores, later were recipients of Nobel prizes. But, to Ceci's knowledge, not one of Terman's "geniuses" has yet received a Nobel prize (Ceci, 1990: 62).

When do we use the Concept of Intelligence?

We invoke the concept of intelligence when one person evaluates the action of another. The use of the term intelligence refers to evaluated action or conduct. Intelligence is neither behavior, nor something only "in the head." It includes actor, action, observers, and evaluation, within a context. We (twentieth-century Euro-centric humans) tend to utilize the concept of intelligence only in certain circumstances. We tend not to use the concept of intelligence when we are considering abilities and skills that *all* humans possess. Rather, we invoke the concept of intelligence when we have observed differences between individuals in intellectual performance that can be evaluated in terms of its worth (or lack of worth), and we believe that we have ruled out all competing explanations of these performance differences, such as differences in motivation, prior experience, or training. That is, when we feel that we have taken care of all rival explanations of individual differences in the performance or conduct, we then conclude that it is proper to conceptualize something that exists "deep within a person" that we call intelligence, and that differences in how much (capacity) each person possesses of this valuable commodity explain the performance differences. Lewontin (1976) has described this as the "bucket theory of the mind," and an elegant and detailed critique of this approach is seen in Mancuso and Dreisinger (1969).

These "deep within the person" differences are viewed by some authorities as innate, inherited, or "hard-wired at conception," and as quite fixed or unalterable over the life of an individual. This approach of eliminating all rival hypotheses is standard procedure in psychological experimentation and research. In the case of intelligence, however, it is embedded within the very concept we wish to investigate. To advance our understanding of human performances that we regard as intelligent, we should use terms and concepts that are not biased toward certain interpretations. The traditional psychometric approach to the study of intelligence shifts the analysis from certain kinds of performance to *differences* in performance. One effect of shifting to an explanation of differences is that we also shift to the comparative enterprise of identifying and predicting differences in ability and success. The comparative approach leads inevitably to the creation of competition. An alternative approach would be the development and utilization of procedures dedicated to making all people more intelligent, a generative model of intelligence, rather than a comparative–competitive model (Andersen, 1978). This alternative to the comparative–competitive model, the generative model of education, which utilizes "testing" only for analyzing *how* a student thinks, and attacks problems, will be presented later.

We should also notice how *contextual* is our use of the terms "intelligent" and "intelligence." We invoke these terms as an evaluation of a person's action within a given context – what is properly called conduct, not behavior (Sarbin, 1982). In a social world, our performances or actions are evaluated by others, although people can, of course, be judges of their own actions. We evaluate some actions as intelligent, some as stupid. This approach "re-locates" intelligence. It is not seen as only "in the head" or in the actions of a person. *It is in the total context*: in the actor, the action, the observer, the context. Intelligence, or intelligent conduct, then, is clearly a social construction, dependent upon the social, cultural, and immediate context for its definition and proper use. It should be mentioned that much of the work of psychologists is the evaluation of conduct, not simply the analysis of behavior, and that four major areas of research in psychology are remarkably similar to four basic folkways in which we evaluate others in our daily life. These are: lazy–energetic, crazy–sane, stupid–smart, and good–bad. The corresponding research areas in psychology are: motivation, mental illness, intelligence, and morality. The strong "prescriptive-bias" (Gergen, 1973) in many of our psychological concepts is reflected in these folkways.

The Various Definitions of "Intelligence"

The definitions vary across cultures, within cultures, and over time. No stable, universal meaning is assigned to the term "intelligence." Multiple definitions clearly betray the status of intelligence as a social construction. Intelligence as a term referring to the general faculty of understanding dates back to the fourteenth century, and intelligence as a term to compare people began in the sixteenth century (Williams, 1983). An etymological dictionary informs us that "intelligence" derives from the Latin words "inter" (between), and "legere" (to choose). So, "intelligence" would be a matter of choosing, or judgment.

Studies carried out over the past 70 years indicate that experts disagree as to the nature of "intelligence." Sternberg (1990) presented a detailed analysis of various definitions of intelligence, as suggested by the title of his book: *Metaphors of Mind: Conceptions of the Nature of Intelligence.* He categorizes these definitions of intelligence in terms of: (1) looking inward (a focus on processes within the person); (2) looking outward (how culture and socialization affect conduct; and (3) looking both inward and outward (a systems approach). I propose two, rather than three, basic metaphors of intelligence: first, intelligence as "doing abstract problems in one's head" (the internal definition), and second, intelligence as the evaluated quality of one's interactions and relationship to one's environment (the contextual definition). These two definitions are not just different, but diametrically opposed, and reflect the basic division in how intelligence is conceptualized. The internal (essentialist) definition is employed by psychometricians and hereditarians, who could be called the "believers" in genetically-determined intelligence. The contextual definition is employed by a broad range of theorists and researchers, often called "environmentalists," who could be called the "skeptics" of the genetic-determinist position (see Asch, 1952).

The metaphor of "doing abstract problems in one's head" is the one typically used by psychometricians. This metaphor takes on a concrete form when an individual being tested is alone in a room with only one other person, the IQ tester, answering questions and solving problems and puzzles presented by the IQ tester. Each person must work totally alone, and must not talk with or help anyone else, for any help or interaction is regarded as cheating, not as cooperation. The self-contained individual (Sampson, 1988) is seen in pure form in the utter aloneness of the individual in the examination room.

This "epistemic oasis" (Maier, 1989) is rare in our daily lives, but there does exist a very familiar social situation. This is the typical testing situation that we find in a variety of institutions: education, business, industry, the military, government, etc. All the testing situations are remarkably similar. The tests may be called achievement tests, ability tests, tests of basic skills, or whatever. Only the names have been changed. The basic dynamics of the situation remain the same: self-contained individuals, whether tested individually or in groups, are to work totally alone with no interaction whatsoever with another person, doing problems "in one's head." This similarity in the testing contexts of the IQ test and other tests, such as achievement tests in the schools, produces correlations between the two kinds of tests. Also, the content of IQ tests is "school-related" material, which would produce correlations between IQ tests and tests given in schools. These correlations, then, which are often regarded as validity coefficients for IQ tests are more properly interpreted as reliability coefficients.

The contextualist definition of intelligence, employed by a broad range of skeptics, rejects the privileging of data derived from the testing of isolated individuals in the psychometric laboratory. Contextualists regard intelligence as constructed from our interactions and relationships with the world. Contextualism is not a simple interactionism or situationism, where the context or situation is seen merely as a support, surround, or elicitor of cognitive processes (Ceci, 1990: 93). Rather, the context and the act are seen as a unity in which each requires the other.

The Social Construction of IQ Testing

It should be emphasized that the terms "intelligence," "IQ," and "IQ score,' are often confused. The term "IQ," of course, stands for "intelligence quotient," and should not be used as a synonym or substitute for "intelligence." It is sometimes necessary to remind ourselves that IQ stands for a quotient or ratio: mental age divided by chronological age times 100. "Mental age" was an invention designed to facilitate the quantification of conduct judged in terms of intelligence. When "IQ" is used as a synonym for "intelligence," the connotation is that an IQ test score *can* be regarded as a valid measure of "intelligence," even though it is most uncertain what an IQ test "measures." When the term "IQ" is used as a substitute for the proper term "IQ test score" or "mental test score," a crude reification of IQ occurs. (This will be discussed in more detail below.) Because of the frequent improper use of the term "IQ" and its reification, coupled with the circular definition of intelligence as "what the IQ tests test," it is necessary to discuss at some length IQ tests, IQ test scores, and the shift to statistical definitions of intelligence, such as the concept of "g," derived from factor analysis.

The opposition between contextualist and internalist-psychometric constructions of intelligence is seen clearly in their contrasting interpretations of what occurs in the testing situation. The internalists see the ideal testing situation as one where all the (independent) variables have been controlled, except the inferred inner processes ("intelligence") of the subject, whose responses to standardized stimuli can be unambiguously scored as right or wrong (Danzinger, 1990). The IQ tester, like the laboratory experimenter, seeks to control all variables except one. The contextualist assumes that all variables cannot be controlled. Rather, the entire context must be considered, the roles, thoughts, the setting, as well as the expectations of the participants in any human situation.

The Role of the IQ Test Subject
We are all familiar with the division of roles in the testing situation. The test "subject" has the passive and reactive role, more of an object than a subject, an object that must produce isolated responses on demand, rather than a subject that interacts with his or her world in ways which reflect the choices and self-reflection of an agent in charge of his or her reality. The test subject is to sit still, pay attention, listen carefully to a stranger, follow all directions given, keep one's mind focused on the task at all times, and try to do one's very, very best. The tester, on the other hand, is clothed in great institutional power and authority (Scheibe, 1979). The testing occurs on the tester's "turf," the tester has the active role, commanding the situation, giving instructions, coding the responses as good or bad, right or wrong. The tester, of course, controls all the information obtained in the session, writes up the test results, with the authority to transform the responses obtained into one of the most powerful icons in our society: the IQ or mental test score.

From the point-of-view of the test subject, a mysterious process occurs involving the use of this icon. It is recorded in a semi-secret information system, usually in the "cumulative folder" in a public-school system. The IQ score is indelibly entered in this file, not in ink which disappears after a reasonable length of time.

Few social situations have a greater imbalance of social and institutional power than that found in the testing situation. It is not a solid foundation upon which to build a general theory of human intelligence. Unless, of course, one wishes to regard "intelligence" as doing abstract problems in one's head while under the surveillance of a stranger draped in great authority, who will later enter one's score into a semi-secret bureaucratic information system which may affect one's future educational and occupational life.

Mental Sets (Response Sets) and the Famous "g."
A good training ground for taking IQ tests would be to live one's childhood in the typical environment of an affluent, middle-class family

where there are many books and toys, but especially one where the entire family sits down together each evening for dinner. The adults would probably control the pace and content of the conversation. The adults are to be listened to, and children may enter into the conversation. Children would learn the intricacies of ascertaining the intentions and meanings of adults, and children would learn the fine nuances and distinctions to be made in responding that can lead either to approval or disapproval from adults. In the IQ testing situation, this kind of interaction between child and adult is called "rapport."

In the IQ testing situation there is a great concern about establishing rapport. The test subject should be in an optimal state: paying attention, being motivated to do well, and so forth. This is a very important problem, but much more is involved than the degree of rapport between the test subject and test administrator. It seems quite plausible to regard the mental set (motivational state and attention-focusing) of the test subject as analogous to the response sets that have been found in the personality testing area, such as the yea-saying and social desirability response sets. Also, the behavior of the hypnosis subject has been described in terms of the mental sets of attention-focusing and intense role involvement (Andersen, 1963; Sarbin and Andersen, 1967).

In ability testing, it is quite plausible that there is a mental set of the test subject which is a complex composite of such conditions as: familiarity with, and a feeling of comfort in, the testing situation, high motivation, careful attention to the directions given by the examiner, and a familiarity with the proper attitude and language to use in responding to the examiner. This mental set would function over a wide range of IQ test items.

It is also plausible to regard this mental set as being the elusive "g factor," first hypothesized by Spearman (1923) and regarded by Jensen as the "Rock of Gibraltar in psychometrics" (Jensen, 1969: 9). To Spearman, Jensen, and many other psychometricians, this "g" is the essence of an individual's general intelligence, and is regarded as a kind of internal force, or mental power which lies behind intellectual functioning.

I propose that we "re-locate" this "g," that we take it out of the head of the test taker, and relocate it in the dynamics and social interaction of the testing situation. This "g" doesn't actually exist in any particular place, but if we insist that it must have some location, it would be "located" in the overall context, particularly the effort, striving, and involvement of the subject in his or her interactions with the examiner in the testing room. This "g" then, can be thought of as the actual strivings and involvement of a highly motivated test subject, not as some mysterious inner entity.

The Role of the Subject Historically
It may be helpful to look at the IQ testing situation in a historical context. In a superb scholarly work, Kurt Danzinger wrote of three models of "constructing the subject" in psychological research. The first model is the Wundtian, Leipzig model. Here the division of labor between the roles we now refer to as "experimenter" and "subject" was totally different, with very different labels. Wundt's laboratory was a community of investigators. There was a switching of roles, and the persons enacting various roles in the experiments were social equals. In the second model, the Paris clinical-hypnosis model of investigation, there was a great social distance between the experimenter-hypnotist, such as the famous neurologist Charcot, and the patient-subjects, often poor charwomen or peasant women. The powerful and authoritative male hypnotist, Charcot, was in total control during public demonstrations. In control, not only over the female patient-subjects, but also his many assistants and students. In the third model, the Galtonian, a series of individuals were tested in a psychometric (anthropometric) laboratory by test administrators, who observed their individual performances and recorded their scores, and summarized these scores as aggregate statistical data (Danzinger, 1990).

The present-day model of IQ testing avoids the Wundtian model, and depends more on the Paris and Galtonian models. Similar to the Paris model is the great difference in social status and irreversibility of roles of investigator and subject, and similar to the Galtonian model is the brief encounter of "strangers in a strange land," the testing of performance only on a pre-selected set of standardized tasks, and the transformation of scores into aggregate statistical form.

The Role of the Subject in an Epistemic Oasis
The interaction of test subject and investigator has been described as an "epistemic oasis" (Maier, 1989). Here the investigator intersperses a series of questions with manipulations of various objects, such as modeling clay, into various shapes, pouring liquids into various containers, and arranging coins in rows of various lengths but with the same number of coins. Maier is referring to the Piagetian type of experiment. After each manipulation of the objects, a different question may be asked of the subject (child). The experimenter interprets the child's responses as indicating an awareness or lack of awareness of relevant and irrelevant transformations of the objects. In the Piagetian model the experimenter is focused on the internal processes of the child. Has he or she attained conservation? The child, however, may be attending to the actions of the experimenter, assuming that each manipulation of the objects by the experimenter "means something." The child, then, would probably also assume that

a different answer would be appropriate after each manipulation of the objects (Maier, 1989). The conclusions reached by the child, then, derive from the child's understanding of the meaning of an adult's interaction with him or her in that particular social situation. However, the experimenter usually ignores the meaning of these social interactions, and focuses instead on inferred inner cognitive processes. This is again an example of the contextualist versus the internalist definition of intelligence, or epistemic conduct.

Creata or Data? The Creation of IQ Scores

The "raw data" provided by subjects in IQ-testing situations are numerical markings tied to specific performance actions by the subjects. These markings undergo transformation into quantitative forms (summary averages, norm-based score abstractions, etc.) and later into global, numerical abstractions called IQ or mental test scores. This is a process of creation and construction, and not just a process of "discovery" or "obtaining what is given." These scores, then, should *not* be called "data," that which is given, but "creata," that which has been created or constructed according to transformational processes inherent within statistical principles used in the abstracting procedures. A whole grab-bag of creata has been produced by the very investigators who are generally unaware that "intelligence" is a construction. Recognizing that "intelligence" is not something given in nature, but constructed, challenges the ontological basis of the internalist, hereditarian, and psychometric approaches. A conscious constructionist approach threatens the Social Darwinian, ideological foundations that Galton and his heirs have struggled so vigorously to establish over the past century (Andersen, 1978; Rutherford, 1986).[1]

The reification of the concept of intelligence, and the interpretation of certain statistical concepts as if they represent "laws of nature," are, thus, often used to mask the human decisions and social processes involved. It is not difficult to find in the literature frequent reification of IQ test scores as "IQ" (Jensen, 1969; Herrnstein, 1971). An illustrative example is the assertion: "IQ is normally distributed." In this statement, IQ test scores have been magically transformed into IQ, with the connotation that IQ is something that really exists within the brains (minds) of individuals. Second, the assertion that IQ is normally distributed suggests that the distribution is due to natural processes. What is not mentioned is that IQ test items were constructed to produce a normal distribution: test items were written and rewritten, some items thrown out, new items added, until bell-shaped distributions were obtained. These particular distributions of IQ test scores were painstakingly created, and cannot be said to be due to any "laws of nature" concerning the actual distribution of human cognitive abilities. These distributions are creata, not data. And IQ? IQ test scores do exist, but not IQ. IQ is found in that land populated by Easter bunnies, unicorns, tooth fairies, and other mythical creatures.

Science as a Social Enterprise

Science, at its best, is a democratic debating society, but it is often not at its best. The hallmark of science is its social, dialogic character, not its technical and methodological aspects. One particular confusion concerns the concept of objectivity, *which is a social and public process and product, not a personal quality or characteristic.* The basic rule in this debating society is that everyone should speak and write clearly when communicating with others about their observations, analyses, and conclusions. The others, in turn, can criticize, agree, revise, extend, or attempt to replicate what the other has done. This idea of objectivity is that with many different points of view focused on one problem or issue, the result may not be perfect or certain, but it is what can be achieved now, in this world, with presently-existing and fallible human beings.

This approach to objectivity involves a full-blown acceptance of subjectivity at the individual level, but objectivity is obtained at the public level through a social process. What is important here is the different points of view, not just different individuals debating one issue. A thousand individuals, all of whom are committed to one theoretical position or point of view, provide only one point of view, not a thousand. We might call this the "Fire-Spotter Theory of Objectivity," where the very different viewpoints of fire-spotters sitting in different towers at different locations must clearly report their *different perceptions* of where the fire is, in order to locate correctly the one-and-the-same fire. These "different locations" may also be different positions in the social, cultural, professional, or academic worlds. Because the hegemony of the psychometric view of intelligence is now being challenged with research from many other disciplines, and because of the many different voices involved in the debate, greater objectivity may be achieved.

An opposing approach is that the essence of objectivity is technological or methodological, where human subjectivity has been reduced or eliminated, so that decisions and interpretations can be made in a mechanical fashion. A derivative of the mechanical view of objectivity is the idea that a part of a social process can be abstracted out, defined as a variable or stimulus, and the overall context ignored. An example of this would be, once again, the IQ testing situation. The tasks and problems presented to the test taker in this situation have been carefully constructed with the goal of eliciting only responses that can be unambiguously scored as right or wrong (Danzinger, 1990: 160). Three very important aspects are thereby neglected: first, the overall context, second, the interaction between test administrator and test subject, and third, the particular thinking processes employed by the test subject which resulted in the answers. Regarded by some as "objective," this form of abstraction rips out of a total context only one part or process, ignores the overall context, and converts into quantitative form responses to standardized stimuli.

The social (intersubjective) view of objectivity and the mechanical (remove all human subjectivity) view of objectivity are diametrically opposed. In the social view, qualitative research methods attempt to capture all or most of the important processes that occur in any social event, and are then recorded carefully and reported to others in a way that *retains the quality of the actual events*. Such methods would be more objective than quantitative research procedures wedded to a mechanical view of objectivity.

At times we might think that the mechanical view of objectivity is the proper one. Examples would be rulers, gauges, and the many counting and measuring devices that we use in our lives. But, in these examples, we have *delegated* to these mechanical instruments the chores of measuring and counting. We make this delegation, and our trust in them continues, because of our belief that these gadgets are doing their job properly. If a gauge or other instrument gave us faulty or unreliable information, we would replace it immediately. The items on so-called "objective tests" may or may not be giving us reliable information. The fact that these items can be mechanically scored is not, by itself, sufficient to meet a criterion of objectivity. They must give us *both reliable and meaningful* information, just as our dials and gauges are required to do.

The Neglected Alternative to IQ Testing and Mainstream Psychometric Conceptions of Intelligence

Mainstream definitions of intelligence and intelligence testing have followed the work of Galton rather than Binet. Binet's work was focused on the individual style (process) by which a child approaches a problem, rather than the ranking of that child's performance with other children. The Galtonians (hereditarians) developed what could be described as a "doctrine of limited potentiality," which contains a whole series of interlocking assumptions: (1) every person has limits to his or her intelligence; (2) those limits are located *within* the person; (3) intelligence is fixed or unchangeable over time; (4) individual differences in intelligence are fixed; (5) intelligence is an innate biological trait, not a social construct; and (6) intelligence is meaningfully and validly measured by existing IQ tests (Andersen, 1978). This Galtonian doctrine of limited, measurable capacity (potentiality) has led to what may be called the "prediction model of education." IQ test scores, and scores of "achievement tests" and other tests, become predictive statements about a child's intellectual capacity. Thus, the prediction model leads *inevitably* to an enormous amount of testing, labelling, sorting, and tracking (streaming) in the public schools, and to discriminatory and unequal forms of education. Tests are to predict which students will succeed, and which will fail.

An approach that is diametrically opposed to the prediction model can be called "the generative model of education" (Andersen, 1978). The purpose of democratic education is to generate increased abilities (intelligence) in *all* students with every year spent in school. The generative model requires a commitment to the allied theory of indeterminate potentiality. Our current testing and assessment procedures are destructive of this purpose, simply producing scores that are used to rank or compare students against one another, a competitive–comparative kind of information that is not useful to the teacher, student, or parents. Rather than producing static descriptions of inferred capacities and abilities, all testing and assessment procedures must indicate directly to the teacher and student "what to do next" in the teaching/learning process.

Many writers, teachers, and researchers have developed educational methods that fit the generative model. The common theme is that they focus on the *process* of learning, or *how* a child is doing his or her work, and not on the product, or who got the most correct answers and therefore ranks the highest. Sylvia Ashton-Warner (1963) uses a "key vocabulary" method, and Paulo Freire (1974) uses "generative themes." Herbert Ginsburg (1972) uses a Piagetian procedure of dialogue with a student asked to solve a problem. Reuven Feuerstein (1980) utilizes the concept of "mediated learning experience." And, of course, there is the work of Lev Vygotsky (1978), in particular his concept of "the zone of potential (proximal) development," which is what a child can potentially do beyond his or her present level of functioning with the assistance of an adult or more advanced peer.

The generative model of education directs us to look for and develop what a child already knows when he or she enters school. It asks that we look for knowledge and strengths in a school child, rather than emphasizing and recording weaknesses. Children enter school with various cultural and ethnic backgrounds which are not deficits. To generate increased ability in all children requires a respect for all cultural and ethnic experiences that children bring with them into the schools. The ideology of hereditarian, psychometrically measurable intelligence which asserts that some individuals and groups are more intelligent than others is inherently destructive of equal education for all people.

Conclusion: Definitions of Intelligence, Inequality and Democracy

The issue of the uses of the hereditarian position to legitimate inequality is rather obvious.[2] The historian, Vernon Louis Parrington, has provided an eloquent statement of the anti-democratic implications of IQ testing. At the end of his three volume work on *Main Currents in American Thought* he wrote:

> Then the war intervened and the green fields shriveled in an afternoon. With the cynicism that came with post-war days the democratic liberalism of 1917 was thrown away like an empty whiskey-flask. Clever young men began to make merry over democracy. It was preposterous, they said, to concern oneself about social justice; nobody wants social justice. . . . Out of the muck of the war had come a great discovery – so it was reported – the discovery that psychology as well as economics has its word to say on politics. From the army intelligence tests the moron emerged as a singular commentary on our American democracy, and with the discovery of the moron the democratic principle was in for a slashing attack. Almost overnight an army of enemies was marshaled against it. (Parrington, 1927, vol. III: 412)

Finally, there is the issue of the relationship of social constructionism to what we regard as objective science. As discussed previously, the mechanical view of objectivity which requires the removal of human subjectivity seems to be a mistaken view. The intersubjective, social view of objectivity, in which all voices and views are to be considered, and where objectivity is seen as a social, collective achievement rather than a personal quality, is entirely congruent with social constructionism. As I see it, social constructionism is not a denial of our common reality, but asks us always to be aware of our different perceptions and interpretations of that reality.

In the short history of the systematic investigation of "intelligence," the attempt to create an objective science of intelligence by taking the short-cut of quantification, operational definition, and statistics, has led us down a dead-end street. The "individualistic bias" also has constrained our thinking. The most important kinds of intelligence are truly social and collective, and not properties of individuals. We learn much from others, from our culture. We pass on to the next generation knowledge that was unthinkable in prior generations. Who would have guessed, 400 years ago, that sons and daughters of peasants would read and write, and would count, not only up to 200, but with little machines, any number imaginable. Maybe, when we get smart, we all get smart together. If the ability to survive is the measure of intelligence, then we will soon discover whether we are all very smart, or very, very stupid.

Notes

1. Many ideas in this paper come from discussions over the last 30 years with my friend and colleague, Eldred E. Rutherford. It is impossible ever to know who should claim authorship of these ideas; I believe that many of them originated with him.
2. An early critic of the hereditarian position was F.C. Constable (1905). His little-known book is a surgical dissection and destruction of Francis Galton's study of eminent men. There are many fine recent critiques. Some of these are: Kamin, 1974; Block and Dworkin, 1976; Evans and Waites, 1981; Gould, 1981; Marks, 1982; Lewontin et al., 1984; Rose, 1985; Mensh and Mensh, 1991.

References

Andersen, M. (1963) Correlates of hypnotic performance: an historical and role-theoretical analysis, PhD dissertation, Berkeley, CA: University of California.

Andersen, M. (1978) The use of IQ tests in blaming the victims: predicting incompetence rather than generating intelligence, *San Jose Studies*, 4 (November/December): 73–96.

Asch, S.E. (1952) *Social Psychology*. Englewood Cliffs, NJ: Prentice-Hall.

Ashton-Warner, S. (1963) *Teacher*. New York: Bantam Books.

Block, N. and Dworkin, G. (1976) *The IQ Controversy: Critical Readings*. New York: Pantheon Books.

Ceci, S. (1990) *On Intelligence . . . More or Less: A Bio-Ecological Treatise on Intellectual Development*. Englewood Cliffs, NJ: Prentice-Hall.

Chase, A. (1977) *The Legacy of Malthus*. New York: Knopf.

Constable, F. (1905) *Poverty and Hereditary Genius*. London: Fifield.

Danzinger, K. (1990) *Constructing the Subject: Historical Origins of Psychological Research*. New York: Cambridge University Press.

Evans, B. and Waites, B. (1981) *On Unnatural Science and its Social History*. Atlantic Highlands, NJ: Humanities Press.

Fancher, R. (1985) *The Intelligence Men: Makers of the IQ Controversy*. New York: Norton.

Feuerstein, R. (1980) *Instrumental Enrichment: An Intervention Program for Cognitive Modifiability*. Baltimore: University Park.

Freire, P. (1974) *Pedagogy of the oppressed*. New York: Seabury.

Gergen, K.J. (1973) Social psychology as history, *Journal of Personality and Social Psychology*, 26: 309–20.

Gill, A. (1978) The misuse of genetics in the race–IQ controversy, *San José Studies*, 4 (November/December): 23–43.

Ginsburg, H. (1972) *The Myth of the Deprived Child*. Englewood Cliffs, NJ: Prentice-Hall.

Gould, S.J. (1981) *the Mismeasure of Man*. New York: Norton.

Herrnstein, R.J. (1971) *IQ in the Meritocracy*. Boston: Little, Brown & Co.

Hofstadter, R. (1955) *Social Darwinism in American Thought*. Boston: Beacon Press.

Jensen, A. (1969) How much can we boost IQ and scholastic achievement? *Harvard Educational Review*, 39 (Winter): 1–123.

Jensen, A. (1980) *Bias in Mental Testing.* New York: Free Press.

Kamin, L. (1974) *The Science and Politics of IQ.* New York: Lawrence Erlbaum (Wiley).

Lewontin, R. (1976) The fallacy of biological determinism, *The Sciences*, March/April: 8–9.

Lewontin, R., Rose, S., and Kamin, L. (1984) *Not in our Genes: Biology, Ideology, and Human Nature.* New York: Pantheon Books.

Maier, R. (1989) Two identities of psychology. Paper presented at the 3rd Conference of the International Society for Theoretical Psychology April 17–21, 1989, Arnhem, The Netherlands.

Malthus, T. (1803) *An Essay on the Principle of Population*, Book IV, chap. 5, 2nd edition. Appeared in Allan Chase (1977), *The Legacy of Malthus.* New York: Alfred Knopf.

Mancuso, J. and Dreisinger, M. (1969) A view of the historical and current development of the concept of intelligence. *Psychology in the schools*, VI: 137–51.

Marks, R. (1982) Legitimating industrial capitalism: philanthropy and individual differences, in R. Arnove (ed.), *Philanthropy and Cultural Imperialism.* Bloomington, IN: Indiana University Press.

Mensh, E. and Mensh, H. (1991) *The IQ Mythology: Class, Race, Gender, and Inequality.* Carbondale, IL: Southern Illinois University Press.

Minton, H. (1987) Lewis M. Terman and mental testing: in search of the democratic ideal, in M. Sokal (ed.), *Psychological Testing and American Society.* New Brunswick, NJ: Rutgers University Press.

Minton, H. (1988) Charting life's history: Lewis M. Terman's study of the gifted, in Jill Morawski (ed.), *The Rise of Experimentation in American Psychology.* New Haven, CT: Yale University Press.

Morawski, J. (ed.) (1988) *The Rise of Experimentation in American Psychology.* New Haven, CT: Yale University Press.

Parrington, V.L. (1927) *Main Currents in American Thought*, 3 volumes. New York: Harcourt Brace.

Rose, N. (1985) *The Psychological Complex: Psychology, Politics, and Society in England 1869–1939.* London: Routledge & Kegan Paul.

Rutherford, E.E. (1986) Care as an empowerment process in a democracy. Paper presented to the American Association for the Advancement of Science, Pacific division, June 11, 1986, Vancouver, British Columbia.

Samelson, F. (1979) Putting psychology on the map: ideology and intelligence testing, in A. Buss (ed.), *Psychology in Social Context.* New York: Irvington.

Sampson, E. (1988) The debate on individualism, *American Psychologist*, 43: 15–22.

Sarbin, T.R. (1982) Contextualism: a world view for modern psychology, in V.L. Allen and K.E. Scheibe (eds), *The Social Context of Conduct: Psychological Writings of Theodore Sarbin*, New York: Praeger.

Sarbin, T.R. and Andersen, M. (1967) Role-theoretical analysis of hypnotic behavior, in J. Gordon (ed.), *Handbook of Clinical and Experimental Hypnosis.* New York: Macmillan.

Scheibe, K. (1979) *Mirrors, Masks, Lies and Secrets: The Limits of Human Predictability.* New York: Praeger.

Shweder, R. (1990) Cultural psychology – What is it?, in J. Stigler, R. Shweder, and G. Herdt (eds), *Cultural Psychology: Essays on Comparative Human Development.* Cambridge: Cambridge University Press.

Sokal, M. (1987) *Psychological Testing and American Society.* New Brunswick, NJ: Rutgers University Press.

Spearman, C. (1923) *The Nature of "Intelligence" and the Principles of Cognition*. London: Macmillan.

Spencer, H. (1874) *Social Statics*. New York: Appleton. (Appeared in R. Hofstadter (1985), *Social Darwinism in American Thought*. Boston: Beacon Press.)

Sternberg, R. (1990) *Metaphors of Mind: Conceptions of the Nature of Intelligence*. Cambridge: Cambridge University Press.

Vygotsky, L.S. (1978) *Mind in Society: The Development of Higher Psychological Processes*. Cambridge, MA: Harvard University Press.

Williams, R. (1983) *Keywords: A Vocabulary of Culture and Society*. New York: Oxford University Press.

8
Some Constructionist Observations on "Anxiety" and its History

Richard S. Hallam

When we follow through the implications of the social constructionist assumption that anxiety is a *construct*, and relinquish the view that it is an *entity* of which the emotion word is a mere representation (Harré, 1986: 4), a whole new set of questions arise. These include the ontological question (for example, in what sense does "anxiety" exist, if at all, before it is construed by a human community), the question of meaning (for example, how does the anxiety construct relate to other presuppositions about mind, to moral valuations, and to social practices), and the questions of function and intentionality (for example, what purposes are served by references to anxiety in human communication). Questions of a more empirical kind can also be asked such as "how does the developing child acquire this type of emotion reference?" This chapter interprets the meaning of the anxiety construct in a broad social context. There are two subthemes; the first is the relationship between scientific and lay discourse about anxiety; the second is the way unspoken assumptions about anxiety in scientific models tacitly reflect, and thereby help to sustain, a value-laden view of "our human nature."

One approach to meaning is to study texts or discourse in specific contexts (see, for example, Lutz, 1990, who links everyday discourse on emotion to gender and power). My approach is more general and consists of an attempt to relate the anxiety construct to authoritative reflections on the way the symbolic resources of western culture have originated and changed, and can be seen to relate to wider social conditions and practices (for example, Taylor, 1990). The main difference between these two approaches is in the type of source material they employ, that is, the difference between focusing on primary material, such as conversation, versus the use of secondary material such as historical analyses and other attempts to interpret social meaning. The distinction is one of emphasis only, given that the symbolic resources individuals draw upon in constructing meanings and expressing them through discourse are already "in place," deeply entrenched within culture and language (Bruner, 1990: 11).

It is this feature of being tacitly and deeply grounded that challenges any attempt to reveal the presuppositions that lie unquestioned behind lay discourse, and also, as I shall argue, within scientific theories of "anxiety." Bruner (1990) has asserted that the quest for meaning arises only when events deviate from what he calls "canonical reality." In other words, meanings that are tacitly shared remain silent. One such widely shared meaning is the idea that anxiety exists as an entity; in other words, that it is a discrete and fundamental component of human nature (Hallam, 1985; Ortony and Turner, 1990). This idea has spawned the search for a scientific theory *of* anxiety. From a social constructionist standpoint, this entity is a reification; the search for it is flawed because what is construed as an entity is taken to *be* an entity. A social constructionist investigation of the anxiety construct does not replace a *theory* of anxiety with a new "model" or "account" of the same reified entity. To examine the way the construct of anxiety relates to other historically situated constructs and social practices is to be engaged in its further social construction (and deconstruction). This chapter should not be interpreted, therefore, as an attempt to lay the foundation of a new social constructionist theory of anxiety.

The aims of the chapter are clearly at variance with (though not incompatible with) the aims of a scientific psychology. However, given that I shall argue that contemporary scientific theories of anxiety are infused by tacit folk psychological beliefs, I intend to treat the former as historical texts, suspending judgment on their correspondence with what we commonly construe as "empirical reality." If the infusion metaphor is apt, the idea of validating theory by showing correspondence with empirical reality is inherently problematic. To illustrate this point with a concrete example, consider the theoretical proposition that an individual experiences "social anxiety" to the degree that a significant image of self that he or she is trying to create for others fails to impress (Schlenker and Leary, 1982). This proposition resonates with common sense; intuitively, it conforms with what we know of social interaction. However, the successful prediction of behavior from a theoretical statement like this is only a limited form of validation. It may be no more than an explicit and carefully worded statement of cultural imperatives. In other words, the extent to which we as cultural participants *make* this true (because we believe it or want it to be true) rather than cause it to be true because we could not as humans do otherwise, cannot be determined easily by empirical experiment.

Although psychological theory rightly aims for universal validity, for the purpose of this chapter, theoretical statements about anxiety will be regarded primarily as cultural texts and only secondarily as pointing to processes and entities whose validity transcends a correspondence with lay discourse and everyday reality.

One species of scientific theorizing is of particular interest from an interpretive point of view. This is the attempt to write a history of anxiety from a universalist, scientific standpoint. These accounts should throw into relief (in the manner of epic cinematic attempts to portray historical events) the contemporary assumptions from which we cannot easily detach ourselves. They provide one means of evaluating the claim to science and universal applicability, as I will argue later.

I have two reasons for writing this chapter. First, as regards scientific theorizing, conceptual analysis may redirect investigation toward new, and more productive, empirical questions. Second, there are arguments for reconstruing anxiety with the intention of influencing lay discourse. This needs further elaboration.

Lay discourse on psychological matters can be seen as fundamentally important in its own right. It is not simply an unsophisticated and unrigorous form of "proper" psychology. In the context of this chapter, lay discourse provides the *object* for discussion (the construct of anxiety) and it is also the *subject* through which new interpretations of the human condition are voiced. Broadly defined, folk psychology is the body of ideas and practices that underlie our regard for each other as persons with a "human nature." These vary in time and place, influencing psychologists as well as everyone else. Psychology as a scientific discipline influences folk psychology through its ability to convince enough people that "human nature" possesses certain "scientifically proven" features. In turn, scientific psychologists unavoidably share tacit folk assumptions and, in their own explanations, look to contemporary sources for their models and analogies (Richards, 1989). The direction of influence between scientific psychology and lay discourse can be conceived, therefore, as two-way. Similarly, the interpretive work of this chapter, if it achieves more than a parroting of lay discourse, does so by taking a critical stance towards it. Put differently, these interpretive efforts are intended to contribute to the social construction of meaning, not study it from a position outside and beyond.

The following thought-experiment is intended to illustrate what might be meant by the previous paragraph. Suppose Cognitive Psychology were to make a leap forward on the scale of Einstein's Theory of Relativity so that we could no longer sustain our current folk understanding of the way we are served by "perception and memory." It seems likely that the need to maintain psychological continuity with our mythic past (that is, how we supposed our minds used to operate) would be irresistible. It would then be one of the tasks of an interpretive psychology to examine critically the scientific claims and to offer a conceptualization of ourselves that would be consistent with this new view of our (biological) "Human Nature" and was also compelling as a source of meaning and value in which to ground our lives. This kind of literature already exists (for example, in the work of writers who have speculated about the implications of split-brain research) although most claims to overturn our everyday folk beliefs (for example, Skinner, 1972) have been vigorously contested.

The first section of this chapter will comment critically on contemporary accounts of the history of "anxiety." The second section will examine tacit assumptions in some contemporary theories of anxiety. Before proceeding to the first section, I will introduce briefly some methodological issues in historical analysis.

Brief Preparatory Comments on Historical Analysis

In his paper discussing what it would mean to write a history of psychology, Richards (1987) drew the distinction, echoed above, between psychology as a discipline and psychology as subject matter. He also noted the serious difficulty of distinguishing them in practice. He marked the conceptual distinction orthographically by using a large P for Psychology, the discipline, and small p for psychology the subject matter, a practice I will follow. With the hindsight of historical distance, many past attempts at Psychology now look more and more like psychology. Nevertheless, contemporary Psychology and also folk psychology continue to assert or unquestionably assume that certain features of human nature are universal.

Although the position I have taken implies that Psychological knowledge is relative, I do not intend to argue for an extreme version of relativism – that only the participants in a discourse understand it and can make sense of it according to their own (relative) criteria. In fact we ourselves can never fully enter the discourse of earlier generations nor would that fulfill our present aims. Rather, the purpose of historical analysis can be seen as reconstructing the past from a contemporary position outside it. This reconstruction, nevertheless, respects the historical evidence; it does not, for example, impute conceptual distinctions to past individuals who would not, on the evidence, have been capable of making them. It will also be forced to make universalizing assumptions, recognizing however, that these assumptions may be relativized at some later time.

Morawski (1984) has outlined three main types of explanatory model in historical analysis. The first is law-like and analogous to natural science explanation. In this model, an essential sameness is assumed in historical patterns so that the causes of past changes are identical to the causes of present changes. Dynamic interaction between the "same variables" accounts for a historical flow. The interaction may follow a natural progression which is evolutionary, cyclical or dialectic. Although Morawski suggests that this type of explanation is rarely used by historians, it seems inevitable that most historians make some assumptions about a universal human nature.

The second type of explanation is rational, that is, based on a consideration of dispositions, beliefs, purposes, etc., when accounting for a unique configuration of circumstances. Where the historical record has been produced for the consumption of a particular audience, the intention behind the record can also be interpreted in this way. This type of explanation raises many problems for an enquiry into psychological constructs because rational explanations are derived from folk models of the mind (for example, the sort of dispositions, reasons, or purposes a person can be said to possess). Sources of rationality have been themselves subject to a process of historical change (Taylor, 1990). One exit from this circle is to reduce complex folk concepts to simpler ones which we feel have validity over a longer time span than the events/concepts we wish to account for. Thus we may be able to provide an intelligible context for extinct emotions in this way. However, the extent to which this move is successful, or even possible, is debatable.

The third type of explanation, the narrative, is a form of abstraction that constructs a story around, or out of, a series of events. Although a narrative theme does not refer to any one person's endeavor (except in the exemplary sense) it is still seen as rational in nature. Its coherence and intelligibility depend on its applicability to the human condition rationally understood. We can apply this to our topic by imagining an idealized individual making narrative sense of new existential circumstances. These new circumstances could be seen to arise historically either through the effects of technical, economic, or institutional change that renders earlier narratives irrational or conflictual, or through changes in prevailing ideas resulting from intellectual activity.

Idealizations such as "Modern consciousness" or "Victorian mentality" contain a narrative element. While there is a tendency to see the idealization (including its narrative element) as an expression of material and social conditions, this removes the individual as an influence on historical change itself. I prefer to make the assumption that individuals play an active role in their own future, implying that a deliberate and reflexive constructive process is at work. This takes place between people, of course, and not in the ratiocinations of an idealized consciousness.

A *purely* narrative historiography would construct a link between a mythically recalled past and a contemporary attempt to make sense of events in the present moment and foreseeable future. On this view, history has a necessary mythic continuity (one that is continually recreated) but one which may perhaps have no ultimate direction or pattern. An extreme skeptic might view Psychology in this way, in other words, as psychology that needs to reinvent itself every few decades.

It is difficult to imagine a form of historical analysis that does not entail each of these three explanatory approaches – natural law, rational, narrative – in some measure. Assumptions about what is natural, timeless, and universal might not be made explicit in the account, but without them the account would be difficult to sustain. For example, it has been argued that any folk model must employ certain a priori conceptual distinctions (Lock, 1981). Moreover, a form of rationality entirely stripped of narrative content, such as symbolic logic, would not by itself constitute a usable historical tool.

This interplay of explanatory approaches can be applied to the writings of Kierkegaard who was so centrally concerned with fear and its relation to selfhood (Cole, 1971). For him, selfhood is a *universal natural* latent power of the organism which does not manifest itself until the historical moment occurs (in a culture but also in the developing individual) when the relation that unites body and soul acquires the ability "to relate itself to its own self." Prior to this moment, we may speak of the individual as an organism living in an age of innocence, governed by its own impulses. Selfhood is a new mode of being in which the individual assumes responsibility for itself. Kierkegaard interpreted the Adam myth, and the end of the age of innocence, as arising from the prohibition of impulses. The *rational* implications of prohibition are: (1) the awareness of freedom to choose; (2) the possibility of choosing to become what is imagined rather than actual (self-actualizing); and (3) the need for reference to norms as a basis for choice.

As a Christian philosopher, Kierkegaard introduced a *narrative* element with the idea of a spiritual quest. People can make use of the power of selfhood to advance their spirituality. There is a qualitative hierarchy of reference norms – the highest, God, represents the idea that all things are possible. In Kierkegaard's vision of the spiritual quest, the self is not permitted to determine its own transcendent norm. In other words, the self cannot be the ultimate source of the norm which it seeks to attain. Given the great moral significance of the choices made by the self, a failure or refusal to choose responsibly is regarded by Kierkegaard as inducing fear, despair or guilt.

Elements of Kierkegaard's analysis retain their persuasiveness today – the question of the qualitative norms that determine self-actualization, for example – while other elements such as the assumption of unity of the self have been re-examined. A historical analysis of the construct of anxiety, therefore, will reconstruct these elements in the light of new assumptions about what is natural and timeless, how concepts are rationally related, and from what sources moral values are drawn.

Historical Analyses of "Anxiety"

In choosing what literature to critique, I have been constrained by the extremely small number of attempts to place anxiety in a historical context. I have selected three examples which allow me to develop a theoretical argument; this section is not intended as a comprehensive review.

Rollo May

Rollo May's book *The Meaning of Anxiety* (1950 [1977]) includes extensive speculation on the history of anxiety which is the aspect of his work I consider here. May states unequivocally that "An individual's anxiety is conditioned by the fact that he stands at a particular point in the historical development of his culture" (1977: 19). He is less clear whether "anxiety" as a cultural category is conditioned by history. As in much literature, the tendency is to take anxiety as a pre-given and to pass it on in a variety of meanings such as (1) the conditions that give rise to some familiar bodily and subjective effects, (2) to those effects themselves, or (3) to the categories the individual employs in perceiving and understanding either the conditions or their effects. By sliding between these meanings, May can talk about "nascent anxiety" in the Renaissance period (because "conscious anxiety" was largely avoided) and it allows him to infer "anxiety" from highly questionable signs such as the bulbous eyes of figures in Michelangelo's paintings.

In his theoretical synthesis, May defines anxiety as a complex condition which involves intellectual, feeling, behavioral and physiological elements. In this respect, he anticipates many theorists who have followed him. Unlike *fear* which he defines as a reaction to a specific danger, he views anxiety as a diffuse apprehension, objectless, and characterized by uncertainty and helplessness. He also ventures to specify the intellectual element. This is an awareness that some value that the individual holds essential to his or her existence as a personality is threatened. May claims that the individual cannot "stand outside his values" and objectify the threat, and is therefore powerless to confront it. In the extreme case, this anxiety is said to be experienced as dissolution of the self. Anxiety itself precludes any attempt to understand it rationally and confront it.

This synthesis already raises some knotty questions. Is "anxiety" the result of a dissolution of a person's values or the result of a perception by a person that his or her values are threatened with dissolution? May's analysis seems to allow for both possibilities although he does not differentiate them. Adopting a Meadian theory of self, it could be argued that both statements are true of "anxiety," one referring to the I, the other to the Me. In other words, the spontaneous, unreflective I produces disorganization and chaos. If this process has not gone too far, it can be objectified as a threatened Me ("I am going to pieces" or "I could go completely to pieces"). May seems to suggest that the perception of this threat adds to the disorganization of the I, a position compatible with contemporary emphasis on vicious cycle phenomena in anxiety problems.

May adopts Goldstein's view (Goldstein, 1939) that, developmentally, "anxiety" precedes "fear," fear being defined as an adaptive response (such as running away) to a known danger or threat. Ultimately though, threat is said to be reducible to "anxiety," a state of the organism in which it is unable to produce any adaptive response, or modify the environment, or for that matter, effectively employ its perceptual or attentional mechanisms at all. This theoretical move, which defines anxiety as a biological state of the organism in which it fails to function adaptively, leaves the definition of adaptation unspecified. The value of this position as a universalizing assumption would depend on whether the concept of adaptation can be applied to different historical contexts. In this interpretation, biological state and social construct are clearly differentiated. How individuals construe a state of "ecological mismatch" of the kind suggested, or whether they construe it at all, or how they respond to it, is a different matter.

There are good grounds for believing that a person's construal of the threatened Me has varied historically and that, formulated in this way, the statement itself is a historical product. The creation of a personal mental space in which an objectified autonomous reasoning self was construed as *possessing* attributes that *could* be threatened, was a development that took place in English culture over the sixteenth to eighteenth centuries (Baumeister, 1987; Logan, 1987; Taylor, 1990). Self words began to flourish in the English language toward the latter half of the seventeenth century. In contrast, the Anglo-Saxon dictionary of Bosworth and Toller (1898) contains only 12 hyphenated self words which relate to attributes of the person. One quarter of them refer to suicide (*self-bana, self-ewalu, self-myrdere*). This suggests that although in this early period the self construct clearly referred to a public identity (presumably subject to shame and dishonour), self-referential acts were directed toward a corporeal body rather than a conceptual Me.

The notion of a self-concept is distinctly modern (*Oxford English Dictionary*, 1st Edition [*OED*], 1934) and so when May develops his analysis and specifies the threat of anxiety as being directed at "self-esteem," "expressing oneself as a person," or "core personality" he is introducing modern assumptions. The *OED* records the first use of self-esteem in 1657. To the extent that meeting the demands of one's environment involves acquiring, proving, and defending this form of self-reference, the individual will be vulnerable to ecological mismatch of this variety. The degree of vulnerability will presumably depend on how easily this form of self-reference is won, how stringently normative standards of selfhood are applied, etc. In this period of Protestant fervour, self-words appeared to give voice to moral disapprobation (for example, selfe-ish, *OED*, 1640). Self-confidence (*OED*, 1653) was often used in the sense of "arrogant or impudent reliance on one's own powers." However, under Protestant influence, self-reference was also being rehabilitated with a positive significance, though one that was grounded in a moral conception of life. Thus Milton (1667) is quoted by the *OED* as follows: "Oft times nothing profits more Then self-esteem, grounded on just and right Well Manag'd."

In May's discussion of the development of individuality since the Renaissance, he introduces a new assumption about the cultural origins of anxiety and develops it as a central problem for mid-twentieth-century life. This is the idea that "isolation of the individual" and "lack of positive value of the community" lead to anxiety. The problem, he argues, is that of combining the value of individualistic self-realization with an older value of interpersonal community, which is endangered by unfettered competition between people. In trying to understand May's thesis that a conflict of values leads to anxiety, we can approach it within his own terms or attempt to reframe his thesis, treating anxiety as a social construct. Within May's terms, social change may be seen to involve the dissolution of practices which sustain the personal identities of certain segments of society; the process may be particularly disruptive when emerging identities and their associated values are incompatible with, or contradictory to, the values associated with earlier identities. For example, capitalist values may have conflicted with the values associated with the medieval guild. For May, sharing and trust are incompatible with competition. According to his naturalistic theory, "anxiety" results from threat to (and presumably conflict within) the values that constitute an individual's sense of identity. Thus, regardless of *which* values are threatened, or what existential dilemmas are posed by historical change, the process will, naturally, produce "anxiety."

A difficulty with this analysis is to produce a definition of anxiety which is stripped of its contemporary connotations and yet remains analytically serviceable. We cannot safely assume that threats to identities in past eras were responded to with anything like the consequences we know today as "anxiety." May's speculations are consistent with what we understand to be "our psychology" but, as argued above, we cannot transpose them to different historical circumstances.

A different way of interpreting May's thesis is to place the *construct* of anxiety within an emerging, secular, and rational view of the world, a world which relies on a mode of social control that emphasizes self-regulation rather than obedience to religious precept or control by extrinsic punishment (Rose, 1990). A new concept of selfhood is a crucial element in this rational scheme. According to this interpretation of the relationship between the anxiety construct and developing individuality, threats to self are perfectly intelligible and, indeed, a *requirement* of effective social control: they are not threats to the construction of identity itself, such that the individual is unable to step outside them and confront them. Individuals who have developed their selfhood in prescribed ways, have had it acknowledged, and have obtained the benefits of so doing, would perceive a threat to their self-identities as quite consistent with their essential values. In the face of this threat, individuals may construe themselves as "anxious" – what the individual values is in danger of not being realized; their fundamental conception of a scale of values is, however, not threatened.

In highlighting a process of construal, I am not disputing that for the individual, the process of social regulation will entail, at times, a variety of psychological, behavioral and physiological consequences experienced as "anxiety." It is simply to point out that when the regulatory processes involved in this form of social control are operating effectively, the individual who deviates will experience the psychological consequences in prescribed ways. When the consequences are construed as anxiety, we are dealing with a response that is placed in the category of involuntary, natural, emotions. Conceptualizing it in this way can be seen to serve ideological functions in as much as the consequences of deviating are commonly attributed not to any defects of a system of regulation (or scale of values) but to natural disorders of individuals for which socially sanctioned remedial help (counselling, pharmacotherapy) is available.

Paul McReynolds

McReynolds (1986) reviews anxiety over the whole span of recorded western culture with the aim of providing a better appreciation of current theory. His contribution will be considered from the point of view of its methodology and conclusions, leaving aside the interesting historical illustrations to his paper. He begins by differentiating between *concepts* of anxiety and the *phenomenon* of anxiety. The latter is said to refer to a natural, inbuilt response of the human organism: "The feeling of anxiety is an intrinsic part of being human" (1986: 131). He assumes that the *way* in which this universal affect is felt and categorized is shaped by culture.

McReynolds offers a cognitive conceptualization of the conditions that give rise to anxiety phenomena. What he calls *primary* anxiety is the natural result of "discrepancies, imbalances, or conflicts, . . . among mental thoughts, feelings, and memories" (1986: 150). Primary anxiety becomes secondary when a spreading number of situations give rise to it as a result of an associative or conditioning process. He suggests that periods of rapid and unpredictable culture change produce "heightened anxiety." This is supposedly a natural consequence of the cognitive challenge of assimilating new world views. Periods of cultural breakdown are said to be associated with increments in individuation, and so, in his view, "feelings of anxiety" are linked to developing "concepts of selfness." The periods of breakdown he mentions are Hellenistic Greece, the Italian Renaissance, the French Revolution, the English Industrial Revolution, and the Modern Era.

McReynolds's historical perspective can be classified as one of natural, cyclical change. He excludes rationality and narrative because "anxiety" is an *automatic* consequence of cognitive discrepancy. Taking this perspective at face value, we would have nothing to learn from History because historical data are employed simply to illustrate a contemporary universalist model. At a more fundamental level, we are asked to take on trust that "anxiety" conceived naturalistically (or phenomenally, as McReynolds puts it) is a universal and unitary response. On his view, as cultural beings, we can only experience this "feeling" through the lens of our own cognitive categories.

A serious difficulty with this position is that we have no other way of referring to some process (or especially, a feeling) as 'anxiety' unless we define it technically, such as a pattern of tension in facial muscles. It is difficult to see how it could be demonstrated on the basis of historical data (1) that cognitive discrepancy gives rise to this unitary response (unless we infer it from the visual arts as May suggests) or (2) that cognitive discrepancy does not give rise to some other form of psychological response.

In conclusion, the circumstances in which the perception of a "natural feeling of anxiety" is conceptualized and enters discourse are left unanalyzed by McReynolds. It would be a gross error, he says, "to assume, as Sarbin (1964) seems to, that because the word 'anxiety' is relatively new, that the general area of human experience to which it points is also new" (1986: 149). McReynolds is taking a position here on the debate about language and reality which is beyond the scope of this essay to examine. However, suppose we go along with this argument and allow that whatever phenomenal response(s) natural anxiety might consist of occur automatically under certain conditions, rather like an eye-blink. Assuming some capacity for self-observation, we might allow that human beings construe this response as worth commenting on and develop a discourse around it. However, Mc-Reynolds gives us no clue as to why this should happen when the word *anxiety* appears in the language. In order to view the introduction of a new word or a change of meaning as irrelevant, one would have to assume that one term for "anxiety" is equivalent to another because it refers to the *same* natural feeling. It is true that there is a sense in which we would want to claim that certain objects of experience (such as trees) have always been available to humans but this does not justify the assertion that the *experience* of trees has remained the same. There is even greater room for doubting sameness in the referents for a word such as "anxiety" which is more obviously endowed with a social significance.

Reference to Sarbin's linguistic perspective on the anxiety construct has already been made and it is to an expanded account of his contribution that we now turn.

Theodore Sarbin

Sarbin (1964, 1968) was concerned to point out that theorists who posited anxiety as a mental state that intervened between environmental stimulus and behavior were thinking unscientifically. He regarded this sort of explanation as a historical mistake occasioned by the literal interpretation of metaphor. His etymological analysis of the term revealed that anxiety derived from Middle English *anguish* which in turn came from Old French *anguisse* meaning a choking sensation in the throat.

Anguish represented a state of spiritual suffering and was therefore an aspect of religious faith. Sarbin claims that an analogy was drawn, on the basis of bodily sensations, between proximal events for which there was a clear distal cause (for example, choking sensation due to a chicken bone) and proximal events for which no distal cause was evident. When the "as if" quality of metaphor was dropped, it was taken literally and attributed to a state, property, or disposition of a substantive entity. Anguish was attributed to the workings of an invisible, immaterial Spirit which inhabited the empty spaces of the body. This concept was later transformed into the reified Mind of which anxiety became a property.

The purpose of Sarbin's historical analysis was to make a point about the ontological status of "anxiety." He drew upon the familiar linguistic process of employing metaphor as a shorthand to talk about complex antecedent and concurrent conditions for which we lack a precise conceptual vocabulary. The point can be taken or rejected regardless of any quibbles about his etymology. Moreover, he does not suggest that we can or should do without figurative language in scientific thinking. The point is not to take tropes literally. Sarbin advances his own metaphor of cognitive strain which is similar to the notions of ecological mismatch and cognitive discrepancy mentioned earlier. Cognitive strain is a stimulus for cognitive accommodation and is conceived as vital for efficient cognitive functioning. Sarbin regards threat as an inability to accommodate to cognitive strain, a state of not having answers (or having incompatible answers) to vitally important questions.

The chief implication of Sarbin's argument is that we should revert to regarding reference to "anxiety" as metaphorical – as a way of communicating, in a shorthand way, about a more complex dis-location in a person's life, but not the manifestation of a unitary *state* of anxiety or inbuilt emotion (Hallam, 1985).

Tacit Assumptions in Contemporary Models of Anxiety

I will address contemporary models with the same questions used to orient the reader in the previous section – what are the universalizing assumptions, the sources of rationality, and the narrative element? These are weighty questions and my comments should be taken as no more than a preliminary sketch of some of the issues.

I have already noted the ambiguity of the concept of threat as a universalizing assumption. Apart from the technical definitions noted earlier, "threat" is also a folk construct – people "feel threatened" when they perceive they cannot meet anticipated demands or cope with harmful events. However, the lay person may have as much difficulty in specifying the precise nature of "threat" as of "anxiety." Con-temporary models of anxiety are largely a description of the conditions in which people tend to feel threatened in the lay sense. When attempts have been made to elucidate "underlying threats" from people who complain of an anxiety problem such as panic, it has been found that most of them can be grouped into a limited number of themes (for example, see Beck et al., 1985). These are the threat of death and illness, of loss of personal control (over mind or body), of looking foolish, of being criticized or rejected by others, and of material insecurities.

It would be wrong to infer that these threats *naturally* produce "anxiety" in the sense that they would universally do so. The form that these threats take is culturally specific and socially constructed. This is more obviously true of some (such as the threat of insanity) than of others, although even the threat of death is closely linked to cultural values. The threats can be said to represent the negative face of modern moral values and expectations. They are not (now) seen as examples of divine retribution or as an opportunity for Stoic resignation. The values that appear to be threatened here are the opportunity to lead an untroubled ordinary life, to possess the faculties to live life as a story, to shape that story in a way that is personally satisfying, to receive one's just deserts, etc. These are values that have historical sources (Taylor, 1990) and they imply a narrative for the conditions of contemporary life.

The ideological content of models of anxiety is revealed in statements about the causal origins of threat and how a person should be encouraged "to cope with it." The psychological literature on coping and mental health has a tendency to conceive of the social environment as a "state of nature" – as intrinsically uncivilized and populated by stressors that are likely to be perceived by the *individual* as uncontrollable and unpredictable (Stam, 1987). Nevertheless, it is the individual who is perceived as having the capacity to exert control – but within the confines of what is defined socially as "possible" and "rational." For example, social institutions, such as the Economy, are seen as operating autonomously, beyond personal control, according to their own (mysterious) self-regulating mechanisms.

Lasch (1984) has characterized the mode of life of individuals in contemporary North American Culture as "Survivalism." He states: "Everyday life has begun to pattern itself on the survival strategies forced on those exposed to extreme adversity" (1984: 57). The perception of everyday reality as unfavorable or hostile interrelates with a narrative of the individual struggling against tough odds. When the struggle falters, the individual may attribute failure to the intrusion of "anxiety," an emotion to which humans in adversity are "naturally" prone. The contemporary emphasis on coping and competence can be understood against this backdrop.

The solution according to Bandura (1977; Evans, 1989) is for the individual to develop a strong sense of self-efficacy, the antithesis of a proneness to anxiety. And in the guise of talking about the scientific locus of causality for human behavior, Bandura (1978) has powerfully expressed his ideological commitment to self-efficacy by stressing the importance of causality located in the person. In other words, he appropriates the rhetoric of Science to reinforce a certain set of values.

It is worth examining Bandura's arguments in more detail. It is useful to spell out several conceptual questions: (1) where causality is really located, for example, inside or outside the organism (within some scientific vision of the Real); (2) where the individual believes causality to be located, for example, in the personal or extra-personal sphere (within a vision of Cosmology and the Moral Order); and (3) what sources, powers, or forces a person believes he or she is drawing upon when causality is attributed to the self.

Bandura (1978) dismisses the search for *ultimate* environmental causes of behavior as an "idle exercise" based on his assumption that behavior, cognition, and environment reciprocally and simultaneously determine each other (his doctrine of reciprocal determinism). This conceptual move frees him to stress the importance of personal causation because this aspect might as well be stressed as any other. For example, he stresses the freedom people have to construct social institutions that act as mechanisms of benevolent reciprocal influence.

The doctrine of reciprocal determinism passes over question (1) altogether and conflates the natural and social order. Whatever Physicists might be up to, Psychological events are generally believed to have a spatial and temporal location. It is difficult to see how we can avoid segmenting behavioral–environmental interactions when considered from the point of view of physical causation. Thus, even though cultural influences are ubiquitous, they still have to be reproduced in material form through physical transactions between people and with the environment.

Extending the doctrine of reciprocal determinism to historical events would imply that questions of assigning *ultimate* causal priority to any one class of determinants also amounts to no more than an idle exercise. If we concede this, we are still left with the problem of weighting or prioritizing different causal factors. To stress the cognitive is arbitrary, given that the doctrine of simultaneous and reciprocal determinism appears to rule out the possibility, in principle, of weighting causal factors. To fall back on what *appears* to be causal (for example, a person's thoughts) is to use the answers to questions (2) and (3) above as a basis for scientific assertions, that is, to rely on lay beliefs about the locus of causality as the foundation for a scientific model of causality. On the contrary, these beliefs are no more than culturally accepted assertions about highly valued powers of causality that are perceived to reside in the person. These beliefs and values are tacit within Bandura's model and therefore fail to be discussed.

A similar criticism can be made of the "terror management theory of self-esteem" in which the construct of anxiety is central (Solomon et al., 1991). This model does not distinguish between statements that describe what people assert (psychology) and assertions the authors are putting forward as Psychology. The core assumptions appear to be that: (1) anxiety is an aversive motivational state; (2) an awareness of mortality causes anxiety; (3) a culture provides protection and hope of immortality on condition that individuals adhere to cultural values; (4)

the individual is esteemed and esteems him/herself to the extent that he or she shares the values of the culture; and (5) anxiety is experienced by those individuals who fail to acquire or maintain the protective buffer of self-esteem. The authors note that a culture that operates on this basis is not particularly conducive to mental health. Curiously, they go on to say that "this is not a political judgement."

What the authors are naively claiming is that their theory is a neutral interpretation of their empirical observations as scientists. One is led to question what empirical psychology is about. Any mirror held up to society (and even more so, one that shows it to be a reign of terror) is likely to impact on cultural values. Perhaps the authors assume that individuals do not rationally examine their values or do not value them because they are intrinsically valuable, but simply value whatever it is that other individuals esteem them for valuing. The narrative suggested by their theory is the person as fugitive, driven by the fear of death and goaded by the disapproval of fellow humans. The theory works well as satire.

Conclusion

This chapter has attempted to show that the anxiety construct is a product of small p psychology. Theorists appear to have ignored Sarbin's suggestion (Sarbin, 1964) that it be dispensed with as a scientific construct. The strength of popular belief that anxiety is a fundamental feeling or emotion can be taken to indicate that it is part of our canonical reality. According to Sarbin, there has been a transformation from metaphor to myth. It was suggested earlier that resistance to the unveiling of this myth has come from at least two quarters: (1) the key role that "anxiety" plays in a system of social control based on self-regulation, and (2) the uncritical adoption of empirical methods for validating Psychological hypotheses. A more promising set of Psychological constructs may develop from abstract conceptualizations of adaptation and ecological mismatch. As regards therapeutic approaches to "anxiety problems" people may benefit more from seeing these in a much wider social context and questioning their adoption of this form of self-reference as an involuntary natural emotion.

Note

I have been helped enormously by comments on earlier drafts of this chapter from Mary Boyle, Paul McReynolds, Kieron O'Connor, Graham Richards and the editors.

References

Bandura, A. (1977) Self-efficacy: toward a unifying theory of behavioral change, *Psychological Review*, 84: 191–215.

Bandura, A. (1978) The self system in reciprocal determinism, *American Psychologist*, 33: 344–58.

Baumeister, R.F. (1987) How the self became a problem: a psychological review of historical research, *Journal of Personality and Social Psychology*, 52: 163–76.

Beck, A., Emery, G., and Greenberg, R. (1985) *Anxiety Disorders and Phobias*. New York: Basic Books.

Bosworth, J. and Toller T.N. (1898) *Anglo-Saxon Dictionary*. Oxford: Clarendon.

Bruner, J. (1990) *Acts of Meaning*. Cambridge, MA: Harvard University Press.

Cole, J.P. (1971) *The Problematic Self in Kierkegaard and Freud*. New Haven, CT, and London: Yale University Press.

Evans, R.I. (1989) *Albert Bandura: The Man and his Ideas – A Dialogue*. New York: Praeger.

Goldstein, K. (1939) *The Organism; A Holistic Approach to Biology*. New York: American Book Co.

Hallam, R.S. (1985) *Anxiety: Psychological Perspectives on Panic and Agoraphobia*. London: Academic Press.

Harré, R. (1986) *The Social Construction of Emotion*. London: Routledge.

Lasch, C. (1984) *The Minimal Self: Psychic Survival in Troubled Times*. New York: W.W. Norton.

Lock, A. (1981) Universals in human conception, in P. Heelas and A. Lock (eds), *Indigenous Psychologies: The Anthropology of the Self*. London: Academic Press.

Logan, R.D. (1987) Historical change in the prevailing sense of self, in K. Yardley and T. Honess (eds), *Self and Identity: Psychosocial Perspectives*. Chichester: Wiley.

Lutz, C. (1990) Engendered emotion: gender, power, and the rhetoric of emotional control in American discourse, in C. Lutz and L. Abu-Lughod (eds), *Language and the Politics of Emotion*. Cambridge: Cambridge University Press.

McReynolds, P. (1986) Changing conceptions of anxiety: a historical review and proposed integration, in C.D. Spielberger and I.G. Sarason (eds), *Stress and Anxiety, Vol 10*. Washington DC: Hemisphere.

Morawski, J.G. (1984) Historiography as a metatheoretical text for social psychology, in K.J. Gergen and M.M. Gergen (eds), *Historical Social Psychology*, Hillsdale, NJ: Lawrence Erlbaum.

May, R. (1950) *The Meaning of Anxiety*. New York: Ronald Press. (Republished, 1977, New York: Washington Square Press.)

Ortony, A. and Turner, T.J. (1990) What's basic about basic emotions?, *Psychological Review*, 97: 315–31.

Richards, G. (1987) Of what is the history of psychology a history?, *British Journal for the History of Science*, 20: 201–12.

Richards, G. (1989) *On Psychological Language*. London: Routledge.

Rose, N. (1990) Psychology as "social" science, in I. Parker and J. Shotter (eds), *Deconstructing Social Psychology*. London: Routledge.

Sarbin, T.R. (1964) Anxiety: reification of a metaphor, *Archives of General Psychiatry*, 10: 630–8.

Sarbin, T.R. (1968) Ontology recapitulates philology: the mythic nature of anxiety, *American Psychologist*, 23: 411–18.

Schlenker, B.R. and Leary, M.R. (1982) Social anxiety and self-presentation, *Psychological Bulletin*, 92: 641–69.

Skinner, B.F. (1972) *Beyond Freedom and Dignity*. London: Jonathan Cape.

Solomon, S., Greenberg, J., and Pyszczynski, T. (1991) Terror management theory of self-esteem, in C.R. Snyder and D.R. Forsyth (eds), *Handbook of Social and Clinical Psychology: The Health Perspective*. New York: Pergamon.

Stam, H.J. (1987) The psychology of control: a textual critique, in H.J. Stam, T.B. Rogers, and K.J. Gergen (eds), *The Analysis of Psychological Theories: Metapsychological Perspectives*, New York: Hemisphere.

Taylor, C. (1990) *Sources of the Self: The Making of Modern Identity*. Cambridge: Cambridge University Press.

III
THE DECONSTRUCTION OF POPULAR CONCEPTIONS

9
Genius: A Social Construction, the Case of Beethoven's Initial Recognition

Tia DeNora and Hugh Mehan

Ranking individuals according to certain identifying features is fundamental to nearly every aspect of social life. In the course of day-to-day interaction we refer to others as characterized by varying degrees of such qualities as intelligence, talent, good looks, and so on. This informal way of talking is recapitulated in a variety of formal settings. In hospitals, courts and schools, people are said to be deviant, mentally ill, educationally handicapped or gifted. In both formal and informal settings, we speak a language of attribution. Our words depict individuals as "possessing" certain traits or states.

This language is also common within a large segment of social science. Individual attributes are routinely (though often implicitly) treated as unproblematic, and explanatory energies are devoted instead to specifying the factors (biological, psychological or social) that somehow "shape" or "determine" identity. Thus, for most of the time in the course of our various practical and social scientific engagements we remain relatively unreflective about the process of how individuals come to be recognized for what they "are."

In recent years, these recognition processes have become the focus of investigation. In so-called "constructivist" research, the language of attribution is viewed as a topic – as opposed to a resource – for sociological inquiry (Zimmerman and Pollner, 1970; Ibarra and Kitsuse, 1993). In this chapter, we adopt some of the tools from the constructivist perspective and apply them to one kind of extraordinary identity, creative genius, in order to consider how it is socially organized and collaboratively produced. We do this by presenting materials from a case study of Beethoven and the social bases of his initial success during his first decade in Vienna (DeNora, 1989, 1993). Along the way we consider the literature on the sociology and social psychology of genius to date, and conclude by summarizing some of the implications of our case study for a more general understanding of creative ability and its social distribution.

Constructivism and Identity

In our view, the construction of identity occurs on two semiotic planes simultaneously. The first of these is cultural. Identities participate in and are sponsored by particular ways of classifying individuals into types and categories. This is to say that there can be no recognized cases of, for example, "handicapped children," if there are no practical and linguistic ways of delineating the characteristics of the categories "handicapped" and "child" (Ariès, 1979; Foucault, 1980). Thus, an awareness of the ways in which identities are culturally configured in and through historically located discursive practices (Weedon, 1987) is crucial for the sociology of identity.

Appreciation of the cultural construction of identity is crucial, then, because the classifications, imageries and frameworks which cultures provide help to organize the ways we experience phenomena. These categories shift and change through times and across cultural groups. Deviance for instance is now characterized as a mixture of environmental and biological factors. (Some would argue that the biological category is gaining the upper hand in recent theorizing.) Previously in western societies, deviance has been seen to be the result of spirit possession, witchcraft and the devil's work. Because of these historical and cross-cultural shifts, "reality" cannot be perceived as independent from the culturally specific instruments through which it is registered (Mehan et al., 1986; Woolgar, 1988).

Yet focus on cultural construction is not enough. In line with some poststructuralist social theory, we conceive of "culture" as providing multiple, ambiguous, and often contradictory sets of constitutive rules. There are, for example, a variety of ways of constituting the meaning of femininity in our society, and at least some of these versions come into conflict (Coward, 1984). Moreover, individuals may adopt or impute to others a variety of contradictory subject positions from scene to scene and moment to moment, sometimes even within the same utterance (Frazer and Cameron, 1989). For this reason we think it is important to explore how and under what circumstances particular individuals come to employ or be regularly associated with particular cultural categories or frames (rather than others) and how, in this process, cultural frameworks are articulated, strengthened and revised.

This leads us to the second plane on which we approach the problem of identity: the interactional. In addition to the cultural construction of the categories of identity, we are interested in the specific ways that connections are established between individuals and the categories for which they are said to stand. How is it, for example, that an individual's deeds are recognized as the product of genius rather than simply as talent? As originality rather than incompetence? Further, how does our perception of particular details about a person come to be organized? Why do we look at them through one cultural prescription and not another, and what, in concrete terms, does it mean to speak of perception as culturally organized? How, in other words, is a particular version of identity constructed, reinforced and made to stick? In what ways can we understand particular cases as interacting and affecting our conceptions of the general categories they are seen as representing? And finally, how does an identity, once established, come to affect the kinds of things that an individual can do or "get away with"? As we will see below, all of these questions are vital to our understanding of just how it was that Beethoven came to be (and still is, for the most part) viewed as a genius during the early nineteenth century.

Genius in Society

Our interest in genius arose out of earlier work on the classification of pupils in schools (Mehan et al., 1986). That research documented some of the ways in which appelations such as "disability" or "intelligence" or "disruptive" are mediated by a range of factors extrinsic to the student's own behavior and school performance. The point was not to deny the reality of "difficult" pupils' behaviors, but rather to document just how the extent of ambiguity and contradiction is managed in order for students' identities (in this case, as "disruptive" or "learning disabled") to be made apparent. For all practical purposes, the identity "handicapped" is interactively produced in conjunction with ways of viewing and doing within the school, including grouping, testing and tracking practices. As a result, we cannot fully understand the nature of learning abilities without simultaneously attempting to follow the range of socially distributed resources and constraints that contextualize school decision-making. Before turning to a consideration of genius in society, it is worth developing this point in greater detail.

To be classified as mentally handicapped is, at least implicitly, to be ranked on the lower end of a continuum of identity within the school. By formal and informal institutional means of assessing ability (such as IQ and psychological testing and classroom teachers' observations), a student's scores or performances are deemed inferior. This is not to suggest, as sociological realists tend to do, that the student is in some "freestanding" or decontextualized way, less able than his or her peers. There is not a world of troubled children out there waiting to be identified. Nor is it to suggest that his or her identity is a result only of labels ascribed to him or her. Rather it is to observe that, according to formal and informal ways of processing that student within the culture of the school, including but not limited to labeling practices of officials, a "handicapped" student could have been perceived along different lines. Under different circumstances – different principles of classification, different interpretive procedures and measures, different assessors and circumstances of assessing, and different resources available to the one being assessed – that student's place on a continuum could vary. Identity, in other words, is not "in" individuals but emerges "out of" the relations between individuals, their acts and instruments.

Identity, in short, is a symbolic production; it could potentially have been otherwise. For this reason, then, the issue of whether a school's assessments of students can meaningfully be exported to settings outside the school is simultaneously an issue of how far the authority of that institution's way of seeing (which is simultaneously a professional ideology) should extend – whether in other cultural contexts the school's way of processing individuals can be imposed legitimately.

We believe these same issues apply to the topic of genius in society. Simply put: under different circumstances individuals recognized as geniuses could be evaluated differently; different ways of evaluating would in turn be consequential for the fields or contexts in which they occur and for the relations of individuals and groups within and between these fields. For example, within both scientific and artistic fields (as we shall see below) the notion of "genius" is a resource for the constitution of professional authority. It serves as a pretext for the classification and ranking of activity within these fields and for ranking these fields in relation to others. In this sense, the cultural category of genius provides a strategy for the construction of authority.

The reality of genius, as of mental handicaps, exists then, only within a framework of ways of classifying and ways of acting. In this sense, then, the reality of genius is socially produced and sustained. We can inquire into the ways in which it is put together; how genius is socially constructed.

In what follows we discuss the case of Beethoven's initial recognition as a genius, during the decade in which he embarked on and began to consolidate a Viennese career, first as a pianist in private aristocratic salons and then as a composer of large-scale works. The point of this discussion is not to report our findings in detail; we have done that elsewhere (DeNora, 1989a, 1989b, 1991a, 1993). Rather, we wish to highlight how we think genius or exceptional talent is open to a constructivist perspective, and we wish to observe a few of the ways in which the recognition of extraordinary talent is reflexively linked to the context in which it occurred in a particular historical case.

Case Study: the Construction of Beethoven as a Genius

The case of Beethoven's recognition as an extraordinary talent is a particularly good one for constructivist analysis. First, the case has a high profile: Beethoven is conventionally viewed, both by contemporary music scholars and by a wide range of the general public as the archetypal genius. The image of Beethoven – scowling and disheveled, as he is depicted in numerous portraits and busts – has had a major impact on the iconography of genius (see Comini, 1987), and it is familiar to many people who are otherwise unacquainted with the world of "high culture" music. Moreover, Beethoven's continuing reputation is due to retrospective celebrations and appropriations of this imagery, where the composer's greatness has come to function as a resource for other cultural-political agendas. Up to the present, Beethoven has been invoked as an "ally" by numerous individuals and groups: musicians pursuing professional agendas (such as Wagner), political regimes (the Fifth symphony was appropriated as a symbol of western democracy during and after World War II), and segments of, for example, gay and ethnic communities who claim the composer as a member.

Beyond Beethoven's continued prominence as a cultural figure, however, his case is interesting because his success and identification as a musical master had a significant impact on conventions of music consumption and on the criteria according to which music was evaluated during the late eighteenth and early nineteenth centuries. During this time, the form of Beethoven's success and celebration was unique. From the start of his career in Vienna, his music was experienced, both by his supporters and his opponents, as in contrast with conventional criteria of musical worth. Beethoven was, in other words, a highly controversial composer. Extant accounts of his music's reception by his contemporaries during these years refer to Beethoven's "different" and sometimes "shocking" music. Thus, the work of aligning Beethoven with categories of musical value should be of special interest to the social scientist because Beethoven's success was accompanied by a transformation of musical criteria. Musical values were altered, so as to "fit" the rather idiosyncratic, from the late eighteenth century Viennese perspective, shape of Beethoven's talent. Initially criticized for writing music that was over-complicated and full of (unpleasant) surprises for the listener, Beethoven was eventually discussed as someone who should be allowed to "go his own gait."

What makes this process especially significant, then, from the music historical point of view, is that it is in and through the articulation of Beethoven as an extraordinary figure that we can account for the initial emergence of a discourse of musical genius. Because Beethoven's works had an impact upon the settings in which they were projected, the study of his construction as a genius provides an opportunity for following the reflexive relationship between the cultural and inter-actional planes on which identity is constructed. Just how, then, did this occur?

In most music historical accounts, Beethoven is portrayed as an uncompromising figure, able, as one introductory music appreciation textbook puts it, "thanks to his genius and to his uncompromising personality to make himself into a pure composer and . . . force the aristocracy of Vienna to support him at it, more or less on his own terms" (Kerman and Kerman, 1976: 190). In fact, we can point to indications of how an important segment of the aristocratic Viennese music world during the 1790s was initially receptive to Beethoven. As with other forms of recognition and success, genius requires a retinue of support personnel (Becker, 1982).

First, Beethoven was able to become a musical star at this time because the general category of musical "star" began to emerge as an artifact of the changing organizational basis of music patronage. During the 1770s and 1780s, aristocrats were disbanding their *Hauskapellen* (private house orchestras staffed by resident musician/ servants) and were turning instead to the sponsorship and co-sponsorship of private, quasi-public and, to some extent, public musical events. This by no means meant however that the market for music expanded; indeed, if we examine concert programs of the period, we find that musical life tended to coalesce around a select few, "star" composers. For the majority of musicians, the shift from private to quasi-public sponsorship was not beneficial. Moreover, the backbone of Viennese musical life was composed of private rather than public concerts, of music in aristocratic salons.

As the music and economic historian Julia Moore has shown, this meant that those composers who were well-connected to aristocrats, and especially to the court, fared best. They were able to enjoy the benefits from publications and public performances of their works while retaining the security of private patronage. In this sense, then, it is meaningful to speak of an organizational predisposition for musical celebrities during the 1790s.

During these years, a preoccupation with the idea of musical greatness emerged. In Vienna this seems to have originated with one particular patron, Baron Gottfried van Swieten, a kind of "super-patron." He was described in a Viennese musical yearbook of 1796 as follows: "when he attends a concert, our semi-connoisseurs never take their eyes off him, seeking to read in his features, not always intelligible to everyone, what ought to be their opinion of the music" (Schönfeld: 1976: 72–3). Describing himself in 1798 as, "oppressed by new evidence of decadence in the arts," van Swieten devoted most of his time to, as he put it, "Handel, the Bachs and those few great men of our own day who, taking these as their masters, follow resolutely in the same quest for greatness and truth." In the 1780s it seems that van Swieten's outlook was considered somewhat eccentric and, if we are to infer from one aristocrat's diary entry, a bit boring. During the 1790s, however (and even before Beethoven arrived in Vienna), van Swieten's enthusiasm for musical "greatness and truth" was increasingly shared by other aristocrats, some of whom were to become Beethoven's primary patrons after 1793 (see DeNora, 1991). Thus, the structure and culture of musical life in Vienna during the early 1790s was conducive to the emergence of a "great" (that is, highly celebrated and "serious" talent). How then, did Beethoven initially fit into this category?

Beethoven's entry into Viennese musical life was eased because of his social position in his native town, Bonn. Beethoven was the son (and grandson) of important electoral court musicians at Bonn (which was one of the largest and most prestigious court *Kapellen* in the empire). He had been exposed to and taught by numerous "important" musicians in the course of his apprenticeship, and, perhaps most significantly, he was patronized by important members of the Bonn aristocracy, in particular by Count Waldstein who had recently come to Bonn from Vienna and who could provide Beethoven access to some of Vienna's highest and most musically active aristocrats. (Indeed, if we diagram Beethoven's expanding Viennese network during these years (see DeNora, 1989, 1993) we find that the majority of Beethoven's aristocratic contacts were made via introductions provided by his closest patron during these years, Prince Karl Lichnowsky, a regular attender of van Swieten's private Sunday morning concerts where the music of Bach and Handel was played.)

Because of his Bonn contacts, Beethoven could be introduced to Vienna as a geographically "foreign" musician (with the allure that this frequently entailed) while simultaneously benefiting from the fact that, in terms of aristocratic patronage networks, he was a more like a "local" talent. (For example, the Bonn Elector, under whose auspices Beethoven initially went to Vienna, was the Emperor's uncle.) Shortly after his arrival in Vienna, then, we find Beethoven attending van Swieten's private concerts and living more or less as a member of Prince Lichnowsky's family. Lichnowsky was one of the most important Viennese patrons with ties to van Swieten, and also a previous close patron of Mozart. An additional resource during these years was that there was some confusion over the meaning of the "van" in Beethoven's name (Ludwig van Beethoven) which was mistaken by some to denote aristocratic birth (as if it were the Dutch equivalent to the German "von"). Though Beethoven was not an aristocrat (his father and grandfather were both musicians; his mother was the daughter of the overseer of food at the Bonn court), the confusion over his social status meant that he was sometimes able to pass as an equal in aristocratic settings (see Solomon, 1978; DeNora, 1989a).

In short, Beethoven's situation was hardly typical of the average musician. At a time when proximity to and patronage by key music aristocrats was crucial to success, Beethoven was, from the very start of his career, placed in the hands of some of the best known and most powerful music patrons in Vienna – patrons, moreover, who were becoming interested in the idea of musical "greatness and truth" who were receptive to and indeed, actively searching for, an heir to what had been newly discovered as the "spirit of Mozart." Beethoven's Bonn patron and friend, Count Waldstein, for example, said exactly this when he wrote the following in Beethoven's autograph book on the eve of the composer's journey to Vienna:

> Dear Beethoven: The Genius of Mozart is still mourning and weeping the death of her pupil. She found a refuge but no occupation with the inexhaustible Haydn; through him she wishes once more to form a union with another. With the help of assiduous labour you shall receive Mozart's spirit from Haydn's hands.

Every major Beethoven scholar hails this message as prophetic, yet it can be more convincingly read as a statement of a project. From the start of his Viennese career, and irrespective of his actual music (that is, in terms of his social connections and location in the social space of the Viennese musical world), Beethoven was an extremely likely candidate for the partially prescripted role of the "next" Mozart.

This is by no means to suggest that Beethoven's success was wholly predetermined. The history of Beethoven's recognition as a "great" composer is more complex. It is complicated by the fact that, during the 1790s, Beethoven's music was received as in opposition to Viennese stylistic conventions and these differences were simultaneously seen by some (and especially early on) as evidence of Beethoven's musical ineptness. For example, as his pupil Carl Czerny put it, Beethoven's critics:

> accused [him] of mistreating the piano, of lacking all cleanness and clarity, of creating nothing but confused noise the way he used the pedal and finally of writing willful, unnatural, unmelodic compositions, which were irregular besides. (1956: 309)

Yet, when Beethoven's music was recognized as great, it was for these same stylistic characteristics. Moreover, his close circle of patrons seem to have encouraged him, during these early years, to develop his works along its idiosyncratic lines. In addition, they actively shaped the forums in which Beethoven's works were presented. They also acted, in behind the scenes ways, to assure that the public image of Beethoven's reception and success was positive; in some cases this meant that their patronage of the composer took on the characteristics of public relations work such that, as one contemporary put it, "hearers not only accustomed themselves to the striking and original qualities of the master but grasped his spirit and strove for the high privilege of understanding him" (Thayer, 1967, I: 164). Through this work, Beethoven could more easily become, as the music history sources put it, "a force in music"; he could more easily become an authoritative bearer of an alternative aesthetic rationale.

In general, this work consisted of a variety of ad hoc processes that helped to align Beethoven with the outward and more material "signs" of great talent and success. It involved lodging Beethoven under authoritative mantles that could then work to shelter him or shield him from "misinterpretation." For example, between the years 1792 and 1796 a series of stories was elaborated around the notion of Beethoven as Haydn's "favorite" pupil and heir (see DeNora, 1989, 1993). These stories provide a clearly selective account of the relationship between teacher and pupil. Other equally persuasive accounts of the Haydn–Beethoven relationship were suppressed. Had these accounts been developed and publicized, they would have presented Beethoven in a very different light. (For example, the extant documentary materials lend themselves to alternative accounts of the Haydn–Beethoven relationship in which it is characterized by ambivalence and by skepticism on Haydn's part.) Lodging Beethoven under the auspices of the, by that time, unimpeachable Haydn provided a source of authority for Beethoven's talent and it provided a set of "contextualization cues" (Gumperz 1982; DeNora 1986) or conventions for interpreting the meaning of Beethoven's works. Also during the 1790s, Beethoven's closest patron during these years, Prince Lichnowsky, secretly underwrote the publication costs for Beethoven's first major publication. In conjunction with other members of his family, he purchased 53 of the 247 subscription copies of that publication. Such a practice enabled Beethoven to appear to outside observers as an "already" successful composer whose first major publication was lucrative (for further discussion of this particular practice see DeNora, 1993). What must be emphasized here is that this patronage practice was by no means standard during these years; in the history of Lichnowsky's efforts we can therefore see the emergence of a new kind of patron, one akin to the nascent arts producer of subsequent years.

Beethoven's increasing presence in Vienna's music world, therefore, was due at least in part to the entrepreneurial activities of his musically powerful patrons. In a context where elites still exercised considerable control (something that distinguished Vienna from London during these years), Beethoven's musically powerful patrons could mobilize conventional assumptions and imageries of how reputations were made to Beethoven's advantage. They did this by backgrounding the history of how Beethoven came to "evidence" conventional signs of success and esteem – the circumstances of how his "successful" first publication was achieved, for example – and by pushing to the fore the achieved signs of Beethoven's success severed from the contexts of their production. This strategy left outsiders (that is, those outside of Beethoven's intimate circle of aristocratic patrons) to draw "their own" (culturally conventional) conclusions about just what such signs meant and how they had been achieved. While these readings were by no means automatic and the kinds of inferences about Beethoven varied, they were biased in Beethoven's favor because the strategies of presenting Beethoven exploited cultural habits: like the magic trick that depends upon attention being focused on some things while deflected from others, Beethoven's successful image (which served as a sign of his prodigious talent, his genius) was built upon a selective presentation and consumption of signs in conjunction with habits and conventions of music reception that allowed these signs to become indices of Beethoven's fundamental quality of musical genius.

Through these and other practices, then, during the middle 1790s a culture of success was built up around Beethoven; an increasing body of circumstantial evidence of Beethoven's worth was created and pieced together which, in turn, could be used to dramatize his plausibility (and therefore) strength as a powerful musical figure.

In turn, these signs of authority became resources for Beethoven's own impression management. Beethoven could and did trade on his emerging image in order to further strengthen his artistic claims. For example, he used his increasing authority as a musical figure to demand more attention from his listeners even to the point of telling one count who talked loudly during a performance that he, "would not play for such swine" – something which, in the days when musicians were still conceived of as servants, would have been a radical departure from concert protocol. He could and did effectively persuade the major music journal of the time to give him more flattering reviews (with the threat of withholding his compositions from their parent company, a music publisher – see DeNora, 1989: ch. 7). He could also, given the credibility he had built up, embark on what his contemporaries recognized as his ever-more daring stylistic ventures after the years around 1803. It is important to underline here that the perception of Beethoven's works as worthy was sustained and nurtured in Vienna specifically; Beethoven's reception abroad was for many years problematic.

Thus, Beethoven's initial success and recognition as a great musician – a genius – entailed an aesthetic reorientation, a redefinition of the categories of musical value that distanced them from an emphasis on lightness of texture, clarity and "pleasingness," in favor of an emphasis on difficulty, complexity, expressiveness and originality. To follow Beethoven's success therefore, is to follow the ways in which an alternative aesthetic "paradigm" was initially articulated. Beethoven's recognition as a talented musician entailed a reflexive relationship between his work and the aesthetic under which his works made sense. His success, emerging out of and conditioned by the circumstances of his reception and the strategies according to which his talent was displayed, strengthened these new criteria. Through his success and the success of his style, Beethoven provided an increasingly powerful figure on which the new aesthetic and the new notion of artist as one who "goes his own gait" could be draped and made to look fashionable.

Genius as Social Construction: an Under-Explored Topic

We hope we have been able to allude, through the case study presented above, to some of the ways in which we believe genius can and should be explored as a social construction. We have tried to illustrate how formal and informal ways of talking about identity privilege a language of attribution, and how this language provides an impoverished way of talking because it obscures the range of socially distributed resources and constraints that contextualize the recognition and ranking of individuals. Our case study was introduced to highlight some of these resources, how they were marshaled and deployed. We hope to contribute to a shift in discourse or way of accounting for genius, from one that places genius within people to one that places it between people, in socially organized contexts that can include power relations, strategies, and devices.

To our knowledge, there has been relatively little exploration of genius as socially constructed. Indeed, the ideology of genius – that some individuals are endowed with extraordinary gifts enabling them to penetrate and radically transform the logic of their particular intellectual creative field – remains, in spite of attempts to deconstruct it, powerful and persuasive. Many of us believe, for example, that we "know" greatness when we see it. In so doing, we tend to conflate our own experience as members of society with the things that constitute our experience as real. We maintain genius as a mysterious phenomenon.

If anything, professional academics may be more susceptible to the ideology of genius than others. To say, for example, as one recent academic writer has, that "no amount of analysis has yet been able to explain the capacities of those rare and gifted individuals who can produce creative work of lasting quality and value" (Murray, 1989: 1), is to take a stance that is congruent with professional academic, expert, and "learned" ideology. It is not surprising, therefore, that there have not yet been ethnographically or historically grounded explorations of genius as socially constructed.

This is not to say, however, that the topic of genius has been ignored within the humanities and social sciences. On the contrary, over the past few years, the topic has been taken up by literary theorists (Battersby, 1989; Murray, 1989), intellectual historians (Regis, 1988), and social psychologists (Bloom, 1985; Horowitz and O'Brien, 1985; Sternberg and Davidson, 1986; Radford, 1990). These studies have enhanced the understanding of genius and, in at least three ways, they are congruent with our own project as we have presented it above.

First, considerations of the ways in which aestheticians and literary theorists have considered the topic have revealed the ways in which our modern idea of genius – as autonomous extraordinary powers of creativity – was articulated during the eighteenth century (Murray, 1989). Thus, we can understand genius as a part of a historically located discourse, a way of imagining talent and ability as socially distributed within specific spatial and temporal settings.

Second, we can begin to consider the ways in which the social distribution of genius is skewed (Battersby, 1989). Why, for example, should great geniuses be predominantly male? Or why should it be that the major musical geniuses are predominantly Germanic and, furthermore, dead for at least a century? Asking questions such as these makes it possible for genius to be reconceived as a conceptual and ideological resource in the sense that to identify an individual as a genius is simultaneously to legitimate one way of doing things as opposed to others, and with it, to legitimate those individuals who are its partisans.

Finally, social psychologists (Bloom, 1985; Horowitz and O'Brien, 1985; Feldman, 1986; Sternberg and Davidson, 1986; Radford, 1990) have described some of the material and social factors that help to foster talent early on, pointing to the presence of, among other things, a devoted and determined parent, training at home where discipline is imposed, supportive mentoring, and the selection of a particular talent at the expense of others. While this work has concentrated predominantly upon the development of child prodigies, the lessons it offers – that the cultivation of talent is a cooperative affair – merge with our more general understanding of "art as collective action" (Becker, 1974, 1982) and with sociologically oriented understandings of the factors that can affect school performance. Helpful as these studies have been, in our view and in light of our own work on the construction of handicaps and genius, they do not go far enough. Social psychological studies of the "prerequisites" of exceptional talent are useful in that they contribute to our understanding of some of the resources that cultivate exceptional talent. We believe that these studies are important for the ways they begin to demystify talent by grounding it in terms of the factors that nourish it and we have observed the usefulness of this perspective in our consideration of Beethoven's social position, his musical family, and his ties to an important *Hofkapelle.*

Yet there are numerous 'talents' who are never recognized as geniuses, and for this reason we believe that social psychological studies do not go far enough. Such studies stop short of a full blown consideration of how the material and social resources that condition talent come to interact with the factors that help to condition that talent's reception, that help to transform talent into perceived genius. Social psychological studies of talent, moreover, are applied retrospectively and because of this they can account for exceptional ability only after it has been recognized and ranked. In Beethoven's case, for example, we saw that his recognition as a "great" talent was dependent upon a kind of ongoing aesthetic entrepreneurship and on presentation strategies capable of transforming musical evaluative criteria in Beethoven's favor. For Beethoven to be received as a genius, interpretive work had to occur; over time, as Beethoven's presence and perceived legitimacy in the Viennese music world increased, Beethoven's own musical efforts became conditions for realizing the criteria against which they were measured. Through this reflexive process, little-by-little over time, musical standards changed and Beethoven's reputation was enhanced. Thus, because social psychological studies of early and exceptional ability leave issues relating to the reception of talent unexplored, they tend to reinforce (at least implicitly) the language of attribution, and because of this, they also leave in shadow the issue of how some individuals come to be recognized as "gifted" and others do not.

Historical studies of the idea of genius and its social distribution also tend to reinforce the language of attribution, and to reinforce the mystery of genius as a category of being. Murray, for example, suggests that, "in each age and in each art, genius is that which defies analysis" (1989: 1). Here, the idea (or mental container) of genius is conceived of having a particular cultural history, but simultaneously, the idea of genius is posited as little more than a fabric, in which underlying transcendental creative gifts are clothed. Thus, Murray can write about how there have, throughout history, been individuals who possess "extraordinary creative powers, powers which distinguish [them] from men and women of talent and which are certainly beyond the reach of ordinary mortals like the rest of us" (1989: 7). The idea here is that geniuses abound throughout history but that, until the eighteenth century, there were no ideological categories for recognizing them as such.

Battersby's discussion of gender and genius proceeds along similar lines: there are disproportionally few women geniuses; this is not, however, because there were no women geniuses: there were. They were, however, simply unrecognizable within a masculine culture. Genius, then, within both of these views, is something that "always" existed. Identity is still conceived of as "in" the person; cultural lenses simply enhance or suppress our perception of that identity. A metaphor which springs to mind here is the photograph; the characteristics are always "in" particular special individuals; culture categories simply draw out what was present all along in latent form. A "misunderstood" or overlooked genius is, in this view, a genius nonetheless.

We consider both Murray's and Battersby's ways of understanding the cultural history of identity to exemplify "weak" versions of constructivism. Others have made similar arguments before and we simply wish to index them here (Woolgar, 1983). In these weak versions, an "underlying" reality is posited; that reality is then depicted as "shrouded" or mediated by cultural "ways of seeing" which the analyst then attempts to undermine in pursuit of "the truth." Here, construction is understood as a series of transparencies that come to "color" the real state of affairs. To "place a construction upon something," as the phrase was used in the eighteenth century, is to conceive as separable that "thing" and the construction or "overlay" of meaning in which it is clothed.

This "weak" constructivist way of conceiving of reality tends to belittle the power of the social. It does this through a kind of misplaced concreteness. For example, in Battersby's (1989) attempt to sensitize us to a hitherto unrecognized proportion of "gifted" or "genius" women, she conceives of her constructivist problem as one of recognition rather than constitution. This is to say that gifted women are "out there" through history; it is simply a matter of "revealing" their existence by dismantling the cultural filters that render them invisible. This position does not consider the ways in which the ability to recognize hitherto overlooked instances of the category "genius" (in this case women) is simultaneously transforming the shape of that category: to add to the canon is also to transform it.

Thus, admirable as it may be to argue for the inclusion of otherwise hidden women (or any other previously "overlooked" individual or group) in a canon, such a position by no means constitutes a radical understanding of genius as socially constructed. Rather, it employs constructivism as a tool, as ancillary to some more instrumental project of cultural politics. In Pollner's terms (1991), this type of constructivism elides the reflexive dimensions – endogenous and referential – of identification.

To imply, in other words, that our reception of objects is "merely" media – that reception consists of ways of representing or ways of filtering reality through cultural lenses – is to forgo consideration of the ways that the very boundaries of objects are themselves symbolic and subject to contention (Hesse, 1974; Barnes and Shapin, 1979; see also Luker, 1983, for a case study of controversies over ways of configuring the boundaries of the category "human being"). It fails to recognize that acts of identification simultaneously constitute and reconstitute both objects and classification frameworks. Thus, constructivism is much more than a methodology that can be harnessed to what otherwise remain implicitly positivistic forms of enquiry as these are articulated within the confines of a language of attribution and free-standing objects.

Conclusion

To ask, then, "who are/were geniuses?" or "what factors 'cause' or inculcate genius?" is to travel toward the topic with too much a priori baggage. It is to fail to recognize how in invoking the very category genius we presume a hierarchy of talent and effort as pre-existing our attempts to frame questions about it. It is to employ the language of attribution as a resource rather than to study it as a topic.

Thus, we need to know more about just how the process of genius recognition actually occurs, to follow, as it were "in motion" the reflexive constitution of extraordinary ability as it is put together over time and place. As we hope we have illustrated with the material on Beethoven, this kind of project can only happen through specific case studies: studies that are historical in the sense that they are attuned to the accumulation of reputation over time and space, that are cultural and institutional in the sense that they highlight how conceptual and material resources can be and are mobilized in the process of this accumulation, and that are ethnographic, in the sense that they focus on the structuration activities of particular individuals and groups engaged (whether strategically and unwittingly) in mobilizing and configuring specific social spaces.

Because identity is symbolic – dependent upon the ways in which it is located in and interactively aligned with cultural classifications – it can always be otherwise. In Beethoven's case, had the configuration of interactive strategies, resources and musical criteria differed, he would not have been recognized as a genius and indeed, the shape of the discourse of genius in music would have been tailored along different lines. (Indeed, if we compare music aesthetics as they developed in

London and Paris during the 1790s and early 1800s with Vienna we find quite different conceptions of musical worth in operation.) Thus, Beethoven's identity was, as are all identities, equivocal; it was dependent for its existence upon its relation to ways of thinking, perceiving, talking and acting, and this is something that at least one of his contemporaries remarked on, sometime around 1797: "Whoever sees Beethoven for the first time," Baron von Kubeck wrote in his diary, "and knows nothing about him would surely take him for a malicious, ill-natured, quarrelsome drunkard who has no feeling for music. . . . On the other hand, he who sees him for the first time surrounded by his fame and his glory, will surely see musical talent in every feature of an ugly face" (Landon, 1970: 71).

References

Ariès, Philippe (1979) *Centuries of Childhood*. Oxford: Blackwell.

Barnes, B. and Shapin, Steven (1979) *Natural Order*. London: Sage.

Battersby, Christine (1989) *Gender and Genius*. London: The Woman's Press.

Becker, H.S. (1974) Art as collective action, *American Sociological Review*, 39: 767–76.

Becker, Howard (1982) *Art Worlds*. New York: The Free Press.

Bloom, B.S. (1985) *Developing Talent in Young People*. New York.

Comini, Alessandra (1987) *The Changing Image of Beethoven*. New York: Rizzoli.

Coward, Rosalind (1984) *Female Desire*. London: Paladin.

Czerny, C. (1956) Recollections from my life, *Musical Quarterly*, 42: 302–17.

DeNora, Tia (1986) How is extra-musical meaning possible? *Sociological Theory*, 4(1): 84–95.

DeNora, Tia (1989a) Mozart's spirit from Haydn's hands? The social bases and social consequences of Beethoven's success and vanguard style during his first decade in Vienna, PhD dissertation, Department of Sociology, University of California, San Diego. Forthcoming as *Beethoven and the Construction of Genius*.

DeNora, Tia (1989b) Beethoven et ses protecteurs (trans. D. Vander Gucht), *Revue de l'Institut de Sociologie* (Univ. Libre de Bruxelles).

DeNora, Tia (1991) Musical patronage and social change in Beethoven's Vienna, *American Journal of Sociology*, 97 (2): 310–46.

DeNora, Tia (1993) Beethoven, the Viennese canon, and the sociology of identity, *Beethoven Forum* (2).

Feldman, David (1986) *Nature's Gambit: Child Prodigies and the Development of Human Potential*. New York: Basic Books.

Foucault, Michael (1980) *Power/Knowledge*. New York: Pantheon Books.

Frazer, Elizabeth and Cameron, Deborah (1989) On knowing what to say: the construction of gender in linguistic practice, in R. Grillo (ed.), *Anthropology and the Politics of Language*. London: Routledge.

Gumperz, John (1982) *Discourse Strategies*. Cambridge: Cambridge University Press.

Hesse, M. (1974) *The Structure of Scientific Inference*. London: Macmillan.

Horowitz, F.D. and O'Brien, M., (eds) (1985) *The Gifted and Talented: A Developmental Perspective*. Washington, DC.

Ibarra, Peter R. and Kitsuse, John I. (1993) Vernacular constituents of moral discourse: an interactionist proposal for the study of social problems, in *Reconsidering Social Constructionism: Debates in Social Problems Theory*. New York: Aldine de Gruyters.

Kerman, Joseph and Kerman, Vivian (1976) *Listen.* New York: Worth.

Landon, H.C.R. (1970) *Beethoven: a Documentary Study.* London: Thames and Hudson.

Luker, Kristin (1983) *Abortion and the Politics of Motherhood.* Berkeley: University of California Press.

Mehan, Hugh, Hertwick, Alma, and Meihls, J. Lee (1986) *Handicapping the Handicapped: Decision Making in Students' Educational Careers.* Stanford: Stanford University Press.

Murray, Penelope (1989) *Genius: The History of an Idea.* Oxford: Blackwell.

Pollner, Melvin (1991) Left of ethnomethodology: the rise and decline of radical reflexivity, *American Sociological Review,* 56: 370–80.

Radford, John (1990) *Child Prodigies and Exceptional Early Achievers.* New York.

Schönfeld, J. (1976 [1796]) *Jahrbuch der Tonkunst von Wien und Prag.* Munich: Emil Katzbichler.

Solomon, Maynard (1978) *Beethoven.* New York: Schirmer.

Sternberg, F.J. and Davidson, J. (1986) *Conceptions of Giftedness.* Cambridge.

Thayer, Alexander W. (1967) *Thayer's Life of Beethoven.* Revised and edited by Elliot Forbes. Princeton: Princeton University Press.

Weedon, Chris (1987) *Feminist Practice and Poststructuralist Theory.* London: Blackwell.

Woolgar, Steve (1983) Irony in the social study of science, in K. Knorr-Cetina and M. Mulkay (eds), *Science Observed: Perspectives on the Social Study of Science.* London: Sage.

Woolgar, Steve (1988) *Science: The Very Idea.* Chichester: Ellis Horwood.

Zimmerman, Donald and Pollner, Melvin (1970) The everyday world as a phenomenon, in Jack D. Douglas (ed.), *Understanding Everyday Life.* Chicago: Aldine.

10
Ageism and the Deployments of "Age": A Constructionist View

Christopher L. Bodily

While orthodox sociology tends to be "method-oriented," a constructionist perspective openly acknowledges that *how* sociology is done (methods) is not a separate question from *why* it is done in a particular way (theory). Constructionist efforts are compelled, not by rigid methodological strictures, but by the assumption that as active social agents we are implicated in the knowledge we produce, the language we use, and the structures and institutions within which we live. As Kenneth Gergen suggests, social constructionism "asks one to suspend belief that commonly accepted categories or understandings receive their warrant through observation" and thereby "invites one to challenge the objective basis of knowledge" (1985: 267).

Gergen raises two important points here. First, as a method of inquiry, constructionism requires that we suspend belief in or "bracket" that which is often taken-for-granted. This can be accomplished by transforming routine accounts or "resources" into analytic "topics." While the concept of "age," for example, is often deployed as a resource for explaining certain behaviors, attitudes, or characteristics, it might just as easily be made into a topic by inquiring into the ways "age" is both constructed and deployed. This transformation of resources into topics gives the social constructionist perspective both its critical spirit and power to illuminate processes that are otherwise taken-for-granted.

The second issue raised by Gergen is constructionism's invitation to "challenge the objective basis of knowledge." Constructionists recognize the discrepancy between the informal complexity of the social world and the relatively simple, formal, and "objective" scientific resources that are often used to account for it (Lindblom 1990: 14). Consequently, to preserve scientific *form* the social content of scientific resources are ignored and thereby "objectified." Science, however, "no longer can regard its own practices as the administrative link between reality and language, but must come to see reality as symbolically constructed and must take responsibility for the realities it constructs" (Baker 1990: 233). From a constructionist view, taking responsibility not only involves an honest acknowledgment of the discrepancy noted above, but also involves turning it to our advantage. To utilize the space created by this discrepancy, we must transform the notion of ourselves as passive "discoverers" of a single reality to that of active architects, builders, and custodians of various realities. The constructionist view is often subject to the charge of throwing the baby out with the bathwater. In other words, the argument goes, even if the value of constructionist approaches and ideas were acknowledged (which many are still unwilling to do), it does not warrant forsaking the hallowed traditions of the Enlightenment. This objection, however, is wide of the mark on two counts. First, the only things forsaken by a constructionist perspective are unquestioned authority, a lack of reflection, and perhaps inhumility concerning what we know and how we come to know it. If orthodox conceptions of science can live without these things, then there is plenty of room in the tub. Second, if constructionism can be accused of anything, it would be tossing additional babies into the bathwater. We are currently confronted with such a wide array of approaches to social phenomena that pangs of nostalgia for simpler times-gone-by are understandable. The world of social inquiry is crowded, often divisive, at times frustratingly inconclusive, sometimes bizarre, and genuinely complex – much like the social world itself.

At the very least, a constructionist view prepares us to construct, listen to, and value very different kinds of stories about ourselves and our world – stories perhaps less conclusive, more playful, and imaginative than is customary, but nonetheless potentially illuminating and important. It is in this spirit that the following analysis is presented. Although its narrative structure is at times more like the chronicle of a journey, my departure from conventional forms of scientific discourse is deliberate. The rhetorical strategies of conventional scientific reporting produce an astringent "matter-of-factness" that I hope to avoid. Such affected objectivity would not only betray the rich interpretive possibilities offered by the respondents in the study below, it would also force an abbreviated, idealized portrayal of the process by which the uses of "age" became my topic. Remaining true to the reflective impulse of constructionism, I intend not only to illuminate my topic, but also to illuminate the process of illumination itself.

The Emergence of "Age"

My own interest in the concept of "age" and the subsequent analysis provided below emerged unexpectedly from a research project on which I collaborated in 1990. The initial project was part of a growing effort among healthcare researchers to investigate and assess potential solutions to the "nursing shortage." Our specific focus was the shortage of nurses in long-term care facilities and our aim was to assess the possibility of attracting older, inactive nurses into long-term care settings. Consequently, we conducted a survey of inactive nurses over the age of 50 residing in Illinois.[1] Our rationale for targeting this group rested, in part, on the view that the voices of older, inactive nurses were simply missing from most discussions of the nursing shortage. Given the accumulated experience of older nurses, it seemed more prudent to pursue solutions informed by their voices, rather than amidst their silence.

Our initial research agenda included the investigation of respondents' perceptions of the "nursing shortage," their attitudes toward working in long-term care, their reasons for both leaving the nursing profession and for not currently working as a nurse, and their desire, if any, to return to nursing. Basic demographic data were gathered and we also provided opportunities for respondents to voice more pragmatic concerns such as their training and orientation needs if they were to return to nursing. For the most part, the questionnaire made use of structured or "fixed-choice" questions and the subsequent statistical analyses proceeded in a conventional fashion. The results, although interesting and important, are the subject of another report (see McBride and Bodily, 1990).

My concerns here are with the written comments of the 1,333 people who responded to the survey or what I take to be their active and spontaneous voices. Fixed-choice questionnaires are adequate for gathering demographic or other discrete forms of data and lend themselves nicely to large-scale surveys and their consequent analyses. But they are not without serious shortcomings; most notably, they discourage elaboration and pre-empt the possibility of obtaining unanticipated responses (see Bourdieu 1984: 414–32 and Cicourel 1964: 105–20). Thus, respondents were provided ample opportunity for qualifications and additional comments, and I was determined to follow through by giving these written responses the serious attention they deserve. Anything less would have misrepresented respondents by producing a bias against experiences, attitudes, and concerns outside the grid of choices offered by our survey.

As I began reading the written responses, I was immediately struck by not only the diversity of what was written, but by the sheer volume of writing. Many respondents answered the open-ended questions succinctly in the space provided, while others let their long, thoughtful reflections flow up and down the margins and over the top of the survey questions. While many comments qualified or elaborated upon previous responses, other respondents offered anecdotes, proverbs, poems, newspaper clippings, letters, formative job experiences, stories of frustration, and many other poignant reflections that make up the lore of nursing. It was clear these respondents had a lot to say and the survey provided a discursive space within which they could say it; it functioned as more than a mere tally sheet for demographics and attitudes.

It was also during my first reading that I began to note that the concept of "age" was often used as a reason for not currently working as a nurse. As I continued reading, paying closer attention to the uses of "age," I noted that first, "age" was often mentioned more than once by the same respondent. Second, in all but a handful of instances where the concept of "age" was used – whether it was used as a reason for leaving nursing or for not returning to work – it was used without qualification or further explanation. Its usage was invariably bold, as if the meaning it conveyed was universal and its implications obvious and unassailable. Phrases such as "my age will not permit me" and "because of my age" and "I'm too old" were common. Finally, the uses of the concept of "age" were not always self-directed. Some were directed toward those older than the respondent; for example, one respondent noted that there is "not enough excitement working with old people." Others' uses of "age" were directed at those younger than the respondent; "the young could mostly not care less," for instance.

After reading all the surveys, my rough tally indicated that 744 (55.8 percent) of the 1,333 respondents had used the concept of "age" either by itself or in conjunction with something (health, physical limitations, illness, retirement, etc.), or directed at those younger or older than themselves. It struck me that respondents were giving "age" a lot of explanatory responsibility and it seemed like a good idea to take a closer look at the ways they were using it. Unfortunately, I could not get at what respondents meant by "age" because they did not say, and the questionnaire, of course, did not ask. As a researcher, I was now faced with the choice of how to proceed. One option would have been to simply drop the whole issue, but with the proviso that the next time I found myself involved in a similar project I would see to it that "age" was included among the possible responses to the relevant question-naire items. It occurred to me, however, that even if "age" had been included among the available responses it would merely have legitimated and even encouraged the very unreflective uses of "age" that now concerned me. Another option would have been for me, as a researcher, to use "age" unreflectively and simply conclude that a certain percentage of respondents were, in fact, "too old" to re-enter nursing. But this would entail nothing more than reproducing respondents' discourse and then presenting a generalized version of it as my own analytical conclusion. Although much social science proceeds this way, not much research or reflection is involved in concluding that respondents are too old merely because they say they are too old.[2]

The option that eventually appealed most to me was to transform the various uses respondents made of "age" from an analytical resource into a research topic. In other words, instead of taking "age" for granted, as if it unquestionably explained the various functional limitations and abilities of these respondents, I could make it into a research "topic." I could then not only report on how the respondents made use of the concept of "age," but also look into what might encourage or legitimate such uses. At the very least, it might provide some insight into origins and maintenance of concepts such as "too old" or "over-aged."

The Deployments of "Age"

Since my interest was now in uses of "age," I wanted an accurate accounting of the various ways that respondents deployed this concept. From my initial tally, it appeared that respondents were directing their use of the concept of "age" in one of three directions: inward toward themselves, outward toward those older than themselves, or outward toward those younger than themselves. I collapsed these further by dividing them into instances of either "self-directed" or "other-directed" uses of "age." I defined self-directed usage as *the unelaborated attribution of one's own characteristics, limitations, or abilities to chronological age.* This included the use of the concept of "age" alone (or conceptual substitutes such as "too old"), as well as the use of "age" in conjunction with something such as illness, physical limitations, and health.[3] Other-directed usage generally took two forms: the "age" of patients in long-term care facilities was cited as a reason for not wanting to work in such facilities, or respondents characterized "younger" nurses, or more generally the "young," as somehow less capable, less dedicated, or less responsible than their "older" peers. Thus, I defined other-directed uses of "age" as *the unelaborated attribution of the characteristics, limitations, or abilities of others to their chronological age.* To account for all the respondents, I also included two other categories: (1) those respondents who used "age" but did elaborate or at least hint at what they meant by it, and (2) those who made no use of "age" (or any conceptual substitutes).

Since these usage categories were not mutually exclusive, I also wanted to capture multiple uses of "age" by a single respondent. By registering such multiple uses, I hoped to get a coarse, but perhaps useful, measure of the intensity of usage. I also decided to consider those who offered no written responses as non-respondents and subsequently removed those 49 individuals from my sample.[4] One last refinement came to mind when I recognized that I was interested in the uses of "age" among the entire chorus of respondents' written voices and not just those who completed the questionnaire or responded specifically to the open-ended questions. It mattered less where they made use of "age" than that they did make use of it. In fact, a particularly stark deployment of "age" was offered by those who, in lieu of completing the questionnaire, merely scribbled "I'm too old" across the cover letter or title page. Consequently, I added these which put the total number of respondents at 1,497. Making use of this new conceptual structure, I then embarked on a closer, more refined reading of the written responses. Since my first reading was loosely focused, I no doubt either overlooked some uses of "age," or included a few that, on closer examination, might better fit in other categories.[5]

The first thing I noted was the absolute number of respondents who made some use of the concept of age. Of the 1,497 respondents who provided some form of written discourse, 870 (58.1 percent) made at least one use of "age" without further elaborating what they meant by it. Moreover, by accounting for multiple uses of "age" by the same respondent, I found 1,227 unelaborated uses of "age" distributed among 870 respondents, for an average of about 1.5 uses per respondent. The sheer volume of usage would seem to indicate that the concept of "age" played an important role in the efforts of a considerable number of respondents to orient themselves toward the questionnaire. I was also curious to know if those respondents who provided only one instance of ageism were, on average, younger than those who provided more than one. I am not, it should be noted, suggesting that chronological age causes the deployment of the concept of "age." On the contrary, I think that as we grow older, the concept of "age" simply becomes more readily available as a discursive resource for explaining all sorts of things. Thus, I would expect to find the effects of this increasing availability in the data. My analysis did indicate that the mean ages increased as the number of uses of "age" increased. On average, then, those who provided multiple uses of "age" were older than those who did not.[6]

Of further interest, only 5 out of 1,497 respondents explained (or hinted at) what they meant by "age." In each case, they used it to refer to the possibility of age discrimination by employers. A couple of examples include, "At my age, though I am very active, it would be hard to get a job – age is discriminated against" and "I am no longer working as a nurse because I was retired due to age discrimination – I think a nurse should be allowed to work until she feels a need to retire, as long as she is performing her duties satisfactorily." The three other respondents, while they did bring up the possibility of age discrimination, also exhibited what might be characterized as incipient self-directed usage. Their remarks were, "I am 78. Doubt anyone would have me," "I am too old for anybody to hire me," and finally, "I don't think anyone would have me at age 82. I do volunteer work instead." In each case, their use of the concept of "age" was equivocal. Unlike the two examples above, it is not clear whether these respondents view their age as their own problem – in which case they might think employers justified in not hiring them – or whether they view their age as a problem only because potential employers might do so. In any event, given the attention to age discrimination in the media and elsewhere, I found it remarkable that only five respondents explicitly indicated concern about it. One explanation may be that respondents have so deeply internalized the concept of "age" as a legitimate explanatory resource that reflection is deemed unnecessary prior to disqualifying themselves from opportunities, including employment. Consequently, age discrimination by potential employers, as a possible concern, is pre-empted. It might also be that such a deep internalization of "age" as an explanatory resource would not only prevent respondents from reflecting on and assessing their own abilities, but also might make it easier to accept or rationalize assessments from others, even if unfair or inaccurate.

One last grouping of respondents concerns those who offered notes and letters in lieu of a completed survey. I approached these separately because, at the conceptual level, these respondents were not giving "age" as a reason for no longer working as a nurse, but as a reason for not completing the questionnaire.[7] I also discovered that "age" was being used in ways I had not previously encountered. Some respondents stated flatly that, because of age, their opinions would be of no value. For example, "I do not really qualify as a representative to complete the survey, due to my age" or "I have no opinion, I'm 73 years old." Others apparently did not get the chance to express their views because a third party intervened and used "age" on their behalf. Examples include "This questionnaire is being returned because the person to whom it is directed is 84 and not capable of answering it intelligently" and "My aunt is soon to be 90 years old. I don't think she should be bothered." Aside from being different conceptually, this group also presented methodological difficulties. Since they opted either not to fill out the questionnaire (or someone else made that choice for them), any basis of comparison which might depend on information given in the survey is, of course, lost. Nevertheless, I felt that I should include them. Using the concept of "age" as a reason for not participating in the research project is as relevant here as using it as a reason for not working. Briefly, then, of the 213 respondents who offered letters and notes, 56.8 percent (121) used the concept of "age" (or had it used for them) as a reason for not completing the questionnaire. This is only 1 percent greater than that of the larger group of respondents who completed the survey. Thus, the overall percentage of respondents using "age" was remarkably consistent between the two groups. A notable difference, however, was that there were no instances of what I defined earlier as other-directed usage; in all but four cases, respondents directed their use of "age" toward themselves.

My efforts here should not be viewed as exhaustive, conclusive, or as somehow providing a "definitive" account of the respondents' discourse. Given different interests, other stories might have been told and other accounts constructed. My aim was merely to highlight the empirical contours of the various deployments of "age" and thereby satisfy myself (and potential readers) that such deployments were pervasive enough to warrant further work. Although I cannot speak for potential readers, a total of 1,227 unelaborated deployments of "age" distributed among 870 respondents was enough to keep me interested. I must confess, however, that the sheer volume of such deployments created some interpretive tension. As a professional with a political interest in the well-being of senior adults I was inclined to interpret such uses of "age" as preventing respondents from fairly assessing their own abilities and options, and perhaps unnecessarily limiting their horizons. As a researcher charged with the duty of presenting the specific reasons why respondents were not currently working as nurses, 1,227 unelaborated deployments of "age" appeared as 1,227 missed opportunities. Certainly, each of the respondents who participated in our survey had reasons for not working, but time and again they brought their comments to an abrupt halt, leaving nothing but "age" for me to ponder. As a reader/author with strong constructionist leanings and a paper to write, the concept of "age" appeared to intrude regularly and often impressively into the discursive space created by the survey. I suspended this tension, of course, by moving forward in my role as reader/author.

The Emergence of "Ageism"

> Mostly as I thought about aging, I tried to rearrange my thoughts.
> They were like a closet that hadn't been cleaned out since high school.
> (Schaper, 1989: 43)

What interested me most about the ways the respondents were using "age" was that its meaning was being taken for granted; that is, as if the implications of phrases like "because of my age" or "I'm too old" were sufficiently obvious to require nothing more than a knowing nod on the part of the reader. Somewhere behind the uses of "age" were routine assumptions that the concept was both sufficiently meaningful and readily interpretable so as not to require further elaboration. One respondent, for example, stated, "I am 76 so you can see I am unable to work." Yet, other than the assumption that I (or any other reader) would readily know what it meant to be 76, it was not clear just what I was supposed to "see" from this statement. Should I have seen actual or perceived functional limitations, chronic illness, or perhaps the fear of being "out of touch" with current nursing practices? Or maybe I should have seen anxiety over the possibility of being discriminated against by employers, a lack of interest in returning to work, or even relief that one's working days are past? While these are a handful of possible meanings that might be lurking behind the phrase "I'm 76," there is nothing given by the respondent conclusively to suggest one over any of the others. About all I did manage to "see" was that this was one of hundreds of examples of the unreflective, unquestioned, and unelaborated use of "age" as an explanatory resource.

To give the reader a better feel for how "age" was used, some specific examples include "My age would not be conducive to working," "Age is a factor at this time," "It would be impossible at my age," "I am past the age," "My age is prohibitive," "The age factor," "I wouldn't consider it at 68 years," or simply "I am 64." Even more curious were comments that ruled out health, illness, physical limitations, and other things commonly associated with "age." For example, "[I am] no longer working because of age although in good physical condition," or "I am too old even though I do not look my age or feel my age." Similarly, respondents ruled out other possible interpretations by stating them explicitly in conjunction with "age" – "age and health," "age and physical limitations," or "age and illness" to name a few. If health or other physical limitations were indeed the problem, then I could only wonder why respondents slipped "age" into their comments. What does it add? Not one respondent said that their limitations or ill-health were "due" to age. Instead, "age" was offered in addition to such factors.

Respondents not only deployed "age" in the various ways discussed above, but implicit in such deployments is a certain confidence that I (or any other reader) would interpret it appropriately. Consequently, I began to wonder just what it is that might permit "age" to be so confidently deployed? What might compel respondents to give "age" such tremendous explanatory responsibility, but at the same time not compel them to explain what they meant by it? The most obvious prospect, it seemed to me, was that the unelaborated use of "age" presupposes some larger context or construction from which it gains legitimacy as an explanatory resource. To merely say, for example, that

"I am too old," and then expect this to be routinely accepted as a sufficient explanation, presupposes something deeper and prior to this particular deployment. Concepts of "age" would then be viewed as dependent on or emerging from a larger, more general construction. It was thinking about just such a construction that eventually pointed me toward *ageism*.

Among its other capacities, the structure of ageism, through our continued maintenance of it, legitimates and encourages the unreflective use of the concept of "age." Most commonly, it allows room for using either specific chronological dates (for example, "65 years" or "past the age of 70") or more general typological ages such as "too old," "over-aged," and "the young." Ageism's power comes from our willingness to take for granted what it means to be "65" or "too old" or simply "young." We bundle up various assortments of limitations, abilities, and characteristics and attribute them to different chronological dates and typological ages. Such constellations of abilities and chronological or typological ages are then readily available as self-contained explanatory resources. As Estes explains:

> The major problems faced by the elderly in the United States are, in large measure, ones that are socially constructed as a result of our conceptions of aging and the aged. What is done for and about the elderly, as well as what we know about them, including knowledge gained from research, are products of our conceptions of aging. In an important sense, then, the major problems faced by the elderly are the ones we create for them. (1983: 1)

Although Estes is not addressing ageism per se, and I by no means offer this as a criticism, I should note that ageism is not confined to the elderly. That ageism, in the context of political discourse, is a charge often made against "the young" only adds to the confusion. Discrimination against the elderly is only one manifestation of the entire construction which I refer to here as ageism. The explanation, for example, that someone is "too young to understand" is equally a manifestation of ageism. Again, what the structure of ageism permits is the unelaborated use of chronological dates and typological ages as sufficient explanations. The concepts of "age" that emerge from ageism may be directed at young and old alike and may produce both victims and benefactors. Attributing "wisdom" to someone merely because they are chronologically old emerges as easily from the structure of ageism as attributing "irresponsibility" to someone's chronological youth.

As for our survey, respondents did not explain what they meant by "age" because they did not have to. They knew, as we all do, that they could count on the concept of "age" to summon more than enough images of ill-health and disability, both physical and mental. In other words, and quite understandably, they were merely making use of socially constructed and sanctioned resources that were readily at hand. Given that aging is often portrayed as a slow poison of which the effects are well known, the only information to add is how much has been swallowed. Of course, without the structure of ageism in place and functioning properly, the concept of "age" would simply not have been available to respondents as a ready-made resource – concepts such as "too old" or "too young" would stand naked, demanding explanation.

A Closer Look: The Construction and Maintenance of Ageism

More than two decades have passed since Robert Butler first formulated the concept of "age-ism" in response to a housing conflict he witnessed in Chevy Chase, Maryland. In 1968, public housing authorities had requested the use of a building in a largely white, middle class suburb in order to provide housing for older citizens. The hearings quickly degenerated into a riot as people fought to keep minorities and "all those old people" out of their community. As Gruman explains:

> The Chevy Chase episodes recounted by Butler illustrate the paradoxical fact, central to the aging crisis today, that the old are now seen as new and unsettling, an alien force threatening to the community. And although conceding that a campaign of community education might have prevented some of the alarm, Butler concluded that the rush to judgment indicated the presence of prejudiced stereotypes and myths – bigotry. In a later work, he [Butler] summarized: "Age-ism can be seen as a process of systematic stereotyping of and discrimination against people because they are old, just as racism and sexism accomplish this with skin color and gender." Like racism and sexism, age-ism insists that inherent biological factors determine traits of personality and character. As Butler has observed, one of the greatest handicaps of aging is the decrease in the range of choice, a loss which results not only from physiological and economic limitations but also from the restrictive norms of a biased culture. (1978: 363)

A lot has happened since 1968, not the least of which is the recognition that our aging population will engender changes in our conceptions of both aging and the aged. Surprisingly little, however, has been written about the social construction and maintenance of ageism itself. As the passage above makes clear, "ageism" was introduced into political discourse as a form of bigotry directed at the elderly. Today, over two decades later, it remains largely confined to political discourse and still narrowly focused on negative images and stereotypes. To illustrate, I have provided a few, more recent definitions of ageism below:

> Age-ism can be seen as a process of systematic stereotyping of and discrimination against people because they are old, just as racism and

sexism accomplish this with skin color and gender. (Butler in Gruman, 1978: 363)

[Ageism is] negative bias or discrimination based solely on chronological date. (Gray Panthers in Lueders, 1990a: 4)

[Ageism is] negative discrimination on the basis of age. (AARP, 1986: 2)

Ageism is the negative social response to different stages in the process of aging. (Copper, 1988: 73)

Ageism is any form of prejudice, bias or discrimination that negatively targets a person on that sole basis [of age]. (Lueders, 1990b: 20)

As these examples show, our understanding of ageism has advanced very little since it was first formulated by Butler in 1968. While "ageism" emerged as a discursive political resource for sensitizing us to and mobilizing support against the negative effects of age discrimination, as an analytic topic it has yet to surface. Given the role that ageism plays in many of our conceptions and deployments of "age," it seemed like a good idea to get it to the surface.

As I suggested earlier, most current definitions of ageism limit their focus to negative stereotypes of older adults. In a very important sense, these are not definitions at all, but descriptions of a particular discursive manifestation of ageism. Ageism is a much broader and more deeply situated construction than most current "definitions" allow. It can accommodate not only both negative and positive images, but is, ironically, indifferent to any particular age or age group. Attributing, for example, a lively inquisitiveness to a person's "young age" is simply the reverse of attributing a morose indifference to a person's "old age." Thus, discrimination against the old based on negative images and stereotypes may be one of ageism's most visible and politically potent manifestations, but it should not be confused with ageism itself. This would be analogous to confusing the aftermath of a fire with fire itself. The structure of ageism, like fire, is independent of any particular benefits it might offer or damage it might cause. That ageism has been consistently confused with its various manifestations might explain why its socially constructed and maintained nature has remained largely unexamined.

To get a better idea of how ageism is constructed and maintained, we need to take a closer look at the deep structure of ageism. By "deep structure" I mean both the basic assumptions upon which ageism is built and certain features which allow for the unelaborated use of "age." The continued maintenance of ageism depends on our willingness to keep its deep structure hidden, and occupy ourselves instead with only its most visible consequences or manifestations. Conceptually, then, we need to separate "ageism" as a primary construction from the multitude of its secondary or emergent constructions. These emergent constructions include all the various, unelaborated uses of "age" which circulate as explanations. Negative stereotypes based on chronological age, for example, are constructions which emerge from rather than define ageism. Similarly, it is these emergent constructions which come to be viewed as "destructive," "unjust," "methodologically frustrating," or "politically useful." Ageism itself, while providing the raw material, is prior to the attribution of any particular values to these emergent constructions.

If ageism allows such a wide array of variously valued emergent constructions, and if its survival depends on its existence as a primary construction remaining hidden, then how are we to know if it is implicated in the various uses of "age" that circulate in our society? Fortunately, these emergent constructions all have a telling earmark; namely, as explanations, they evoke a seeming "naturalness" or "mundaneity." Put another way, they have a vernacular or "everyday" quality which makes them convenient, if not irresistible explanatory resources. It is not difficult to experience this first hand. Tell almost any story about a chain of events stemming from someone's forgetfulness and then end it with the phrase, "but, you know, he (or she) is getting old." You will likely get a room full of knowing nods. Tell the same story, but add that the person was 17 years old, and you will likely get people wondering and even openly speculating about what might possibly account for such behavior. It is no great revelation that the efficacy of stories and anecdotes can change dramatically merely by altering the age of the protagonist. In fact, it is remarkable how readily and unreflectively we make "age" available to ourselves as an explanation for all sorts of everyday events. John Kenneth Galbraith highlighted this point nicely in a recent interview:

> Increasingly, I find myself looking at my watch and wondering if I can escape some boring occasion without people saying, "Well, you know, he's getting on in years." When I was younger and sought escape from similar situations, I was thought to be merely rude. Now I'm thought to be old (Galbraith in Lederman, 1990: 6).

According to Galbraith's account, we have the same behavior interpreted very differently depending on his apparent "age." But why does this practice seem so natural? What might account for the mundane power of ageism's emergent constructions?

The ease and seeming naturalness with which we slip "age" into any characterization or explanation, whether of oneself, of others, or even of objects, is what, borrowing from Pollner (1987), I call the mundaneity of ageism's emergent constructions. Explanations emerging from ageism are not limited to old people; in fact, they are not limited to people at all. Take the following examples:

- A child asks why the bananas on the kitchen counter have turned brown and an adult explains, "Because they are old."

- Your car breaks down on the way to work and your co-workers ask why. You offhandedly remark, "It's just old."

- You are at a family picnic and you overhear someone whisper that the "Potato salad tastes old."

In each example above, "age" is used not merely to describe objects, but to explain various characteristics or conditions. The peculiar taste of the potato salad is not referred to as "spoiled" or "poorly prepared," but as "old." Thus, the concept of age functions simultaneously as both a description and an explanation – the car broke down because it is old. Concerning the examples above, it is of little everyday consequence that molecular biologists and car mechanics would necessarily move beyond age to explain these same conditions or events. The mundane association of "age" with such things as decay and disability is introduced early in our lives and then reinforced almost daily. Not surprisingly, then, the jump from broken old cars to broken old people seems quite natural.

The mundaneity of ageism's emergent constructions is largely a consequence of what I consider to be the deepest structural feature of ageism; namely, the assumption that time itself has causal force. Virtually all explanations which rely on the unelaborated use of "age" depend on a deep and unstated assumption that, given the *mere passing of time*, certain things will happen.[8] Without this assumption, the very notions that something could taste "old" or someone could be "over-aged" or "too young" would seem nonsensical. How could someone be "too old" in a world where time is assumed not to have causal force? It would be akin to suggesting that someone was "too heavy" in a world without gravity. At bottom, then, it is the assumption that the mere passing of time produces sufficient grounds for explanations that is the root of ageism. Put another way, ageism is constituted from the unacknowledged circulation of this assumption in our society – it is the "social face" of the assumed role of time as an independent variable in our world.

The social maintenance of ageism is an interesting twofold process. On the one hand, its survival depends on our continued ignorance of or unwillingness to question the assumption that time has causal force. On the other hand, and somewhat paradoxically, this assumption must be widely and regularly reinforced for ageism to function properly. But how is an assumption aggressively reinforced without at the same time increasing the risk of it being brought into the open for discussion and possible critique? A few actual examples of reinforcement may be helpful here.

- A documentary film about Germany speaks of President Hindenberg's death as "succumbing to age."

- The authors of a research article in a respected medical journal remark, "Not surprisingly, the frail subjects – those with multiple disabilities – averaged over 86 years of age, while transitional and vigorous subjects were between 78 and 81 years of age on average." (Speechley and Tinetti, 1991: 50)

- A television commercial depicts a man bumping into a woman in a grocery store. He happens to be holding a box of bran cereal and is embarrassed when she notices it. He laughs nervously, glances at the box, and explains that "his parents are visiting."

- Countless research reports in various journals make unquestioned use of the concept of "age effects" to explain residual variation among dependent variables.

- In the court records of recent guardianship hearings vague references to "old age" are given as professional medical diagnoses. Nowhere in the records does it say how such a diagnosis was confirmed or how "age" might affect the defendant's mental abilities. (Stevenson and Capezuti, 1991: 13)

Note how the passing of time or chronological age is subtly implicated in each of these examples. It not only has scientifically measurable "effects," but we might actually "succumb" to it. According to scientific researchers, it is "not surprising" that 86 years on this planet results in "frailty." Preferring bran cereal is suspect when one is "young" and "old age" emerges as a medical diagnostic category suitable as evidence in a court of law. Taken together, the assumption of chronological age as a sufficient cause is reinforced from several different directions – historical, cultural, scientific, and legal. Yet, questions of just how chronological age might account for such things as death and breakfast cereal preferences are rarely asked. This is the key to social maintenance of ageism. Such questions rarely arise because of the unacknowledged interpretive transformations of chronological descriptions into explanations.

- A doctor *describes* a defendant as chronologically "old" and a judge interprets this as both an "explanation" of the defendant's behavior and as evidence as to why guardianship should be granted.

- A social scientist, after arbitrarily dichotomizing a sample of adults into "young" and "old," proceeds to measure (while attempting to control for any confounding variables) and then *describes* the differences between these two groups. These descriptions of difference are interpreted by readers (and perhaps even the author) as "explanations."[9]

- A narrator of a film *describes* a famous figure at the time of his or her death as "quite old." The audience interprets this as an "explanation" of this figure's death.

- Visitors gather in your living room and you sheepishly *describe* the furniture as very "old." Without a word, they interpret this as an "explanation" of its poor condition.

- A local newspaper reports a car accident involving a 1968 Camero and *describes* the driver as "age 16." Images of a reckless youth are evoked in the reader's mind which serve (in part or in whole) as an "explanation" for the accident.[10]

In each case, what literally begins as a chronologically referenced "description" is socially transformed into a self-contained "explanation." The important point is not whether the person offering the description intends it as an explanation (as many surely do), but that it will invariably be interpreted as such. Once transformed, these "explanations" then circulate as what I referred to earlier as emergent constructions of ageism. The transformation itself is facilitated by ageism or the socially shared and routine assumption that the mere passing of time plays a sufficient causal role in our world. This assumption is widely and regularly reinforced by scientists, doctors, lawyers, authors, friends, relatives – in short, by all of us in our various private and public roles. Moreover, the question of how time or chronological age might play such a role is pre-empted by this transformation. Once a chronological description is transformed into an "explanation," the window for questioning is past. If I, for example, interpret a description of someone as "old" as an explanation for their errant automobile driving, and if similar interpretations are widely circulating and routinely accepted, what would compel me to dig further? In the act of transforming a chronological description into an explanation, I am, at the same time, assuaging my curiosity which tends to preclude further questioning. Thus, as an everyday matter, the deep structure of ageism is simultaneously maintained and removed from view.

If questions are to be posed about precisely how chronological age might explain such things as errant driving, they must be asked prior to the transformation of descriptions into explanations. This transformation can only be forestalled if chronological descriptions are literally and routinely interpreted as simply "descriptions." If a colleague tells me about a recent collision and describes the other driver as "some young kid," I would have to resist the temptation to construct an explanation by linking "young kid" with "collision." I would also have to ignore the fact that my colleague likely intended this explanatory linkage. Thus, by interpreting "young kid" as merely a description of the driver's chronological age relative to my colleague's age, I would then likely raise the question of just how the other driver's age is relevant to the account. If successfully interpreted as a mere description, "young kid" would seem as out of place in this account as would my colleague describing the other driver as "tall." The point here is that in order to raise questions which might eventually lead us to the socially constructed and maintained character of ageism, we have to first circumvent ageism by forestalling the transformation of chronological descriptions into explanations. As an everyday matter this is rarely achieved, which attests to our active, unreflective, and largely unexamined role as the builders and custodians of ageism.

Final Reflections

As an author of a constructionist view of ageism, I hope I have highlighted and uncovered some of the more interesting and important aspects of my topic. As a concerned citizen, however, I share sympathies with those who have an interest in dismantling ageism. Unfortunately, their task has been made more difficult both by confusing ageism with its emergent constructions and by confining it to public, political discourse. In a sense, one leads to the other. By confusing or reducing "ageism" to negative images and stereotypes of the elderly (and the discrimination which results), there is nowhere else to go but headlong into the political arena. Such efforts would be better served by digging at the roots of ageism rather than by chopping at few of its easy-to-reach branches. A deeper circumvention which forestalls the transformation of chronological descriptions into explanations is required. Moreover, by limiting the focus to discrimination based on "negative stereotypes," the opponents of ageism will be forever arriving too late in the game. The very existence of these negative images (or emergent constructions) indicates that the transformation has already taken place. The effective strategy, it seems to me, would be to prevent chronological descriptions from masquerading as explanations in the first place.

It is also important for those who wish to dismantle ageism not to underestimate or overlook the mundane reinforcement of ageism which largely takes place outside the confines of political discourse. For every piece of legislation or successful discrimination lawsuit, there are thousands of people at picnics sampling "old" potato salad, driving "old" cars, telling their children they are "too young" to understand, and being cut off by "some young kid" on the way home. It is through these seemingly innocent reinforcements that the groundwork is laid for the bigotry that concerns the opponents of ageism. Related to this is the apparent logic of the battle against ageism. One of the most visible "solutions" that emerge from this logic is that ageism can be given a good blow by simply encouraging *positive* images of the elderly in the media and elsewhere. What is overlooked here is that positive images are merely the flip side of negative images and that both are emergent constructions of ageism. Attributing wisdom to a person's "old age" involves the transformation of a chronological description into an explanation of that person's wisdom. Moreover, images tend to evoke their opposite, albeit subtly and often unconsciously. The notion that someone's "age" explains apparent "wisdom" opens the possibility that "age" might also explain an apparent "lack of wisdom." The result is that this so-called "solution" actually reinforces ageism. A better strategy would be to contextualize *wisdom* by attributing it to various life experiences rather than merely "age."

As I noted in an earlier section, ageism not only allows for both positive and negative images, it need not involve people at all and may manifest itself in unexpected ways. Take, for example, the following passage from Charles Darwin which was written over 130 years ago.

> The mere lapse of time by itself does nothing either for or against natural selection. I state this because it has been erroneously asserted that the element of time is assumed by me to play an all-important part in natural selection, as if all species were necessarily undergoing slow modification from some innate law. (Darwin 1861: 110f)

Interestingly, Darwin was addressing the very transformation that I spoke of above. His colleagues, it seems, were taking his descriptions of how things evolve over time and transforming them into an explanation (with "time" as the centerpiece). Darwin was concerned that the actual processes which affect natural selection would be pushed aside in favor of the notion that natural selection was the product of time; that is, given only enough time, natural selection is inevitable. He is quite clear, however, that natural selection is neither inevitable nor the product of time. Without environmental and genetic changes, natural selection would not happen regardless of how much time had passed. What I hope this example makes clear is that neither the breadth nor the depth of ageism can be captured by its current and narrowly focused "definitions."

Ageism, by nature of its manifold, deeply reinforced, and often enigmatic structure, is bound to be a lively and equally manifold topic. While I am satisfied with the opportunity here to bring ageism and its emergent constructions to the table as analytic topics in their own right, I also hoped to avoid "over-determining" them and alienating my own account from future discussions. Rather than reaching some sort of conceptual closure, my intentions were to precipitate a more open or reflexive conversation about ageism and the deployments of "age." While much has been said about the "playfulness" and "reflexivity" of social constructionism, something ought to be said about the serious burden it imposes upon us. The shift from passive "discoverers" of a single reality to that of active architects, builders, and custodians of various "realities," means we have no where to turn but to ourselves. Rather than gazing objectively out of windows, we instead find ourselves in an elaborate hall of mirrors – turning one way, then another, but never managing to escape our own reflections. Some joyfully exploit the infinite reflective possibilities and opportunities for self-critique, while others passionately maintain that the mirrors are, in fact, windows and refuse to succumb to what they see as "indecisive and cannibalistic paradoxes" (Baker, 1990: 232). Whatever the approach, we are never free from the responsibility of carrying on. Even while those so inclined wait patiently for the emergence of scientific truth and certainty, decisions still have to be made and actions taken. The constructionist aesthetic simply suggests that we do not hold our breath and carry on with some understanding of how we are implicated in the various realities that constitute our world.

Notes

The author wishes to thank Dr Barbara McBride for the patience, insight, and honest criticism that she generously offered during successive drafts of this paper. The author would also like to acknowledge that portions of this study were reworked from an earlier paper which appeared in *The Journal of Aging Studies* 5 (3) (Fall 1991): 245–64.

1. From a listing of approximately 27,500 inactive nurses in Illinois, a one-quarter random sample (6,891) was drawn. Since the age of those in the sampling frame could not be obtained, questionnaires were mailed to the entire sample, but only those age 50 and over were asked to respond (for reasons given above). We received 1,333 completed questionnaires from respondents age 50 and over. This research was funded by a grant from The Retirement Research Foundation of Park Ridge, Illinois and conducted by the research staff of The Hillhaven Foundation of Tacoma, Washington.

2. Mulkay and Gilbert (1984: 3–6) suggest that most qualitative studies seem to follow these steps: (1) obtain statements from respondents; (2) look for broad similarities between the statements; (3) if there are similarities, take these statements at face value, that is, as accurate accounts of what is really going on; and (4) construct a generalized version of these accounts and present this as one's own analytical conclusion. Thus, by treating the statements of respondents as resources rather than as possible topics of research, the researcher will often miss the distinction between a respondent's "account" of the situation and other possible accounts. For a related discussion concerning anthropology, see also Clifford (1986).

3. On the face of it, those cases where "age" was used in conjunction with something else might appear less problematic, but in fact the meaning of "age" is being taken even more for granted. As I explained earlier, by stating explicitly things like health, illness, or physical limitations, the respondents, unless they are merely being redundant, are actually ruling out some of the factors most commonly associated with "age". In effect, this leaves "age" standing more naked than if they had used it alone.

4. Those defined for the purposes here as non-respondents were not significantly different in any measurable way (demographics, interest in returning to nursing, etc.) from those defined as respondents.

5. Admittedly, some of the uses of "age" that I overlooked were a consequence of my own willingness to use "age" as a resource; that is, as if it were an accurate assessment of respondents' situations. This implies, of course, my own routine assumption that

"age" alone may account for the various abilities, limitations, or characteristics of the respondents.

6. The results of a bivariate regression with the respondents' chronological age and the number of unelaborated uses of "age" yielded $r = .256\,p < .001$.

7. This was in sharp contrast to the other 43.2 percent who, without mentioning their age, generally explained in detail their reasons for not completing the survey. Some felt too "out of touch" with the nursing profession, others mentioned various disabilities and illnesses, and a few simply said they were not interested.

8. The "mere passing of time" includes both specific chronological dates (for example, "75" or "over 60") and more general typological ages (for example, "too old" or "the young").

9. Philip Stafford (1989: 271–2) offers the following passage which draws out a rather severe implication for gerontology if it insists on viewing "age" as its primary theoretical resource: "Social and psychological gerontology, in the main, adopt the bio-medical model insofar as they pursue a quest for what is called 'normal aging' – those sociological or psychological features of old people which remain after all other possible contributing variables have been peeled away. Such 'confounding' variables include gender, class, illness, ethnicity, etc. For the edifice of the discipline of gerontology, the latent fear is that the social and psychological aging may be so residual that the object of study itself evaporates. Wouldn't it be ironic, after all, as Jennie Keith suggests, that 'old people are people.' "

10. Dr Barbara McBride offered this example in a personal discussion with the author. Newspapers provide continual examples of the implicit use of chronological age as an explanatory resource. Regardless of the topic or event being described, the age of individuals is regularly reported. Moreover, when an individual's age is not available, many journalists go so far as to include the phrase "age not available." The implication here is that "age" is viewed as an important explanatory factor requiring its absence to be noted. If it were not routinely interpreted as such, then this raises the question of why journalists include chronological age (or note its absence)? If it is merely descriptive, then wouldn't height, weight, hair and eye color be more useful?

References

American Association of Retired Persons [AARP] (1986) *Truth About Aging: Guidelines for Accurate Communications.* Washington DC: AARP, Special Projects Section, Program Department.

Baker, S. (1990) Reflection, doubt, and the place of rhetoric in postmodern social theory, *Sociological Theory*, 8(2): 233–45.

Bodily, C. (1991) I have no opinions. I'm 73 years old! Rethinking ageism, *Journal of Aging Studies*, 5(3): 245–64.

Bourdieu, P. (1984) *Distinctions.* Cambridge, MA: Harvard University Press.

Cicourel, A. (1964) *Method and Measurement in Sociology.* New York: The Free Press.

Clifford, J. (1986) *Writing Culture.* Berkeley, CA: University of California Press.

Copper, B. (1988) *Over the Hill.* Freedom, CA: The Crossing Press.

Darwin, C. (1861) *On the Origin of Species by Means of Natural Selection.* London: J. Murray.

Estes, C. (1983) *The Aging Enterprise.* San Francisco, CA: Jossey-Bass.

Gergen, K. (1985) The social constructionist movement in modern psychology, *American Psychologist*, 40(3): 266–75.

Gruman, G. (1978) Cultural origins of present day "Age-ism:" the modernization of the life cycle, in S.F. Spicker, K.M. Woodward, and D.D. Van Tassel (eds), *Aging and the*

Elderly: Humanistic Perspectives in Gerontology. Atlantic Highlands, NJ: Humanities Press.

Lash, S. (1990) *Sociology of Postmodernism*. London: Routledge.

Lederman, A. (March 1990) John Kenneth Galbraith: a long life in the public eye, *Gray Panther Network*, 19(1): 6.

Lueders, M. (1990a) Ageism, *The Crone Newsletter*, 2(1): 4.

Lueders, M. (1990b) 'A Culture Conspiracy', *Puget Sound Women's Digest*, April: 20–21.

Lindblom, Charles. (1990) *Inquiry and Change: The Troubled Attempt to Understand and Shape Society*. New Haven: Yale University Press.

McBride, B. and Bodily, C. (1990) *Project ONE-AGE: A Survey of Older, Inactive Nurses from Illinois*. Tacoma, WA: The Hillhaven Foundation.

Mulkay, M. and Gilbert, N. (1984) *Opening Pandora's Box: A Sociological Analysis of Scientists' Discourse*. Cambridge: Cambridge University Press.

Pollner, M. (1987) *Mundane Reason: Reality in Everyday and Sociological Discourse*. Cambridge: Cambridge University Press.

Schaper, D. (1989) *A Book of Common Power: Narratives Against the Current*. San Diego, CA: Luramedia.

Speechley, M. and Tinetti, M. (1991) Falls and injuries in frail and vigorous community elderly persons, *Journal of the American Geriatrics Society*, 39(1) (January): 50.

Stafford, P. (1989) Towards a semiotics of old age, in T. Sebeok and J. Umiker Sebeok (eds), *The Semiotic Web*. New York: Mouton de Gruyter.

Stevenson, C. and Capezuti, E. (1991) Guardianship: protection vs. peril, *Geriatric Nursing*, January/February: 13.

11
Cocaine Careers: Historical and Individual Constructions

Karl E. Scheibe

The history and present state of the human use of cocaine provides a powerful example of how social constructions determine how people act. A white power is the product of a fairly simple chemical extraction from the leaves of the *erythroxylon coca* plant which grows in abundance in the climate of western and central South America. Around this substance are woven the most varied and complex social constructions. It is now common to hear cocaine discussed as a major element in US foreign policy and as a prime determinant of current urban problems. It is common also to hear cocaine described as the most dangerous and psychologically addictive substance available – all of this in marked contrast to the scant regard accorded to cocaine just a decade ago, when it was generally described as relatively innocuous for the individual and trivial as a domestic or foreign relations problem.[1]

Major phenomena, such as wars, epidemics, depressions, and revolutions, produce social constructions from a variety of perspectives – economic, political, religious, medical, psychological, literary, etc. The recent growth in the use of cocaine is such a phenomenon. Cocaine has powerful economic significance in that it forms one of the principal exports and sources of currency for several South American countries.[2] Since the non-medical sale, possession, and use of cocaine is illegal in the United States and in many countries of the world, commerce in cocaine is a major problem in international politics.[3] The criminal problem of cocaine is reflected in the large portion of the time and resources of our criminal justice system devoted to the detection, arrest, prosecution, and incarceration of individuals who are illegally involved with cocaine and other drugs. Since a number of deaths result from cocaine overdose or adverse cardiac reactions to cocaine use, the substance is a medical and public health problem.[4] Procurement and use of cocaine and its crystal form, crack, has been described as the major cause of social malaise and decline in cities across the United States; hence, cocaine is a social problem. The attraction of individuals to the use of cocaine can be regarded both as a psychological and as a physiological problem. How individuals who become addicted to cocaine are to be treated is a therapeutic question, psychological as well as medical.

The major claim of this chapter is that it is useful to regard cocaine in terms of socially constructed careers, and that in two distinct senses.

First, as a conception or object of thought, cocaine has a historical career. Not just the powder, but ideas about the powder made their entry onto the world's stage in mid-nineteenth century and are still with us. The collective history of these ideas and the accompanying use of cocaine comprise, let us say, one kind of career. Just 135 years ago, no one had heard of cocaine (the extract from the coca leaf was named in 1860). The trajectory of the general use and prominence of cocaine is uneven, with a major upswing starting about 1885, a decline just before the Great War, another spurt during the 1920s, and a major and protracted period of dormancy from 1930 until about 1975. Now the use career appears to be in full flower – in Europe where use is thought of primarily as a public health problem, and in the United States where use is viewed mainly as a criminal and law enforcement problem. A sample of current books on the topic reflect the general florescence of concern with cocaine: *The Steel Drug: Cocaine in Perspective* (Erickson et al., 1987); *Cocaine Politics* (Scott and Marshall, 1991); *The White Labyrinth* (Lee, 1989); *The Cocaine Kids* (Williams, 1987); and *Cocaine: White Gold Rush in Peru* (Morales, 1989).

The second sense of cocaine careers relates to individuals rather than historical developments.[5] Individuals who have had experience with cocaine have cocaine careers – careers which vary from the trivial and extremely brief – an experimental sniff – to the monumental and lastingly consequential. Examples of the latter would be Lenny Bias, the Boston Celtics basketball recruit who died in 1986 of a cocaine overdose, or Thomas Henderson, whose career as a professional football player was overwhelmed by his career with cocaine.[6]

It is the objective of this chapter to develop an understanding of cocaine careers in both the historical and individual senses. The method is to examine the history of understandings about cocaine over the past century and to explore evidence of individual use of cocaine as reflected in survey research as well as a series of current case histories of individuals who have had varying forms of involvement with cocaine use.

This twin examination of the historical careers of cocaine as a social construct and the careers of individuals who have used cocaine has as a major aim the demonstration of variety. The guiding assumption is that a proper understanding of cocaine is not absolutist or essentialist, but must be contextual and pragmatic. As William James (1890) argued in his chapter, "The perception of reality," "Every object we think of gets at last referred to one world or another," and "Each world whilst it is attended to is real after its own fashion; only the reality lapses with the attention" (1890: 293). Thus, cocaine is always to be understood as the white powder *cum* observer in a particular context of observation.

The Historical Career of Cocaine

Erythroxylon coca is one of the several gifts of the American continents to the world. Others include chocolate, tobacco and coffee – all of which have addictive properties. From the fifteenth century to the present we have had new material on the world stage to lead us to ponder the phenomena and paradoxes of chemically induced pleasures. Alcohol has a career that extends to the reaches of recorded history, and opiates have been a story in western culture for centuries. About the latter, it is instructive to note that Thomas De Quincey (1822/1956), author of the famous *Confessions of an English Opium-Eater*, acquired his opium by legal purchase in an apothecary shop and that opium was available for legal purchase in the United States until 1914. Cocaine was also a legal over-the-counter drug until that time.

While no one knows when the human use of coca leaves actually began, it is virtually certain that it has been in continuous use among native Andean tribes for at least 400 years. Some anthropologists have claimed that coca was strictly regulated and used only for religious ceremonies in Andean civilizations prior to the Conquest, but that after domination by the conquistadors, the habits of chewing coca leaves became pandemic – an anodyne, let us imagine, for the pain of domination. While the Spanish conquerors at first forbade the use of coca by the natives, they quickly discovered that coca leaf chewing served as a palliative to hunger and fatigue, and thus proved to be a useful adjunct to a regime of slavery (see Morales, 1987; MacDonald, 1988).

It was not until mid-nineteenth century that much attention was given to coca in Europe. In 1860, with the isolation of the now-familiar alkaloid form of cocaine, prepared as a powder, experimentation with the drug began. Most of the early medical experimentation was quite personal. Here is the testimony of an Italian physician after his trials of self-administration:

> Borne on the wings of coca leaves, I flew about in the space of 77,328 worlds, each one more splendid than the others . . . I prefer a life of ten years with coca to one of a hundred thousand years without it. (Paolo Mantegazza, quoted in Erickson et al., 1987: 3)

Very little systematic research was done with cocaine for 20 years or so, and physicians seemed to regard it with either suspicion or indifference.

In addition to its euphorogenic properties, cocaine was found in the 1880s to be a powerful anesthetic, applied topically or injected – and it is still used in this way, particularly for eye surgery. Sigmund Freud claims to have suggested to Dr Carl Kollor that cocaine might be used as a topical anesthetic, and it was Kollor who received credit for the discovery of this use of cocaine in 1884.

The most powerful medical boost for cocaine was provided by Sigmund Freud's famous 1884 paper, "Über Coca," wherein this claim is entered: "I have tested the effect of coca, which wards off hunger, sleep and fatigue and steels oneself to intellectual effort" (Freud, 1884/ 1974: 50). Some recent scholarship has suggested that the intellectual effort required for the production of *Interpretation of Dreams* was supplied in this way (Freud, 1884/1974). Freud attributed truly magical powers to cocaine, suggesting that it can literally substitute for food as a source of energy. Moreover, he did not consider it to have addictive properties. Based on his own experience and that of some patients to whom he prescribed the drug, he offered the following generalization:

> First, cocaine is not likely to cause physical ill-effect, even when consumed over extended periods in "moderate" dose. Second, the use of cocaine, be it once or on a regular basis, never creates a need for a larger dose; on the contrary, in the long run, a certain repulsion for the substance is likely to appear. (Freud, 1884/1974: 55)

Freud's own repulsion to the drug appeared in a way he did not anticipate. Freud's friend and fellow Viennese physician, von Fleishl, became addicted to morphine after an injury to his hand. Von Fleishl used morphine for 10 years to combat chronic pain in his hand and became dependent. Freud suggested that he use cocaine as a way of gaining relief from morphine. While he was able to discontinue morphine, he developed an even more serious and destructive addiction to cocaine. Von Fleischl became delirious and descended into a state of mental and physical deterioration from which he never recovered. Freud then conceded that cocaine should not be used to treat morphine addicts, because the weakness induced by the morphine addiction produces a unique receptivity to the negative effects of cocaine, though for some years he continued to advocate its use as a stimulant, even sending it to his fiancée, Martha Bernays. After 1890, one finds no further references to the curative properties of cocaine in Freud's writings, and at some point before 1900, he stopped using it himself (Freud, 1884/1974).

The evaluative construction of cocaine in late nineteenth-century America was generally quite positive. In 1887, a former Surgeon General of the US Army, Dr William Hammond, published a report of his personal experience with various preparations and dosage levels of coca. He concludes that the drug has great utility in treatment of local pain and in producing a general elevation of the spirits in case of melancholia or depression. He also claimed that cocaine is not habit-forming as morphine is – that it produces no craving, no weakening of will power, and no debilitating aftereffects. He likened the cocaine habit to the habit of drinking coffee. At about the same time, the Atlanta pharmacist John Styth Pemberton included cocaine as an ingredient in his new beverage, Coca-Cola. In 1903, because of rising public suspicions about addictive properties, the cocaine was removed and caffeine was added instead.

While the widespread use of cocaine in this period by artists, intellectuals, and ordinary people testifies to its capacity to enhance mood, stimulate effort and creativity, and forestall pain and fatigue, evidence of certain less favorable consequences began to accumulate as well.[7] The German psychiatrist Albrecht Erlenmeyer published in 1885 a rebuttal of Freud's paper. This was a serious indictment of the effects of prolonged cocaine usage – citing cardiac disturbances, particularly tachycardia as a consequence, as well as mental deterioration, loss of memory, and paranoid psychosis. Beginning in 1890 until his death 30 years later, the toxicologist Ludwig Lewin published a series of lengthy indictments of cocaine use, based on observations of hundreds of patients. His conclusions were that the substance is perniciously addictive and poisonous to the psyche as well as to the body. In 1926, the psychiatrist Hans Maier published a definitive clinical indictment of cocaine use, surveying the clinical and pharmacological literature of the previous 40 years, claiming as negative consequences at least the following: perforated septum, nasal bleeding and irritation, loss of sense of smell (anosmia), tachycardia, hallucinations, phantom bugs ("cocaine bugs" – perceived as working just underneath the skin and thus provoking violent scratching), paranoid delusions, elevated blood pressure, and in extreme cases, heart stoppage. Vivid case studies were supplied in abundance to fortify the generally horrific impression. Maier concludes his work with a statement on the social dangers posed by cocaine and other addictive drugs, and with a plea for the prohibition and elimination of these substances. Note the strong moralistic tone of his conclusion:

> It will be incumbent upon us to protect the youth of our large cities from the temptation of resorting to unhealthy sources of pleasure by training it to acquire healthy recreational habits. This will not be enough. In addition, the medical profession, the authorities, the pharmaceutical industry and the pharmacists, as well as the police and the courts of all countries will have to make a united and concerted effort not only to bring about legislation against the most dangerous drugs, among which cocaine unquestionably belongs, but, above all, to ensure its implementation. (quoted in Nahas, 1989: 224)

The Harrison Act of 1914 included cocaine among prohibited substances, misclassifying it as a narcotic. It is often claimed by those who advocate outlawing drugs that this act succeeded in eliminating cocaine addiction as a serious problem in US society. However, the recreational use of cocaine became popular in the United States throughout the 1920s, and a radical reduction of cocaine use occurred only with the turning of popular opinion against cocaine, and with the economic deprivation brought about by the Great Depression, when expensive and frivolous indulgences could hardly be widespread and when alcohol was both cheap and legal again (see Parssinen, 1983).

The transformation of the societal evaluation of cocaine from a generally harmless and even useful substance to something sinister and harmful was accompanied by shifts in the metaphors used to describe the drug. Montagne (1988) has shown that the imaginative symbolism conveyed in drug metaphors carry both positive and negative meanings (magic bullets, secret killers, chemical vacations, plague, disease, consciousness expander, etc). Cocaine's image in mid-twentieth century America came to be tarnished; it came to be viewed more as poison than as panacea.

Since the heyday of Harry Anslinger, head of the US Federal Bureau of Narcotics from 1930 until 1962, drugs in the United States have been constructed primarily as a criminal and law enforcement problem and only secondarily as a public health issue. Viewing cocaine in this way has produced military and law enforcement efforts to choke off its career. A current examination of the results of these efforts has produced a uniform conclusion of failure. After an extensive examination of facts and data on this issue, including the question of the US government's complicity in cocaine traffic, Scott and Marshall drew this conclusion regarding the US effort at control:

> Instead of addressing the root causes of America's drug demand, however, during the 1980s about 70 percent of federal drug spending went to law enforcement, which even enthusiasts admit can interdict only a small fraction of total drug supplies. Spending priorities must be reversed if any progress toward social healing is to begin. Drug education and support for expanded treatment are essential. . . . Ultimately, the United States must begin to consider and experiment with proposals to take the crime out of drug markets through controlled legalization. (1991: 192)

The heart of this proposal is to change the social construction of the cocaine problem – to stop viewing it as a criminal problem and to conceive of it instead as a public health problem or a problem in social education. Controlled legalization of cocaine would transform the criminal career of cocaine at a stroke. This course of action is supported by the Drug Policy Foundation, which has established itself as a center for debate and advocacy of legalization (see Trebach, 1987). Legalization is strongly opposed by segments of the medical community, based on a fear that decriminalizing drug use would result in massive increases in use with accompanying deleterious effects for individuals and for society (see Nahas, 1989). The construction of cocaine use offered by those who oppose legalization is that the drug is addictive for a large proportion of individuals who try it, and that therefore it should not be made accessible. Those who argue in favor of legalization point out that cocaine is widely accessible now, though expensive and of variable purity and quality. The expense and illegal status of cocaine link it inevitably to the world of crime in two major ways: first, criminal organizations and networks of production, processing, transportation, distribution, and sales are obliged into existence; second, individuals are forced to resort to illegal sources of income – robbery, drug dealing, prostitution – in order to be able to afford regular cocaine use.

Evidence from Survey Research and Case Studies

Some light might be shed on these varied propositions by examining the actual careers of current users of cocaine as reflected in survey data and individual case studies. Relevant questions to keep in mind while examining the careers of users are these: What evidence is there for an inevitable progression or tolerance of cocaine use? What are the reasons and causes of the cessation of cocaine use and how often does complete abstinence occur? How are individuals who use cocaine influenced by its status as an illegal drug? To what extent does using cocaine involve a user with a life of crime of some kind?

The curve representing prevalence of cocaine usage in the United States has a surprising form. The volume of cocaine use can be assessed in a variety of ways – by the volume of product seizures by law enforcement officials, by the number of toxic reactions treated in emergency wards, by frequency of deaths, by survey research using questionnaires and interviews, and by the frequency of individuals who come to treatment centers or outpatient therapists for treatment. All of these measures converge to produce the following generalizations. Cocaine use in the United States was negligible to minor in quantity from 1930 until the early 1960s. While the 1960s and early 1970s are popularly regarded as a heyday for drugs, cocaine use remained relatively minor until the early 1970s – a kind of tag-along to the drug culture. Throughout the 1970s, cocaine use increased and in the early 1980s the increase in prevalence became dramatic. Something of a peak appears to have been reached in 1985–86, and since that time, reports of cocaine use, deaths from acute cocaine intoxication and the like have shown a moderate decline. Just in the past year, I have documented a one-third decline in the proportion of individuals in a drug and alcohol treatment center who report using cocaine. (Typically, just under one-half of the people in drug and alcohol treatment centers report cocaine involvement.) Of course, within the last five years, the smokable crystal form of cocaine, crack, has shown a substantial increase. Even including crack use with cocaine use, the evidence still suggests a leveling off of use and perhaps a slight decline over the past three years. Annual surveys of drug and alcohol use by the Institute for Survey Research at the University of Michigan show that cocaine use among high school seniors peaked in 1985 and has been dropping steadily since then. Bachman et al. (1990) conclude that the reasons for this drop, which parallels an earlier drop in the use of marijuana, have to do with increased perceived risks and social disapproval, which in turn result from public education campaigns about the dangers of cocaine conducted over this period.

Bachman et al. (1990) note that there has been no perception of decreased availability of cocaine among high school students. Studies of cocaine production and supply suggest that virtually no effect of the "war on drugs" is discernable at the level of supply on the street. During the years of the Reagan administration, the US government launched massive paramilitary campaigns to cut off cocaine supply at its source. Billions of dollars were spent to eradicate cocaine production by the napalming of fields and the destruction of processing plants – with no discernable effect. By 1990, Senator John Kerry of Massachusetts, who was one of the main supporters of this initiative, changed his mind, calling for a re-evaluation of the military options (see Scott and Marshall, 1991). One of my own informants has told me that in 1985 an ounce of cocaine cost about $2,000 in New York, while today the same amount can be purchased for $800 – evidence that the supply is not diminished.

Evidence about cocaine use by individuals is easily available from a number of survey studies on drug and alcohol use in the United States. One of the most consistent findings from these studies has direct and inexorable meaning for the question of characteristic cocaine careers. Typically, a survey finding will indicate that about 10 percent of a sample will have tried cocaine at some time in their life, but that only a small fraction of those who try it become regular users or show evidence of abuse or dependence. Surveys conducted over the past decade consistently indicate that something like 25 million Americans have tried cocaine at least once in their lifetime. Yet the number of individuals who abuse or are dependent on cocaine is less than 10 percent of this number (Green, 1978; Chiauzzi, 1991).

Use of cocaine at Wesleyan University has been assessed on two different occasions in the last decade as part of a larger survey of drug and alcohol use. The relevant data from these surveys are presented in

Table 11.1   *Self-reported cocaine use among Wesleyan*
undergraduates for 1986 and 1990 samples, by sex, percentages

Reported cocaine in:			Lifetime	Year	Month
1986	M	(n = 133)	35	21	10
	F	(n = 174)	30	18	8
1990	M	(n = 234)	13	8	1
	F	(n = 266)	8	3	4
Totals	M	(n = 374)	25	13	4
	F	(n = 440)	17	10	1
All		(n = 814)	20	11	2

Table 11.1. Several features of these data are worth noting. First, the aforementioned decline in drug use is reflected. The reported percentage of students who had tried cocaine in their lifetime has dropped by about two-thirds from 1986 to 1990. Second, a consistent sex difference is present in these data – with a higher percentage of men reporting cocaine use for all periods of self-report and for both samples. It should be noted, however, that these sex differences are nowhere near the 3:1 to 10:1 ratio commonly reported for alcohol and opiate use and dependency. Third, and most relevant to the present argument, the percentage of individuals who have tried cocaine in their lifetimes is many times greater than the percentage who have used it in the past month, which use would reflect a pattern of habitual use or dependency. Overall, while 20 percent of all students surveyed reported trying cocaine at least once in their lives, only 2 percent report use in the past month. Clearly, these data do not support the more alarmist views of the inevitable addictive properties of cocaine.

A longitudinal study of cessation of drug use among young people supplies strong support for the idea that cocaine careers for most young people are of limited duration. Kandel and Raveis (1989) report that at ages 24–25, 22 percent of men and 14 percent of women in their sample (n = 1222) were using cocaine. Four years later, 49 percent of the men and 56 percent of the women who had been using had stopped, and the majority had stopped decisively. Their analysis showed that, "Changes in role, specifically the assumption of new family roles, are associated with cessation of drug use for both sexes" (1989: 111). Becoming pregnant was a certain way for women to terminate their cocaine careers. This study also demonstrated that cessation was less frequent for individuals who have been using drugs more intensively and for a longer period of time. Kandel and Raveis also conclude that, "Those subjects who stopped using marijuana or cocaine by their late 20s had been in an environment in their mid-20s that was less supportive of drug use, as reflected in the behaviors and attitudes of individuals in their social networks" (1989: 113–14).

Individual Cases

Over the past eight years, I have compiled case histories of upwards of 250 cocaine-using individuals who were in treatment for alcohol or drug abuse both as inpatients and as outpatients in psychotherapy. For the majority of these patients, (about 85 percent of the 250) alcohol dependence was the primary diagnosis. This is hardly a representative sample of the general population, for all of these individuals were sufficiently troubled by their drug and alcohol use to seek recovery, with the aim of abstinence. A clinical population is obviously biased in favor of increased intensity of substance abuse and accompanying dysfunction or pathology. Even so, a remarkable variety appears in the presented picture of cocaine use and abuse. The following brief case summaries were selected with a view to illustrating that variety.[8]

Case 1. Sarah began to drink heavily and to use marijuana while in 7th grade, at age 12. She is the daughter of two working, professional parents and has a younger brother. Both parents are alcohol dependent. Her grades were poor, and she was often in trouble with the school authorities because of truancy and delinquency. She began to show symptoms of bipolar depression at age 13 and was referred to a psychiatrist for treatment. She was placed on medication (Lithium, Desipramine, Novane) and continued to just get by in school, eventually graduating from high school. In high school, she became a polydrug user, taking cocaine, codeine, and speed in addition to the pot and alcohol she had started earlier. By the time she reached age 23, she had held only menial, low-paying jobs, continuing in psychotherapy and on medications as well as illicit drugs. She had a brief period of confinement in a psychiatric hospital following a suicide attempt. She occasionally resorted to prostitution as a way of earning money to support her drug habit, which came increasingly to be dominated by cocaine. She also stole silver and other valuable articles from her parents' home in order to buy cocaine. Her longest period of abstinence from cocaine was six months, during which period she was under treatment by her psychiatrist for depression and by a psychologist for drug dependency. After six months, she relapsed back into cocaine use, was effectively disowned by her parents, and became a homeless person – using cocaine when she can afford it, using alcohol when she cannot, and periodically attending AA and NA meetings in desultory attempts at quitting.

Sarah always has snorted cocaine – never using crack, freebase, or needles. Her use pattern is controlled by available money. She has never been arrested either for prostitution or for cocaine use or possession.

Case 2. Wayne is a 34-year-old journeyman plumber who has been using cocaine and drinking alcohol since age 20. He comes from a working class home, has three brothers, all of whom have substance abuse problems. He has one son by his first marriage which ended in divorce, and is remarried. His cocaine use quickly became established at about one gram per week, and was always snorted. He used alcohol as a way of moderating the aftereffects of cocaine – typically drinking several beers after beginning to "come down" from the cocaine. This pattern of use persisted for eight years, during which time he continued to work without disruption. At age 28, just after his divorce, someone introduced him to the freebase form of cocaine use. At this time, his use pattern accelerated rapidly, and he began to deal cocaine and to steal money and goods in order to support a voracious and all-consuming appetite for freebase cocaine. He illustrated his amoral drive for cocaine by describing his behavior when his grandfather, who lived in the same household, had a stroke and had to be taken to the hospital by ambulance. Wayne's first act, while the ambulance was waiting for him to accompany his grandfather to the hospital, was to go to his grandfather's room, take the $250 in cash he found there and his checkbook as well – which he used to buy more cocaine. His use of freebase became so all-consuming that he lost his job, his second wife threatened to leave him and herself went into a major depression, while his health deteriorated, and his weight went from 150 to 120 lbs.

At this time, he committed himself to an inpatient drug rehabilitation center – his third such attempt at getting clean. But this time, something happened which effectively ended his cocaine career. He describes the event as follows:

> After detoxing at the treatment center, I began to have migraine headaches – never had migraines before. I was miserable. My roommate was a guy named Mike, also a cokehead. We used to take walks around the grounds during free time. One afternoon, we were sitting on this huge rock overlooking the water – the wind was blowing and there were dark clouds on the horizon. I found myself crying, sobbing without control. All of a sudden it was like something snapped, and I told Mike that I just gave up – that I was helpless to control cocaine, so I surrendered and asked God to help me. I knew from that moment on that I would not use. And up to now, I haven't – haven't even come close to using.

When Wayne got out of treatment, he returned home, and with his wife began attending a fundamentalist Christian church – with much bible study, prayer, and singing. Wayne became a devoted member of the congregation. Soon, he and his wife moved to another city, he became steadily employed as a plumber again, and he has found another church to support his religious beliefs. Two years later he has not used cocaine, alcohol, or any other drug.

Case 3. Liz began using cocaine at age 15, always by snorting and always with beer. In school, she was diagnosed as "hyperactive," and retrospectively her pattern of symptoms fits the current *DSMIIIR* category of Attention Deficit Hyperactivity Disorder (ADHD). At age 16 she dropped out of school, continuing to use cocaine and alcohol quite heavily. At 19 she married and shortly thereafter had a baby. During her pregnancy she did not use cocaine and did not drink heavily. However, she began to use and drink again after the baby was born. The relation with her husband, also a cocaine user, was tempestuous and by age 22 she was divorced. Liz was given a diagnosis of "major depression" and was prescribed Lithium by a psychiatrist. She was admitted to an inpatient alcohol and drug rehabilitation center twice, the second time following a suicide attempt. She was able to stay clean and sober for up to four months after her last rehab program. But when she is discouraged by employment problems, financial problems, difficulties with her boyfriend, or feeling bored and restless, she returns to the town associated with her drug use, makes contacts with old friends, and binges on cocaine – drinking alcohol simultaneously. Alcohol per se seems not to be a problem – but the craving for cocaine sometimes takes control. For one year, she had two-day binges about once every six weeks. After a binge, she felt weak, defeated, remorseful, and yet each time she resolved to try again to abstain. At age 24, she began a relationship with a man who neither drinks nor uses drugs. She is totally abstinent in his presence. Her relapses have gradually become less frequent and less intense.

Case 4. Mel is a 30-year-old truck driver, who has had a major heroin problem since age 18. At one time, he was using as much as 10 bags of heroin a day. He began at age 24 to use cocaine in conjunction with heroin – always snorting the cocaine. While his use of cocaine became progressively heavier, he began to develop a physical aversion or bodily rejection of cocaine about one year after he first began to use it. As soon as he sensed the smell of cocaine, he would have gag reactions and throw up. So he stopped using cocaine entirely, while continuing on heroin. After about five years' complete abstinence from cocaine, he discovered that he could tolerate it if he injected it rather than snorting, even though he professed still to sense the taste of cocaine from its presence in his bloodstream. At this point, his drug use went "out of control." He would shoot up ever greater quantities of heroin and cocaine on extended binges that would last up to 10 days. To support his drug habit, he began dealing in cocaine and heroin, and was eventually arrested for possession and trafficking. After a protracted trial, he was finally acquitted. After the trial, he resolved to enter an alcohol and drug rehabilitation program. After completing the program, he attended NA meetings regularly and participated in regular outpatient counseling. He has resumed regular employment as a truck driver and appears to be well embarked on a program of recovery.

Case 5. Gibson is a successful 36-year-old salesman, married with two daughters. He began to drink excessively in his high school years, and while he experimented with pot, never used drugs extensively until after his marriage at age 27. He began to experiment with cocaine with his wife – arranging elaborately prepared dinners at home, with expensive wines, concluding with both of them snorting cocaine. Initially, his wife went along with these parties, but soon grew concerned about the consequences, for her husband would often become violent and aggressive after a bout of heavy drinking and cocaine use. On one occasion, after he had been drinking and using cocaine, he struck her in the face, causing her to fall and cut her head and face. He called the police, who promptly arrested him. While charges were pending, he began a program of outpatient counseling aimed at establishing abstinence from drugs and alcohol. The charges against him were eventually dropped, and he continued to maintain complete abstinence from cocaine for the next two years. He did not maintain abstinence from alcohol consumption but did not drink to the point of intoxication for this period.

Case 6. Jack is a 30-year-old mason. He had been drinking excessively since high school, and at age 27 his beer drinking had become so much of a problem that he was threatened with termination by his employer unless he did something about it. He had used marijuana periodically since high school, and had tried cocaine twice, but professed not to like it. Recognizing the consequences of his drinking, he began a program of complete abstinence from alcohol with the aid of outpatient counseling. For the first six months of this program, he was completely clean and sober. But then he began to use marijuana with his girlfriend, and shortly thereafter began to snort cocaine. Now, without alcohol, he began to crave cocaine with great intensity, even though he contended that all of the pleasure in its use was derived from the first line he snorted, while he was powerless to stop using until all of his available supply was exhausted. When he used cocaine, he would either do it with his girlfriend or else alone, locking himself in his apartment. He exhibited a pronounced "cocaine paranoia," imagining strange presences just outside his windows, or that law enforcement officers were observing his apartment from parked cars. Cocaine use was irregular, always followed by remorse and by a sense of weakness. Jack maintained his abstinence from alcohol completely. He became a regular user of marijuana, and about once a month, would use cocaine extensively for a 24-hour period. This remains his pattern.

What can we Learn from Cases?
Quite obviously, these case observations about cocaine use can be multiplied at will. Additional cases would add even more to the impression of bewildering variety in the actual cocaine careers of users in the world around us. I have not included in these cases any casual or recreational users of cocaine, but in the course of routine clinical practice many such instances could be cited. A female college student used cocaine once, and never tried it again for it made her face feel numb. A male alcoholic tried cocaine for one month, using it intensively, but then quit as abruptly as he started, for no apparent reason, while continuing to drink. A successful executive uses cocaine at the rate of about a gram every two weeks, and has maintained this pattern for 10 years, with only minor variations. What kinds of generalizations can be drawn about cocaine careers?

First, it is patently obvious that the vast majority of individuals who try cocaine do not become repeated and regular users of the drug. Most cocaine careers are quite brief, with individuals stopping on their own. But a subset of individuals who try cocaine do become addicted to it, and as strongly addicted in a psychological sense as any alcoholic, cigarette smoker, or heroin addict. The longitudinal survey data cited earlier suggest that those who are selected out to assume the career of cocaine addict are characterized by having many friends who also do cocaine, who are part of a delinquent subculture, and whose degree of involvement with illicit drugs is greater. Research also suggests that "hyperactive" individuals are more likely to become habitual cocaine users, perhaps as a means of self-medication (see Horner and Scheibe, forthcoming).

The ways in which cocaine careers are terminated are many and various. In the individual cases cited above, the individuals who have maintained abstinence for an extended period of time (a year or more) have had distinct "bottoming out" experiences – or what Sarbin and Nucci (1973) refer to as "self-reconstitution" processes, characterized at an initial phase by something like a "death–rebirth" phenomenon. The case of Wayne is most illustrative of the conduct reorganization paradigm that Sarbin and Nucci describe as typical of people who succeed in quitting tobacco use. Loss of weight, migraines, loss of job, loss of family, brought about a crisis which was met by an admission of helplessness (similar to the first step in Alcoholics Anonymous), and was followed by a socially supported way of transcending the limitations of a former life-style. The case of Mel also fits this paradigm, for his retirement from a cocaine career was precipitated by an arrest and protracted trial. This trial, while resulting in acquittal, was a humiliation, and was followed by the self-reconstitution processes promoted by NA groups. On the other hand, we have cases of individuals who have not so much retired as moved to part-time status in their cocaine careers, and are moving gradually rather than abruptly to a cessation of use.

Conclusion and Implications

The person who uses cocaine has been variously constructed over time as a dope fiend, a *bon vivant*, a criminal, a sick person, as living on the fast track, and as a fool. The argument here is that construing the user of cocaine as having a cocaine career bears several advantages. First, it calls attention to the variable trajectory of use – recruitment, progression, maintenance, reduction, and cessation. Also, it suggests the multiplicity of influences – economic, political, social, physiological, legal, and even religious – which might alter the intensity and duration of the career. Cocaine use can be viewed to some advantage from each of these perspectives and does not naturally belong to any one of them.

Those in the helping professions might usefully think of trying to help their clients retire from a career that has become noisome to them. In order to do this, one would want to think of the values, pro and con, which accounted for recruitment and maintenance in the career, and to think as well of alternative ways of satisfying the person's needs by pursuing a different career path. In thinking of careers and career change, one must think in a variety of ways – economically, psychologically, socially, etc. Multiple perspectives on cocaine use are more likely to bring about a favorable career resolution than focus on a single point of view.

The same general argument might be made about the historical career of cocaine as it is socially construed. It is unfortunate that cocaine's assignment to the category of "illicit drugs" in the early part of this century has legitimized a military-criminal perspective in viewing the substance. The "war on drugs" is a manifest failure and the paramilitary attempts at eradicating the drug problem by "attacking it at its source" is one of the more ludicrous examples of misguided foreign policy in our nation's history. At the root of this wasteful and destructive effort is a category mistake: cocaine is not necessarily a criminal problem, but it has been officially constructed as such by our society for many decades (see Nadelmann, 1989).

The public efforts in the past 30 years to control tobacco use provide an instructive example of how cocaine use might diminish as a public policy problem. Musto (1987) argues that the previous period of decline in cocaine use, in the first years of the twentieth century, and again at the beginning of the Great Depression, corresponded with public opinion turning against acceptance and use. Now cigarette smoking has become increasingly disreputable as an activity, and millions of smoking careers have been truncated as a result. Public education is only partially accomplished by centrally directed propaganda campaigns. Eventually, the cumulative consequences of warnings on cigarette packages, restrictions on advertising, increase in taxation and price, films and brochures and television announcements, restriction of smoking in public places, and prominent notice given to deaths brought about by tobacco use have their effect on the conscience of the community.

Evidence from the Bachman et al. (1990) studies shows that cocaine's career is now beginning a phase of decline, and for much the same reasons. The availability of the drug is not changed at all – and its price is lowered. But use of cocaine has been much less attractively presented to the public eye over the past six years, particularly since the tragic death of Lenny Bias, and the prominent and graphic notice given to crack, with its associations with poverty, crime, sick babies, and sudden death. Much of the glamour of cocaine use has been removed, and consequently its use has become less attractive as a career.

It is notable that none of the cases cited in this paper has demonstrated any deterrent effect of cocaine's status as an illegal drug, which must necessarily be purchased from a criminal, most likely in a criminal neighborhood. The arguments for and against legalization of cocaine are complex, but it would seem that the time has come to consider carefully the possible advantages of reconstructing cocaine away from its strictly criminal career.

Notes

1. A *Scientific American* article described cocaine as "no more habit forming than potato chips" (Van Dyck and Byck, 1982).

2. "Bolivia, Columbia, and Peru are the source of 95 percent of the cocaine smuggled into the United States. While in industrial societies cocaine is a social evil, in the Andes of Peru, coca and cocaine preparation and traffic are part of the traditional ecological exchange as well as an important source of cash. The infiltration of an underground economy into the indigenous people's lifestyle has brought about a new type of economic dependence. . . . The illegal circulation of 'coca dollars' supports local economies, feeds inflation, and causes changes – such as cocaine smoking – in the social behavior of the indigenous" (Morales, 1987: xv).

3. "U.S. foreign policy toward Latin America during the 1980s can genuinely be characterized as drug diplomacy" (Lee, 1989: 1).

4. "According to the National Association for Perinatal Addiction Research and Education, about 1 out of every 10 newborns in the U.S. – 375,000 a year – is exposed in the womb to one or more illicit drugs. The most frequent ingredient in the mix is cocaine" (*Time*, May 13, 1991: 57).

5. This use of career is parallel to that employed by Goffman (1961) in his famous essay "The moral career of the mental patient." Goffman described a typical progression by which an individual assumes the career of mental patient, noting in particular how difficult it is to escape the career label once assumed. Careers have at least three phases – recruitment, activity, and retirement. And nature and duration of these phases provides the substance for the description of careers.

6. Both of his careers are described in his autobiography, *Out of Control* (Henderson and Knobler, 1987).

7. In the late nineteenth century, many patent medicines contained cocaine, as did the famous Italian wine, Vin Mariani, endorsed by such notables as Thomas Edison, Sarah Bernhardt, the Czar of Russia, the Prince of Wales, and Pope Leo XIII. Evidence suggests that Robert Louis Stevenson's *The Strange Case of Dr. Jekyll and Mr. Hyde* may have been written with the help of cocaine. Stevenson was quite ill at the time of its composition, and had been taking morphine. The prodigious feat of producing 60,000 words in six days is not likely to have been the result of morphine, but rather of a cocaine high. The fantastic content of the story is also compatible with the transformed sense of reality and identity commonly produced by cocaine.

8. Names and other identifying details have been changed in these case summaries in order to protect the confidentiality of the sources.

References

Bachman, J.G., Johnston, L.D., and O'Malley, P.M. (1990) Explaining the recent decline in cocaine use among young adults: further evidence that perceived risks and disapproval lead to reduced drug use, *Journal of Health and Social Behavior*, 31: 173–84.

Chiauzzi, E.J. (1991) *Preventing Relapse in the Addictions*. New York: Pergamon Press.

De Quincey, T. (1822/1956) *Confessions of an English Opium-Eater*. London: MacDonald.

Erickson, P.G., Adlaf, E.M., Murray, G.F., and Smart, R.G. (1987) *The Steel Drug: Cocaine in Perspective*. Lexington, MA: Lexington Books.

Freud, S. (1884/1974) *Cocaine Papers*, R. Byck (ed.). New York: New American Library.

Goffman, E. (1961) *Asylums*. Garden City, NY: Anchor.

Green, B. (1978) The politics of psychoactive drug user in old age, *The Gerontologist*, 18: 525–30.

Henderson, T. and Knobler, P. (1987) *Out of Control*. New York: Putnam.

Horner, B. and Scheibe, K.E. (forthcoming) Cocaine abuse and attention deficit disorder, *Journal of Addictive Behavior*.

James, W. (1890) *Principles of Psychology*. New York: Holt.

Kandel, D.B. and Raveis, V.H. (1989) Cessation of illicit drug use in young adulthood, *Archives of General Psychiatry*, 46: 109–16.

Lee, R. (1989) *The White Labyrinth: Cocaine and Political Power*. New Brunswick: Transaction.

MacDonald, S.C. (1988) *Dancing on a Volcano*. New York: Praeger.

Montagne, M. (1988) The metaphorical nature of drugs and drug taking, *Social Science Medicine*, 26: 417–24.

Morales, E. (1987) *Cocaine: White Gold Rush in Peru.* Tucson: University of Arizona Press.

Musto, D.F. (1987) *The American Disease: Origins of Narcotics Control.* New York: Oxford University Press.

Nadelmann, E.A. (1989) Drug prohibition in the United States: costs, consequences, and alternatives, *Science*, 245: 939–47.

Nahas, G. (1989) *Cocaine: The Great White Plague.* Middlebury, VT: Paul S. Eriksson.

Parssinen, T.M. (1983) *Secret Passions, Secret Remedies.* Philadelphia, PA: Institute for the Study of Human Issues.

Sarbin, T.R. and Nucci, L. (1973) Self-reconstitution processes: a proposal for reorganizing the conduct of confirmed smokers, *Journal of Abnormal Psychology*, 81: 182–95.

Scott, P.D. and Marshall, J. (1991) *Cocaine Politics.* Berkeley, CA: University of California Press.

Time, Innocent victims, May 13, 1991: 56–60.

Trebach, A.S. (1987) *The Great Drug War.* New York: Macmillan.

Van Dyck, C. and Byck, R. (1982) Cocaine, *Scientific American*, 246: 128–41.

Williams, T. (1987) *The Cocaine Kids.* Reading, MA: Addision-Wesley.

12

A Sociocultural Construction of "Depressions"

Morton Wiener and David Marcus

We do not believe that it is reasonable merely to assert that "depression," or for that matter, any other "psychopathology" is a social construction rather than a traditional "disease." On the contrary, we take our task here to outline what would be identified and/or understood differently were one to explore such "events" from *one* sociocultural perspective. Although we will invoke a number of empirical and analytic arguments to rationalize our approach, we recognize that our approach, like every other perspective, proposition, or criterion is embedded in a particular sociocultural matrix. Our own enculturation (that is, language, beliefs, assumptions, and psychosocial history) remain omnipotent and omnipresent in our explication. We anticipate that we may all too often still incorporate concepts and terminology from our earlier enculturation, rather than maintaining a coherent social construction framework. We will try, however, to contrast our perspective with the predominant, traditional "disease" approaches to psychopathology, and to differentiate our perspective from other social construction perspectives as well.

Our general strategy has been to approach the "events" now considered "psychopathological," as if we were cultural anthropologists rather than traditional psychologists, social workers or psychiatrists. This cultural anthropological approach helps us to remember that our "observations" are constructions seen through the lenses of one particular sociocultural matrix.

One way we will try to emphasize this aspect of our approach is to try to use terms that incorporate this observer-inferential orientation in our descriptions, categorizations and interpretations of the psychosocial transactions, rather than using terms that attribute "agency" to the individual(s), or by invoking "inner" states or traits. If we approximate this ideal, our constructions will be understood in the same way that one recognizes that the work of an artist is a representation, rather than as an ostensible discovery by a "scientist." Our representations, as a constructed reality, are only to be understood as *one* way to describe a "world" *within one metaphorical framework.* Our concerns are not whether our constructions are more "real," or even whether they are "better," but whether the representations offer a different, interesting, heuristic, and pragmatic way to view some sociopsychological events now considered "psychopathological."

We do not wish to do battle with the traditional medical-disease tradition once again. Although we are convinced that the concept of "disease" is an ambiguous, imprecise and misused social construction, all of the combatants, including us, continue to talk past each other. In this context, it is important to reiterate (1) that most arguments are about assumption and metaphors, not facts; (2) that the underlying metaphors of "deviance" and of "psychopathologies" have differed in different historical periods (for example, possession by the devil, weakness of character, disease, disorder); (3) that some "pathologies" have been jettisoned within one era, even within a traditional framework (for example, hysteria, neurasthenia, homosexuality), and (4) that defining criteria are often changed to ensure consensus (agreement) among judges, rather than as changes that elaborate the perspective, or to identify additional or more *precise* criteria (for example, *Diagnostic and Statistical Manual of Mental Disorders*, American Psychiatric Association, 1987).

Linguistic difficulties must be anticipated in any effort to explicate a non-traditional view of "psychopathology." When we identify events of concern, we often find it necessary to use the very terms that we are calling into question (for example, "depression," "anorexia nervosa," "schizophrenia"). If the differences between our underlying metaphors and those in the more traditional perspectives are not represented adequately, it will be all too easy for a reader (1) to transform the terms and concepts from our perspective into those of another (for example, social transactions into social interactions; bio-socio-psychological, as a system, into a multi-causal or multi-determination model); or (2) to infer that two perspectives are "different" if a term in a construct is changed, but the metaphor remains. For example, the metaphor of a "defective" individual is maintained, even though a word is changed from "medical anomaly" to "social anomaly."

One Socio-Cultural Transactional Perspective

In part, our perspective has its roots in Ryle's (1949) arguments that "knowing that," "knowing how" and "competencies" are inferences about actions made by an observer, not statements about some special action "in" or "by the person" ("ghost in the machine"). For Ryle, "knowing that" is taken as the knowledge of the facts or information that has been codified, formally and informally in a social group (for example, the capital of New Mexico, or the group's history). "Knowing how" is an inference that a specific act or conduct can be taken as evidence that the person knows the *ways* to participate in the interrelated sets of actions of a specific complex system of actions (for example, playing chess, speaking a language). Knowing the rules of chess ("knowing that") says nothing about "knowing how" to play chess; one is either playing chess (by not transgressing the rules) or is not playing chess, but only moving the pieces. "Competence" in "knowing how" entails a different kind of assessment (for example, playing chess aggressively or defensively, well or badly). Whatever the evaluation (for example, badly), "knowing how" is *not* negated. When we identify different transactions, we are *not* assessing competence; we are identifying the different "games" (or "dialects") the participants are "playing" (using).

Socialization, or better still, enculturation, may be seen as coming to "know how" things are done in the social transactions of one's group. Participants may do them in *different* ways, but each way still remains within the parameters of the social system, the social fabric and the social contract of the group. Some psychosocial transactional actions may be assessed as typical or atypical, as better or less good (for example, adult vs child), frequent or less frequent, honored or sanctioned, but these assessments are criteria other than whether the action is consonant with the social matrix.

A second assumption in our approach is that when an "infrequent" or "unsuccessful" encounter or transaction is identified, the transaction is still to be described and understood in terms of a *mismatch* of the enculturated patterns of the participants in the encounter, or *differences* in the ways the participants have come to perceive or construe the situation. We do *not* invoke constructs of defective, deficient, disrupted, or disorganized actions or people (Wiener and Cromer, 1967; Wiener, 1989; Wiener, 1991). Such attributions of disordered actions and people seem to be entailed even in socially-based (see for example, Miller and Flack, 1991), interpersonally-oriented (Klerman et al., 1984), or personality-based (for example, Millon and Kotik, 1985) perspectives.

Bakhtin (Clark and Holmquist, 1984) and Vygotsky (1986) posit that enculturation and/or socialization includes the incorporation of the language, the transactions, the psychosocial contexts, and the objects which permeate a child's "world." Enculturation, then is the "world" that becomes known, and how to be in it – including the language, the transactions, the contexts, and the objects which are the sociocultural fabric for the group. Within any one group, there may be a variety of social transactional patterns that are evolved by different subgroups (such as, ethnic differences), even for spatially proximal sociocultural subgroups. Again, in our perspective, diversity does not entail defects, deficiency, disruptions, nor disorganization.

We do not deny biology in *any* behavior, act, or transaction. On the contrary, we start with an assumption that every living (that is, biochemical) system is a "transducer" in a larger "physical" system. Every "transducer" is a limiting system. The issue for a social construction approach is not whether a biochemical transducer is an important or even a relevant construct, but whether its contribution to action is pre-eminent in the remarkable diversity of human actions. We assume that whatever the constraints of biology the omnipresent sociocultural world (enculturation) of a human is a more heuristic source, to try to "account" for the kinds and range of actions that occur in typical or atypical transactions. That is, whatever the transducer constraints, the "world," and how it becomes known, incorporated, perceived, transformed, modified, enhanced, emended, mutated, transposed, converted, metamorphosed, recast, or whatever, is presumed to be a construction embodying the sociocultural matrix of that individual. Transactions are in a *socially constructed world*, however and whatever becomes known.

The sociocultural history of a group is itself an enculturation product that has become codified in the language (Whorf, 1956; Sapir, 1964), mores, codes (Bernstein, 1971), beliefs, artifacts, metaphors (Turbayne, 1991); world hypotheses (Pepper, 1942), or whatever else may be considered the social matrix and social contract of a group. What is ostensibly taken as a shared social world may become known somewhat *differently*, as a function of transducer differences, and in the ways different individuals (for example, "active," in contrast to "placid" children, or "blind" versus "sighted" individuals) come to know about the socially constructed world of their group. We understand individual differences in the same way we understand differences in dialects.

In our view, then, individuals become enculturated to their socially constructed world by, and with their group, within the limits of the socially constructed world of their group and transducer constraints or possibilities. The entailment of this premise is that we do not deny individual variability and differences, but again, the objects, events, and transaction patterns for all are still to be understood as being part of a common sociocultural matrix, not as an inner state "pathology." What constitutes "acceptable" actions are considered socio-political criteria, criteria subject to changes over time and as social organizations evolve and are modified.

Although we assume that early enculturation is a prepotent period in the inculcation of a socially constructed world, we also believe that enculturation is a continuing and dynamic activity. Transactions (as participant or observer) in different settings, contexts, and/or with different individuals are some of the possible sources for the ever-changing enculturation, and for the evolving of *different* transactional patterns. Variability of transactions by, and among individuals, is presumed to be part of living. It is difficult to imagine *identical* actions over any time span, or over different spaces by any living system, even for everyday transactions. Despite differences in kinds of transactions – unusual or "infelicitous" instances (Austin, 1962), those that are sanctioned or considered honorific (for example, bravery, altruism) – the same "explanatory" concepts or categories are invoked.

In contrast to traditional and some social construction approaches in which the individual is the focus, we are concerned with the mutual interdependent actions of the participants in their encounters. In this orientation, social actions are considered as trans-individual events (like language, communication or the history of a group). Given the entrenched tradition of viewing individuals and their "inner" states as the units of analysis, we find remarkably few terms in our language that denote or entail transactions among individuals (for example, marrying, debating, cooperating, disagreeing). This limitation of our lexicon makes it difficult to identify the *kinds* of social transactions of interest to us, when we attempt to re-examine the events subsumed under "psychopathology." Unfortunately, we have had to resort to hyphenated terms like helpless–helpful, or powerless–empowering, to specify the simultaneous, mutually interdependent transactions of interpersonal transactions. The concept of a "field" (Lewin, 1935) or a "system" (Bertalanffy, 1951) is very difficult to articulate in the language of a culture in which attributes of individuals are identified as the causal agents of all actions, and components of complex systems are described in static relationships.

We, like some others (for example, Uzgiris, 1989), try to transcend this tradition by using the term "transaction" instead of "interaction." A transaction is *not* what individuals do sequentially, but a designation of the *concurrent, interdependent, mutual activities* (for example, arguing, conversing, playing, fighting). In our usage, it is the shared action, not who is doing any aspect of the mutually interdependent actions. In a way, we are trying to extend an approach (suggested by Schafer, 1976) to describe actions rather than states or traits of participants.

The approach offered here is not about *social origins or "causation,"* or about a "dysfunctional" system (such as, family, group), or the labelling of deviancy. Instead, with this approach we attempt to shift the focus to the description of the kinds of sociocultural transactions that are identified and deemed significant for a group, as well as the social consequences of such actions by and for the group. We make no claims to "objectivity," or claims about ontology, rather with this perspective we may know a different and heuristic way to study all kinds of transactions among humans, including those now deemed psychopathological.

"Psychopathology"

In a series of papers, the constructs "anorexia nervosa" (Marcus and Wiener, 1989), "depression" (Wiener, 1989; Marcus and Wiener, 1991), and "schizophrenia" (Wiener, 1991) were re-analyzed from our psychosocial transactional perspective. The focus of our analyses was on what and how things are done, including how things are "said" (for example, requesting, pleading, demanding, asserting) with whom, in what contexts.

Two kinds of arguments were invoked to justify a reconsideration of the traditional diagnostic categories, "depression," "anorexia," and "schizophrenia." The first was to identify the imprecision, inconsistencies, ambiguity, overgeneralization, and contradictions in these traditional "diagnoses." The second was to show that each of these "diagnoses" subsumed several (in these cases five or more) very different kinds of psychosocial transactions. That is, the transactions subsumed within each of these diagnoses included very different kinds of instrumental sociocultural acts by the participants, with each participant acting in complementary and interdependent ways. It became apparent to us that there are often greater socially patterned similarities among psychosocial transactions *across* diagnostic categories, than *within* diagnoses.

Despite our efforts to demonstrate first, that each of the diagnoses incorporates sets of quite different psychosocial transactions, second, that the same kinds of transactions designated as psychopathological are considered as non-pathological when they occur with some individuals, or when they occur in other social contexts, or third, that analogous or similar psychosocial transactions in different eras, or under special conditions are deemed to be "evidence" of special merit (for example, "Joan of Arc") rather than pathological, the rejoinder by traditionalists is that we have only identified subsets of the traditional "pathologies."

Diagnoses of Depressions

At this point, it may be helpful to concretize our psychosocial transactional framework by applying it to the construct "depression." In our reconstruction, we will outline first, some of our differences with traditional psychiatric approaches to "depression" (*DSM III R*); second, some conceptual consequences when changes are introduced into the traditional framework, but the traditional metaphor is maintained; third, some of the social contexts in which "depressive" behaviors are identified; and fourth, how these "deviant" social instrumental action patterns seem to be maintained by participants in the transactions.

Wiener (1989) tried to show that the term "depression" (as it has been used traditionally and codified in *DSM III R*), first, is subsumed in a number of diagnostic categories (for example, major depression, dysthymia), second, includes heterogeneous sets of interpersonal actions, third, is a disjunctive system of signs and symptoms (namely, "A," or "B," or "C," etc.), and fourth, includes different sets of "signs" and "symptoms" (that is, syndromes) for the same diagnosis, and some syndromes within a diagnosis requiring polar opposite sets of signs and symptoms. For example, an individual who reports depressed mood (says he is "sad"), who manifests psychomotor retardation, reports low energy, hypersomnia and weight gain, is diagnosed with major depressive syndrome, as is an individual with psychomotor agitation and reports insomnia, weight loss, feelings of worthlessness, and indecisiveness. Although these two people do not share a single action in common, and in many respects appear to be behavioral opposites, both are identified as belonging to the same diagnostic category, just as in another era "madness," poverty, and "criminality" would have been seen as belonging to the same category (Foucault, 1965).

Wiener (1989) also tried to show that if the social transactional matrices were examined carefully, (even in instances of two "depressives" ostensibly reporting the "same" signs and symptoms), radical differences in their social actions can be identified, despite what may appear to be *identical behaviors or verbalizations.* For example, in one psychosocial action pattern the statement "I feel helpless" may be understood as one person reporting that he or she is *incompetent* and *unable* to accomplish anything without assistance. If seen as part of a different action pattern, the same statement may be understood as the person believing that he or she is *powerless* to act because another will not permit the actions. By shifting the focus to the social import of these communications, at least five different psychosocial transactional patterns were delineated, each including one of the participants who would meet the traditional diagnostic criteria for a "depressive disorder."

With this shift of focus from symptoms to psychosocial transactional patterns, not only do individuals who had been assigned to the same category begin to look different from each other, but similarities among individuals assigned to different diagnostic categories become apparent. For example, "depressed" individuals reporting negative self-evaluation (that is, worthlessness), withdrawal from interpersonal contact, and a need for punishment seem to have far more in common with some individuals diagnosed as "anorectic," that is, one who fasts and is concerned with self-denial and self-punishment (Marcus and Wiener, 1989), than either have with individuals describing a "powerless" ("depressed") pattern or other anorectic syndromes.

Identification of such apparent similarities across diagnoses is not the same as saying, for example, that "anorexia" is really a "latent" or incipient, or masked type of "depression." Numerous theorists and researchers working from traditional perspectives have attempted to broaden the construct of "depression" beyond its already diffuse and imprecise construction with this type of reasoning. In the past, "masked" or "latent depressions" have even been posited for instances where the diagnosis of depression is made after an explicit acknowledgment that "depressive symptomatology" is absent. For example, Zigler and Glick (1984, 1988) argued that "paranoid schizophrenia" is *really* "camouflaged depression." Other researchers (for example, Hudson et al., 1984; Walsh et al., 1985) argued that "eating disorders" are actually "affective disorders." There are also a number of other claims in which "depression" is inferred in the absence of the "criteria" for diagnosing it. For example, since so-called "antidepressant medications" have been shown to relieve the distress of some individuals labeled "depressed," when they also "help" others who are not labeled "depressed" (for example, alcoholic, anorectic, anxious), the conclusion is often drawn that these other diagnosed individuals must also be suffering with an underlying, masked or latent "depression." That "depression" is not a single member class can also be a conclusion, if one considers that some "psychotherapies" designed specifically for "depression" (for example, Beck's cognitive therapy; Shaw and Beck, 1977; Wright and Beck, 1983; Klerman's interpersonal psychotherapy (Klerman et al., 1984)), have also been found to be "effective" for many others who apparently do not "qualify" for that diagnosis. (See Wiener, 1989, for a more detailed and extended explication of these kinds of arguments.)

Descriptions of individuals considered "depressed" have also been the basis for many thought-provoking theories (for example, Freud, 1917/1968; Bibring, 1953; Lewinsohn, 1974; Coyne, 1976). However, from our view, each of these traditional reconstructions of "depression" still retains the many apparent limitations and contradictions identified in the codified formulations (that is, *DSM III R*). Some of these limitations may be demonstrated by considering the history and development of one of the most influential and sophisticated models that have come to be associated with "depression" – the "Learned Helplessness" theory proposed and modified by Seligman and his associates (Seligman, 1975; Abramson et al., 1978; Peterson and Seligman, 1984; Abramson et al., 1989).

The Learned Helplessness Paradigm

The Learned Helplessness paradigm is not being used as an exemplar here because we consider it to be a particularly problematic model or an "easy target." On the contrary, this model is used because it appears to us to be very thoughtful, and is rooted in an empirical-experimental psychology. Furthermore, it is one of the few paradigms to be revised radically by its proponents, even at the height of its influence (Abramson et al., 1978). However, the reformulation itself is instructive and can be used to demonstrate some of the limitations that can be identified when one makes radical changes, but does not bring the traditional root metaphor of "depression" into focus.

Seligman first explored "helplessness" in dogs to examine the effects of non-contingency on learning (Overmier and Seligman, 1967; Seligman and Maier, 1967). Dogs that were subject to inescapable shocks in a harness failed to escape from shocks when placed in a shuttle box (a different physical context). Dogs that could control the shocks (by some actions) while in the original harness typically also escaped the shock when in the shuttle box. Seligman (1975) noted similarities between the "helpless" dogs and depressed humans and suggested that Learned Helplessness might serve as a model for human depression. He cautioned that "learned helplessness need not characterize the whole spectrum of depression, but *only* those primarily in which the individual is slow to initiate responses, believes himself to be powerless and hopeless, and sees his future as bleak" (1975; emphasis added). Note here the connotation of "multiple kinds" of depressions.

Two problems became evident rather quickly. First, the empirical data could not be replicated with humans. Some investigators had tried to use humans in analogous studies (for example, Hiroto and Seligman, 1975), but a number of problems were identified with these analogues (for example, Cole and Coyne, 1977). Among the key differences between the human and animal studies were that the human subjects, unlike the dogs, were never truly "helpless," that is, they could always escape the aversive stimuli by withdrawing from the experiment. In addition, to state an obvious but crucial difference, animals do not use speech nor other social actions that humans do as parts of transactions with experimenters. However, reformulation also occurred in large part when it became evident that the original "helpless" (or more appropriately from our analysis, "powerless") explanation did not incorporate many of the (different) self-deprecating actions encompassed in the category of human "depression." Abramson et al. (1978) at that point shifted the focus of the Learned Helplessness model away from concern with contingency versus non-contingency to an emphasis on attributional or explanatory style (for example, powerless). The model also became less "behavioral" and more "cognitive" (an approach that presents other kinds of issues but would take us too far afield were they to be pursued here). Instead of questioning the construct "depression," these investigators assumed the difficulties were in the model.

Suppose it were possible to repeat the original "learned helplessness" experiments with human beings (clearly an unethical and unacceptable option). However, were we to do so, we would also introduce some additional, minor variations in the experimental contingency conditions. With our changes, we believe a number of very different social action patterns (all now considered "depressed") might have become apparent. What might the original model have looked like with these changes?

Imagine children subjected to inescapable shocks (or any other uncontrollable, aperiodic aversive stimuli) over a period of time, without any contact with another person. This hypothetical context is the closest to Seligman's classic experimental design with the dogs. What might these children come to do? Eventually they, like the dogs, would become almost inert. We would see this as an appropriate action in a world where terrible things happen and no action is possible to effect changes. "Hopelessness" (rather than helplessness) would be a more reasonable description of the responses of the children in that condition.

However, what might be the outcome if the design were altered slightly? Suppose the children could not turn off the shocks themselves, but by "appealing" (for example, by look, cries, pain-responses, and/ or verbal reports) to an experimenter who was nearby (an older, stronger other) the shock was terminated. That is, every time a child appealed for help, acknowledged that he or she was incapable of terminating the shock, or even just looked at the experimenter with a "pleading" expression, the pain was eliminated by the bigger, stronger other. How might this matrix be manifested in other social matrices? It is our contention that here the children would be in a world in which helplessness-helpful transactions would be prominent (in contrast to the earlier hopeless context in which there were no others available). They might act as if they were incapable of accomplishing these or other actions by themselves. Their transactions would include patterns in which "assistance" would be required from others, taken as stronger, smarter, or more competent than they (much as we may do with taller people whom we consider more competent to reach for objects on higher shelves in a cabinet).

A third variant of the "shock" paradigm is one in which the "shocks" would only be terminated if the child acquiesced to the experimenter's request that the child apologize for some (unspecified) mistakes, imperfections, transgressions, or misdeeds. Every time the child apologized or made self-deprecating remarks the shock would be terminated. Under such conditions, it seems likely that these children would come to identify transaction matrices as requiring actions and words that define that participant as a transgressor of the arbitrary "rules," as unworthy and/or worthless.

Finally, (although these are far from an exhaustive list of possible variations), one could create a condition under which the child comes to believe that the termination of the shocks would occur only if the child acted in ways, or said things that could be understood that the child is "acknowledging" that the experimenter is "nice" and "kind." No help is offered if the child fails to acknowledge this state of affairs. The experimenter determines which actions are to be taken as appropriate acknowledgment. The child can then be said to be behaving in a powerless way, required to conform in a placating, non-critical, or ingratiating manner, to any wishes of, or demands or requests by the other. The child is *powerless*, to do anything except to conform to the arbitrary actions of the other. It would seem reasonable to believe that the world for some such children would be one in which powerful others are viewed as "unreasonable" or "unfair" and that complaints to powerful others will be counterproductive. "Non-assertive" actions and aquiescence are likely for the children in this condition, as the anticipation of unpredictable punishment and disapproval becomes generalized.

If such analogous conditions were part of a child's social matrix, children in all four of the hypothetical conditions could be expected to behave in ways that are consistent with most of the diagnostic criteria for "depression," and to receive high scores on "objective" tests, called "Depression Inventories." Even though all subjects might endorse the same items on a depression inventory, such as "I can't make decisions at all anymore" (Beck Depression Inventory, Beck, 1967), the statements describe quite different social transactions associated with each of these different constructions of the child's world. Individuals from a "Hopeless" context would be communicating something on the order of "there is no point in doing anything because nothing will change anyway." For an individual from a "Helpless–Helpful" matrix the same statement would entail a world in which others must be depended upon to make decisions because, "I do not know how to manage responsibility." Individuals from a "Worthless–Judgmental" matrix would in their endorsement be specifying a world in which their decision will not be good or worthy enough. Those from the "Powerless–Powerful" matrix would be saying that their world is one in which they are not permitted to make decisions without con-sequences.

Interestingly, 13 years after Seligman connected helplessness in dogs to human depression, and 10 years after the first reformulation, from contingency to cognitive attribution, some of Seligman's colleagues (for example, Alloy et al., 1988; Abramson et al., 1989) introduced a differentiation between "helpless" depressions and "hopeless" depressions. With the benefit of hindsight, it would seem that the entrenched traditional metaphor of "depression" contributed to a "delay" in identifying even these two different patterns. We may wonder how long it might be before "learned worthlessness" and "learned powerlessness" or other identifiable variants are assigned as subsets of "depression," given the significant differences in the kinds of psychosocial transactions evident for these individuals and groups.

Social Matrices that Maintain "Depressions"

In another paper (Marcus and Wiener, 1989), the term "improvisational script" was invoked to describe the ritualized transactional patterns in the encounters between members of a family. This term is readily generalizable to the transactions among members of sociocultural groups. This concept seems analogous to Sarbin's (1989) use of "situated actions." In our view, all transactions are considered to be improvisations, but the social significance of the contents remain constant and predictable. Further, although we believe that all transactions among members of the same sociocultural group are predictably consistent, we also believe that those who have a long, intimate shared history (for example, family members), are likely to evolve some foreshortened exchange patterns of their own, much like a private dialect. In any case, it is important to reiterate that all transactions are considered to be improvised, even if the particular words and contents may vary across situations and participants. This regularity and predictability in the participants' coordinated, interrelated patterns is what we mean by "script." Script, then, incorporates the notion of a shared social history, or what can be considered a "social contract" among members of a social community and it can be seen as an exemplification of that "social contract." Further, if one were to explore transactions of the same group members over time, it is possible to identify "themes" that become focal and repetitive in particular social contexts.

Our analysis of the Learned Helplessness paradigm was an attempt to demonstrate how different social matrices could engender different transaction patterns, all of which are now construed as "depressive." In this exemplification we focused attention primarily on the subject, without apparent concern about the other's participation in the event. The concept of "improvisational script" shifts that focus to what all individuals are doing together as part of a shared action and away from how one person attributes, perceives, or otherwise experiences the world differently. For example, instead of speaking of the "Learned Helplessness" of a person, we are specifying a "Helpless–Helpful" transactional pattern or improvisational script. Instead of "Learned Powerlessness" we can consider a "Powerless–Empowering" transactional pattern, as a mutual interdependent action. Helplessness, Powerlessness, and Worthlessness do not occur in social vacua.

Up to now we have presented some imagined social matrices which may be thought of as the kinds of social matrices from which the "depression" scripts could come into being. Although the thought experiment we described could never be carried out, the conditions described can be seen as analogues for child rearing matrices that are not uncommon.

Based on clinical "experience," the different description of "depression" (for example, Spitz, 1946; Seligman, 1975; Blatt and Schichman, 1983), and the descriptions available in the literature about parents' styles of raising children and "depression" (for example, Schwarz and Zuroff, 1979; Crook et al., 1981; Whiffen and Sasseville, 1991), it is possible to identify some equivalent exemplars. The helpless–helpful transactions may come into being with parents who identify themselves as caring, but may be considered by others as "overprotective." The child comes (inadvertently) to be in a world where they do not "acquire"[1] ways to act independently of their socializing agents or to consider themselves competent or mature. These children also seem to view others as more competent, effective or efficient than they. As reported in the literature on the ways parents raise their children, some caretakers also provide helpful responses (which may include attention and affection), when the child acts in ways that are consistent with a Helpless–Helpful script. Were the child to react in ways we might consider "independent," the script also includes statements like, "You don't let me help you anymore," or "You aren't really taking care of yourself, you need someone who knows how to take care of you."

Seligman (1975) speculated that a "Hopeless" script (in our terminology) might arise if children come to "learn" that their actions have no effect (possibly because of an uncontrollable tragedy like the death of a parent, or because of non-responsive caretakers). In an often cited report, Spitz (1946) noted instances of hospitalized infants who became non-responsive to changes in their immediate environment as a function of non-attentiveness by others.

A "Worthless" script may arise in families who focus on idealized or perfect behavior from children, and less than perfect conduct becomes associated with a critical script. Self-deprecatory statements become associated with support and a script of "try harder," "you can succeed if you really try," etc. Cameron (1947) reported an extreme case where a woman was *required* to ask her parents for punishment when she misbehaved, and to thank her parents afterwards.

Where caretakers have a low threshold for disagreement, non-immediate compliances, or complaints, "Powerlessness" is likely to arise. The child participates in scripts where no direct question or complaint to a parent is permissible, but may find access to another who appears to be a sympathetic listener (for example, others in their world, siblings, friends). In these latter transactions, the child comes to learn that a second other will empower the child, and will empathize about how "mean" and "unfair" the original caretaker was.

These descriptions do not by any means provide an exhaustive account of how the different scripts may evolve. Individuals may incorporate such scripts within a variety of other possible socio-psychological contexts. Children in some families or situations may be part of such transactions more often than others, even to the exclusion of some of these scripts. However, it is important to underscore our belief that these kinds of scripts are part of the sociocultural patterns for all members of the group. Individuals in the group *know how* to act within these transactions, even though many of these scripts may only occur for them in a limited number of circumstances. For example, Helpless–Helpful scripts may arise when individuals are ill, Hopeless patterns when individuals are in "mourning," and Worthless patterns after a significant "failure."

Even if one accepts that these kinds of scripts arise as part of one's enculturation during childhood, it still leaves the question of how members of a group continue to engage in these patterns after they leave the family. To address this issue, Marcus (1989), in an experimental paradigm, explored whether members of a community participate in predictable ways in these scripts. Female subjects met with a female confederate[2] who had been "trained" to enact each of the three different "depressed" improvisational scripts. In the Helpless script, the confederate used a "childlike" tone, seemed "immature," and "sad," (head bowed, relatively inert posture) spoke of such things as not being able to make friends, understand what was required of her in class, etc. In the Powerless script, the confederate "sounded" querulous (as if close to tears), and "complained" that others (for example, her professor, her roommates) were "mean" and "unfair" to her. In the Worthless script, the confederate appeared somewhat withdrawn, while criticizing herself for not working harder in school or being more effective with others, emphasizing her sense of worthless-incompetence.

The female subjects were randomly assigned to one of the three experimental conditions, and met with the confederate for approximately 10 minutes. The subjects were told that they were meeting with another student to help us learn how people get to know one another. Analysis of the experimental subjects' actions during their transactions with the confederates showed that they "knew" and used the "socially correct" response to each of the confederate's different presentations; they "knew how" to do the appropriate kinds of improvisational scripts. Subjects who were faced with the confederate while she enacted the Helpless script, responded by trying to be helpful. They gave advice, pep talks, and on occasion even offered to perform the "difficult" task for the confederate. Subjects in the Powerless condition typically responded by trying to empower the confederate, agreeing with the confederate that she had been mistreated and participated in criticizing the unfair other. Subjects in the Worthless script responded with questions about the confederate's high standards and emphasized the confederate's previous accomplishments. Furthermore when subjects were asked to give their impressions of the confederate using the Impact Message Inventory (Kiesler, 1987), their attributions about the confederate differed depending on the script; three very different descriptions of the confederate were invoked by the subjects.

Marcus (1989) also hoped to demonstrate that members of the social community recognize and "know how" (in Ryle's, 1949, sense of the term) to participate in these different "depressive" transactions, much as one learns to answer when a question is asked, or to act "politely" or "aggressively," in particular socially identified contexts. Further, if the responses of the subjects are examined, one can recognize how the larger community helps to maintain the different "depression" scripts of the confederate. The findings were that our subjects seemed to know the exact "socially appropriate," complementary script for each transaction. For example, as members of the same sociocultural group, it seemed "natural" for us to hear suggestions by the subjects, like "have you thought about getting help?" during a Helpless transaction. However, this response would seem "inappropriate" for either the Powerless pattern (such as, "My teacher/mother/friend, is so mean or unfair") or the Worthless pattern (such as, "Even if I am getting A's, I must work harder"). In the same way, there does not appear to be any intrinsic basis to account for a Worthless statement (such as, "I should know as much as my roommate") not being followed by a "you are worthwhile" response (such as, "You are as good as he, it's mean to say you are not"). Responses like "It sounds like you are being too hard on yourself," or "What about all of the things you do better than he." Each of these seems so "appropriate" in these kinds of transactions. Given that these sorts of rejoinders sound so natural and "automatic," it is reasonable to conclude that they are an integral part of our social contract.

We believe these scripts including the postural and gestural variations that usually co-occur with them are also acquired in the same ways one acquires an "accent," or ways of dressing, walking and sitting in contexts and situations. We have come to believe that no one is explicitly taught these scripts (unlike, for example, children being "corrected" not to stare at someone who seems to be different). Instead, they seem to arise from a variety of cultural contexts (observations of others interacting, television, books, etc.). Because such responses seem "natural" and because they are so pervasive, it is easy to overlook their contribution to the maintenance of the "social contract."

Conclusions

Social psychologists have demonstrated again and again (for example, Nisbett et al., 1973; Storms, 1973; Ross et al., 1977) that *observers* consistently overestimate "dispositional" or "internal" factors when asked to account for *another person's* conduct, but almost invariably invoke the *situations* as explanations to account for *their own* actions. Our argument is that traditionalists engage in this fundamental attribution "error" when they invoke constructions like "psychopathology" and "depression" to classify or explain infrequent, non-normative, non-typical, or even unusual conduct of their targets. In contrast, we have argued for a perspective in which all human actions in their contexts are focal and are to be understood in terms of the sociocultural matrices in which they occur. With this shift in perspective, from explanations focusing on the individual to descriptions of sociocultural transaction patterns and their sociocultural contexts, comes a fundamental change in how one might study "psychopathology" and how non-normative (that is, low frequency psychosocial transactions) might be modified. (See Marcus and Wiener (1991) for one exemplification of the ways one might use to "change" an inculcated pattern.)

If our viewpoint were adopted, it would first be necessary to replace a "symptom" based account (*DSM III R*, APA, 1987) with a transactional taxonomy that would arise from a careful sociocultural analysis. Earlier work by Leary (1957) and Kiesler (1983), for example, may serve as starting points for developing such transactional taxonomies. More generally, "clinicians" would have to listen to their clients in a different manner, focusing on themes and improvised scripts instead of "symptoms." However, given the longstanding tradition of a "person"-oriented approach and the incorporation by the general population of the traditional "paradigm" (Kuhn, 1972), or "disciplinary matrix" as reformulated recently, differences in conduct will continue to be explained by professionals and the public by invoking notions such as defect, deficiency, disruptions, or person disorganization. We do not expect that the general population, or professionals will find it easy to incorporate a perspective that focuses on a sociocultural construction of these kinds of events – a view embedded in a very different paradigm and world view of human action.

Notes

1. See Wiener et al. (1980), for a discussion of this problematic construct, "acquisition."
2. Because more females are "diagnosed" depressed, it seemed appropriate to limit the experimental sample to females.

References

Abramson, L.Y., Metalsky, G.I., and Alloy, L.B. (1989) Hopelessness depression: a theory-based subtype of depression, *Psychological Review*, 96: 49–72.

Abramson, L.Y., Seligman, M.E.P., and Teasdale, J.D. (1978) Learned helplessness in humans: critique and reformulation, *Journal of Abnormal Psychology*, 87: 49–74.

Alloy, L.B., Abramson, L.Y., Metalsky, G.I., and Hartlage, S. (1988) The hopelessness theory of depression: attributional aspects, *British Journal of Clinical Psychology*, 27: 5–21.

American Psychiatric Association (1987) *Diagnostic and Statistical Manual of Mental Disorders* (Third edition revised). Washington, DC: Author.

Austin, J.L. (1962) *How to do Things with Words*. London: Oxford University Press.

Beck, A.T. (1967) *Depression: Clinical, Experimental, and Theoretical Aspects*. New York: Hoeber.

Bell, R.M. (1985) *Holy Anorexia*. Chicago: University of Chicago Press.

Bernstein, B. (1971) *Class, Codes and Control*. London: Routledge & Kegan Paul.

Bertalanffy, L. (1951) Problems of general systems theory, *Human Biology*, 23: 302–12.

Bibring, E. (1953) The mechanism of depression, in P. Greenacre (ed.), *Affective disorders*. New York: International Universities Press.

Blatt, S.J. and Shichman, S. (1983) Two primary configurations of psychopathology, *Psychoanalysis and Contemporary Thought*, 6: 187–254.

Burke, K. (1945) *A Grammer of Motives*. Englewood Cliffs, NJ: Prentice-Hall.

Cameron, N.A. (1947) *The Psychology of Behavior Disorders*. Boston, Houghton Mifflin.

Clark, K. and Holmquist, M. (1984) *Michael Bakhtin*. Cambridge, MA: Harvard University Press.

Cole, C.S. and Coyne, J.C. (1977) Situational specificity of laboratory-induced learned helplessness, *Journal of Abnormal Psychology*, 86: 615–23.

Coyne, J.C. (1976) Toward an interactional description of depression, *Psychiatry*, 39: 28–40.

Crook, T., Raskin, A., and Eliot, J. (1981) Parent–child relationships and adult depression, *Child Development*, 52: 950–7.

Foucault, M. (1965) *Madness and Civilization* (R. Howard, Trans.). New York: Vintage Books.

230 The Deconstruction of Popular Conceptions

Freud, S. (1968) Mourning and melancholia, in J. Strachey (ed. and trans.), *The Standard Edition of the Complete Psychological Works of Sigmund Freud* (Vol. 14). London: Hogarth Press. (Original work published 1917).

Hiroto, D.S. and Seligman, M.E.P. (1975) Generality of learned helplessness in man, *Journal of Personality and Social Psychology*, 31: 311–27.

Hudson, J.I., Pope, H.G., and Jones, J.M. (1984) Treatment of bulimia with antidepressants: theoretical considerations and clinical findings, in A.J. Stunkard and E. Stellar (eds), *Eating and its Disorders*. New York: Raven Press.

Kiesler, D.J. (1983) The 1982 interpersonal circle: a taxonomy for complementarity in human transactions, *Psychological Review*, 90: 185–214.

Kiesler, D.J. (1987) *Manual for the Impact Message Inventory*. Palo Alto, CA: Consulting Psychologists Press.

Klerman, G.L., Weissman, M.M., Rounsaville, B.J., and Chevron, E.S. (1984) *Interpersonal Psychotherapy of Depression*. New York: Basic Books.

Kuhn, T.S. (1972) *The Structure of Scientific Revolutions* (2nd edition). Chicago, IL: University of Chicago Press.

Leary, T. (1957) *Interpersonal Diagnosis of Personality*. New York: Ronald Press.

Lewin, K. (1935) *A Dynamic Theory of Personality* (D.K. Adams and K.E. Zener, trans.). New York: McGraw-Hill.

Lewinsohn, P.M. (1974) A behavioral approach to depression, in R.J. Friedman and M.M. Katz (eds), *The Psychology of Depression: Contemporary Theory and Research*. Washington, DC: Winston.

Marcus, D.K. (1989) Depressions and the response of others reexamined from a psychosocial transactional perspective. Unpublished PhD dissertation, Clark University, Worcester, MA.

Marcus, D.K. and Wiener, M. (1989) Anorexia nervosa reconceptualized from a psychosocial transaction perspective. *American Journal of Orthopsychiatry*, 59: 346–54.

Marcus, D.K. and Wiener, M. (1991) A psychosocial transactional approach to psychotherapy with depressed individuals, *Comprehensive Mental Health Care*, 1: 195–208.

Miller, D.R. and Flack, W.F., Jr (1991) Defining schizophrenia: a critique of the mechanistic framework, in W.F. Flack, Jr, D.R. Miller, and M. Wiener (eds), *What is Schizophrenia?* New York: Springer-Verlag.

Millon, T. and Kotik, D. (1985) The relationship of depression to disorders of the personality, in D.E. Beckham and W.R. Lieber (eds), *Handbook of Depression: Treatment, Assessment, and Research*. Homewood, IL: Dorsey Press.

Nisbett, R.E., Caputo, C., Legant, P., and Marecek, J. (1973) Behavior as seen by the actor and as seen by the observer, *Journal of Personality and Social Psychology*, 27: 154–64.

Overmier, J.B. and Seligman, M.E.P. (1967) Effects of inescapable shock on subsequent escape and avoidance learning, *Journal of Comparative and Physiological Psychology*, 63: 28–33.

Pepper, S.C. (1942) *World Hypotheses: A Study in Evidence*. Berkeley, CA: University of California Press.

Peterson, C. and Seligman, M.E.P. (1984) Causal explanations as a risk factor for depression: theory and evidence, *Psychological Reports*, 91: 347–74.

Ross, L., Amabile, T.M., and Steinmetz, J.L. (1977) Social roles, social control, and biases in social-perception processes, *Journal of Personality and Social Psychology*, 35: 485–94.

Ryle, G. (1949) *The Concept of Mind*. New York: Barnes and Noble.

Sapir, E. (1964) *Culture, Language and Personality*. Berkeley, CA: University of California Press.

Sarbin, T.R. (1989) Emotions as situated actions, in L. Cirillo, B. Kaplan and S. Wapner (eds), *Emotions in Ideal Human Development*, Hillsdale, NJ: Erlbaum.

Schafer, R. (1976) *A New Language for Psychoanalysis*. New Haven, CT: Yale University Press.

Schwarz, J.C. and Zuroff, D.C. (1979) Family structure and depression in female college students: effects of parental conflict, decision-making power, and inconsistency of love, *Journal of Abnormal Psychology*, 88: 398–406.

Seligman, M.E.P. (1975) *Helplessness: On Depression, Development and Death*. San Francisco, CA: Freeman.

Seligman, M.E.P. and Maier, S.F. (1967) Failure to escape traumatic shock, *Journal of Experimental Psychology*, 74: 1–9.

Shaw, B.F. and Beck, A.T. (1977) The treatment of depression with cognitive therapy, in A. Ellis and R. Grieger (eds), *Handbook of Rational-Emotive Therapy*. New York: Springer.

Spitz, R.A. (1946) Anaclitic depression, *Psychoanalytic Study of the Child*, 2: 313–42.

Storms, M.D. (1973). Videotape and the attributon process: reversing actors' and observers' points of view, *Journal of Personality and Social Psychology*, 27: 165–75.

Turbayne, Colin M. (1991) *Metaphors for the Mind: The Creative Mind and its Origins*. Columbia, SC: University of South Carolina Press.

Uzgiris, I.C. (1989) Infants in relation: performers, pupils, and partners, in W. Damon (ed.), *Child Development: Today and Tomorrow*. San Francisco, CA: Jossey-Bass.

Vygotsky, L. (1986) *Thought and Language* (A. Kozlin, trans.). Cambridge, MA: MIT Press.

Walsh, B.T., Roose, S.P., Glassman, A.H., Gladis, M., and Sadik, C. (1985) Bulimia and depression, *Psychosomatic Medicine*, 47: 123–31.

Whiffen, V.E. and Sasseville, T.M. (1991) Dependency, self-criticism, and recollections of parenting: sex differences and the role of depressive affect, *Journal of Social and Clinical Psychology*, 10: 121–33.

Whorf, L. (1956). *Language, Thought and Reality*, Cambridge, MA: MIT Press.

Wiener, M. (1989) Psychosocial transactional analysis of psychopathology: depression as an exemplar. *Clinical Psychology Review*, 9: 295–321.

Wiener, M. (1991) Schizophrenia: a defective, deficient, disrupted, disorganized concept, in W.F. Flack, Jr, D.R. Miller, and M. Wiener (eds), *What is Schizophrenia?* New York: Springer-Verlag.

Wiener, M. and Cromer, W. (1967) Reading and reading difficulty: a conceptual analysis, *Harvard Educational Review*, 37: 620–43.

Wiener, M., Shilkret, R., and Devoe, S. (1980) Acquisition of communication competence: is language enough?, in M.R. Key (ed.), *The Relationship of Verbal and Nonverbal Communication*. The Hague: Mouton.

Wright, J.H. and Beck, A.T. (1983) Cognitive therapy of depression: theory and practice. *Hospital and Community Psychiatry*, 34: 1119–27.

Zigler, E. and Glick, M. (1984) Paranoid schizophrenia: an unorthodox view, *American Journal of Orthopsychiatry*, 54: 43–70.

Zigler, E. and Glick, M. (1988) Is paranoid schizophrenia really camouflaged depression? *American Psychologist*, 43: 284–90.

13
Constructing Family: Descriptive Practice and Domestic Order

James A. Holstein and Jaber F. Gubrium

Both conventional social science and persons in everyday life treat the family as an object, a fundamental unit of society that some call its bedrock or most important institution (see Bernardes, 1985). Family forms confront us as concrete realities, undeniable entities that we encounter in everyday life. Social constructionism, however, maintains that "the objectivity of the institutional world, [as] massive it may appear to the individual, is a humanly produced, constructed object-ivity" (Berger and Luckmann, 1966: 60). Yet, while the constructionist perspective asserts that social forms have no ontological status apart from the activity that produces them, constructionists have shied away from the practical deconstructive challenge posed by the assertion. "Deconstructing" social institutions – working backward from taken-for-granted social realities toward the social processes that produce them – emphasizes ordinary, local practice over the more general, cognitive processes of social construction that are typically analyzed.

This chapter has a distinctly *social* emphasis as it refocuses the constructionist "gaze" onto the everyday discursive processes through which family is constituted. It reconceptualizes family in terms of descriptive practice – that is, the mundane (Pollner, 1987) communi-cative process through which realities are produced and made meaningful. From this viewpoint, family is a way of interpreting, representing and organizing social relations as much as it is a distinct object or concrete set of social ties (Gubrium and Holstein, 1990, 1992). It is a category *used* to define social bonds, part of a discourse for constructing domestic order. Family usage links category to experi-ence, creating practical understandings of domestic reality.

The view is clearly constructionist in its assumptions and aspira-tions, but several features distinguish it from other applications of the general perspective. While deriving from phenomenological initiatives (Schutz, 1970) and sharing the premise that actors interpretively produce everyday realities, the approach to family presented here reflects the ethnomethodological tradition (Garfinkel, 1967; Heritage, 1984; Pollner, 1987) more than, for example, Berger and Luckmann's

(1966) version of constructionism. The latter is primarily concerned with the cognitive *principles* governing the world of meaningful objects. It focuses on the structure of the life world in a general sense, considering how that world is constituted as a stable entity, what comprises that world, and how meanings shape, and are shaped by, it. Emphasis is on the *cognitive* processes of "universe maintenance." In contrast, ethnomethodology highlights the *social procedures* through which individuals produce and sustain social order, underscoring the constitutive interactional practices that link principles to experience.

For Berger and Luckmann, social institutions, once constructed, are virtually self-maintaining in the absence of problems or challenges; institutions "tend to persist unless they become 'problematic'" (1966: 117). Ethnomethodology, however, construes institutional realities as ongoing, locally-managed accomplishments. Rather than treating institutions as self-sustaining, it focuses on how constitutive actions continually determine and re-determine their institutional realm, with context and activity being reflexively related (Heritage, 1984). An ethnomethodologically-informed "constructionist" approach to family, then, emphasizes *interactional practice* as the basis for family meaning and domestic reality. It is more concerned with the articulation of domestic meanings – family usage – than with the "finite province of meanings" that comprises family (McLain and Weigert, 1979) or the cognitive principles that sustain "the" family as a social form. This is not to say that the "objective" significance of family as a social form is discounted. To the contrary, concern for the way domestic realities are interactionally produced and sustained leads to consideration of how the abstract entity "family" is locally conditioned, used, and interpreted to be a social object – a "thing" in its own right.

Durkheim (1961) referred to social forms like the family as "collective representations." By this he meant that social objects abstractly represent the organization of adherents' lives. As pre-existing, experientially-acquired frameworks for organizing and making sense of everyday life, collective representations might be likened to Schutz's (1970) "schemes of interpretation." Grounded in biography, they simultaneously reflect and perpetuate culturally promoted and shared visions of, and orientations to, social reality. Assimilating the Durkheimian understanding to a constructionist perspective prompts the examination of the ways that family as a social form is articulated with concrete social relations. Durkheim proposed that "publicly standardized ideas (collective representations) constitute social order" (Douglas, 1986: 96). The following constructionist analysis of family pursues this lead, examining the interpretive, representational work that bridges ideas and experience to produce domestic reality.

Family Discourse and Descriptive Practice

As they construct aspects of their everyday realities, people *use* family as a category to define social ties. Family discourse provides a way of making sense of and organizing social relations, conferring upon them (or withholding) domestic, familial meaning. Carol Stack's ethnography of an urban African-American community, *All Our Kin* (1974), provides several examples of how family usage constructs domestic linkage. Consider how one of Stack's informants, Billy, constitutes her family as she states:

> Most people kin to me are in this neighborhood . . . but I got people in the South, in Chicago, and in Ohio too. I couldn't tell most of their names and most of them aren't really kinfolk to me. . . . Take my father, he's no father to me. I ain't got but one daddy and that's Jason. The one who raised me. My kids' daddies, that's something else, all their daddies' people really take to them – they always doing things and making a fuss about them. We help each other out and that's what kinfolks are all about. (1974: 4)

Billy constructs her network of kin (and non-kin) by selectively applying family terminology, assigning meaning to the social ties between community members. She recognizes the stable and enduring relationship with the man that raised her by calling him "daddy," but casts her biological father outside her circle of significant others by labeling him "no father to me." By assigning family status, she not only announces what persons mean to one another, but she simultaneously designates their interpersonal rights and obligations. Her talk instructs her listeners in how to understand and interpret the concrete meaning of those relations. It is practical, not merely descriptive.

Indeed, family usage is rhetorical, a means of both tacitly and explicitly advocating particular understandings of persons' attachments and responsibilities to one another. A dispute over family "visitation rights" elucidates several aspects of family's rhetorical use (*Milwaukee Journal*, February 7 and 8, 1992). In February of 1992, a woman claiming to be the primary caregiver to a six-year-old girl sought a court order allowing her to visit the child after the girl's biological mother refused to let the other woman see the child anymore. According to the biological mother (who has been separated from the child's father since before the child was born), the woman had been a "live-in nanny," merely someone who was employed to help take care of the child from the time she was born until she was four-and-a-half years old. The woman, however, disagreed:

> It angers me to be called a nanny because I cared for that child 24 hours a day. I put her to bed every night. I walked the floor with her when she was sick. It was me who had to take her to the hospital on more than one occasion. (*Milwaukee Sentinel*, February 8, 1992)

Resisting the categorization as a mere employee or "baby-sitter," the woman noted that the child had always known her as "Auntie." Further, she claimed, "I was more of a mother to her than she [the biological mother] was. I love this child and I'm trying to protect her. I'd do anything for her, anything a mother would do" (WTMJ-TV, February 7, 1992). She went on to allege that the biological mother was a neglectful, bad parent.

Note the strategic use of the terms "nanny" and "mother" in this exchange. Their use is clearly rhetorical as well as descriptive. The biological mother used "nanny" to persuade others to understand the relationship the woman had with the child as more-or-less impersonal; it cast the woman as an employee, not kin. Laying rhetorical claim to being "more of a mother" to the child, the woman countered with a rhetorical claim to virtual familial intimacy and responsibility. The overt pronouncement of being "more of a mother" escalated the woman's claim that she was an important figure in the child's life, suggesting that her ties with the child were stronger than those between the biological mother and the child. And her report that the child called her "Auntie" further argued the existence of a functional, if not biological, kinship bond.

Family rhetoric can thus be used to convey the sense in which attachments grounded in nurturance and concern supersede even those of biological kinship. The claim is not uncommon. Many disputes have emerged recently involving homosexual couples who claim they are entitled to "family" rights, benefits and recognition by virtue of their deep commitment to one another. Similarly, a religious order recently petitioned the State of Wisconsin to be granted spousal "survivor's benefits." A member of the order had been a state employee, and when she died, the order claimed that, as the "family" of a deceased employee, the order was entitled to her "death benefits."

Constructing family, then, is a practical activity with myriad possible objectives. It involves diverse interactional processes that purposefully locate aspects of everyday experience within specified domestic categories. We use phrases like "He's like a brother to me" to convey the depth and permanence of a relationship. Labels like sorority "sisters" and fraternity "brothers" underscore the meaning of affiliation. Even street gangs and prison inmates use terms like "family," "brother," "sister," "mother," and "father," to descriptively organize their relations with one another, and represent their solidarity vis-à-vis outsiders. Family discourse thus conveys apparently shared ideas – collective representations – about domestic life that attach particular meanings to diverse social ties. In connecting family, domesticity, responsibility, caring, sharing, and the like, family discourse articulates a configuration of concern that relates what we think, know, and feel about our social relations.

While constructing family is a social, public enterprise, the image produced is decidedly private. That is, the common view is that family's inner workings and domestic matters are beyond the purview of outsiders. Lasch's (1979) poignant formulation of the family as a "haven in a heartless world" typifies the tendency to assign family and related domestic matters to a "secret" realm where activities and relations are, or should be, sheltered from public scrutiny and regulation (Skolnick, 1983). Typically, family constructions reflect this "private image" (Gubrium and Holstein, 1987), a set of assumptions about domesticity that are embodied and used in public pronouncements and interpretations to reify the family for the "outside" world, but define domestic relations as "inside," therefore *private*.

The first assumption holds that family is a separate and distinct domestic order, an entity in its own right. Families are taken to be real, things or groups endowed with tangible, consequential features like boundaries, members, and distinctive outlooks, themes or "personalities." A second assumption holds that domestic order is located within households. While family members carry on their lives in diverse settings, the private image assumes that the most authentic familial experiences are encountered in homes. Finally, if the natural order of the family lies within the household, then members have privileged access to it. This is the third assumption of the private image, that domestic affairs can be truly understood only by insiders, or from within the household. In practice, the private image is used to discern and define the familial. Its assumptions guide the construction of domestic order, giving family and its concrete realizations the distinctive shape and character that is collectively recognized and reproduced.

Models of domesticity are not automatic in their application, however. Not just anything or anyone is called "family." Family is not constructed out of "thin air." Descriptions must make sense; they are accountable in that they must convince socially-defined competent observers that the circumstances in question warrant attributions of domesticity. It may seem more feasible, for example, to speak of a communal living group as "family" than to apply the term to some other group whose intra-group relations are clearly less involved or more impersonal. Still, it is interpretive *practice* that constitutes domestic ties, not some "objective" state of affairs. Thus, it is possible (even plausible) to refer to a 12,000 student university as the "Marquette Family," or to label a corporate foodstuffs conglomerate the "Beatrice Family." Discourse and actual interpretable occurrences, then, are mutually constraining and elaborating (Bilmes, 1986). Social relations take on their familial character as they are descriptively constituted, while, simultaneously, description and categorization orient to "what everyone knows" about family in order to be compelling.

Family discourse is also situationally and historically delimited. As circumstances and their available discourses vary, so do the potential meanings of our relations with others, as well as the meaning of family itself. Social historians have noted that family and domesticity are recently "invented" interpretive structures, and that family imagery varies notably from one era to the next, and across cultures (Ariès, 1962; Shorter, 1975). For example, as late as the Middle Ages, the German language had no word for the private group of parents and children that we currently understand as family. The root form of the word "family" was something like "house," referring to the totality of cohabiting persons, including kin, servants, slaves, and other boarders (Mitterauer and Seider, 1982). As Nicholson states,

> What existed prior to the sixteenth century was so different from what emerged later so as not to even properly warrant the label of family. Indeed, prior to the early modern period, there was not even the concept like ours of family. (1988: 4)

Variations in family usage are culturally grounded as well, some collectivities applying domestic labels where others would not, and vice versa. In short, family's meaning and usage are responsive to context; the discursive production of domestic order is situationally conditioned.

Analyzing family from this perspective calls for the deconstruction of versions of domestic reality into the diverse discourses, interactional processes, signs, and circumstances that constitute them. The aim is to display the ways in which everyday relations and experience are publicly recognized and organized as "family" matters. The following sections consider several aspects of family construction, focusing first on family as a practical undertaking, or discursive project. We then examine the practical semiotics of family, considering the organization of signs used to represent the domestic. Next, we turn to the social distribution – particularly the organizational embeddedness – of family discourse, and conclude by raising some issues for constructionist family studies. To illustrate our arguments, we draw upon research in a variety of human service settings where "family" is an enduring category of concern.

Family as a Discursive Project

As a social construct, family does not simply emerge as a description of inherently meaningful domestic circumstances. Rather, it is a resource – a concept, image or metaphor to be *used* – for responding to interpretive challenges regarding the status and meaning of social bonds. Family meaning, for example, comes into practical view when the quality or depth of one's social relations are questioned. Such occasions draw family from the invisible background of everyday life into the interpretive foreground, a discursive "project" assembled to meet the interpretive demands of the situation at hand (Gubrium, 1988).

Family may be constructed in response to varied challenges regarding the *affectional, custodial,* or *durational* grounds of inter-personal relations. Questions like the following often provoke the articulation of family's presence, form, and function: Who cares about other people? Who takes care of others? For how long? The circumstances where family is made relevant are diverse. Consider, for example, what was accomplished through family usage in the midst of a labor-management dispute. In 1989, employees of Eastern Airlines walked off the job to protest what they felt were harmful changes in corporate policy instituted by new owner Frank Lorenzo. In asserting that Lorenzo disregarded the well-being of the company as well as its employees, one worker lamented that "This company used to be a family" (*New York Times*, March 12, 1989). "Lorenzo's not part of the Eastern family," said another employee. "He doesn't care about the airline." Family, here, is invoked to denote the mutual caring and concern that had once been characteristic of the corporation. At the same time, descriptively situating Lorenzo outside the family rhetori-cally underscores Lorenzo's lack of care and concern. The point is not that the workers were right or wrong in their characterizations of the situation, but rather that family discourse provides a practical resource for depicting social relations whose status has been called into question.

Concern about the sentimental character of social relations is especially likely to evoke images of family's presence, form, and function. For example, consider the questions that prompt elabora-tions of the meaning of family in a support group for psychiatric patients and significant others (Gubrium and Holstein, 1990). During a particularly impassioned discussion, the father of a 22-year-old son diagnosed as schizophrenic questions his son's filial sentiments, casting doubt on the son's feelings for his parents. The father complains that despite all he and his wife have done for their son, the son is indifferent and ungrateful.

> You're always willing to drop in any time they toss you out of the [transitional living] home, but you never show us any appreciation at all. You don't keep in touch. You won't even talk on the phone. Or when you do, you're just plain disagreeable. . . . You don't care about your mother's feelings, you don't feel for her at all. Do you realize what she goes through, worrying about you. You know, you don't give us a damn thing. You could be a stranger. No consideration. No warmth. Nothing. You only act like a son when you need us. Where's your family loyalty, anyway? (1990: 58)

The son is initially defensive, blaming the parents for driving him away. Then he softens, becoming more conciliatory, almost apolo-getic, as he tries to establish the ways in which he is, in fact, a son:

Come on. You know that I care. It's just hard for me. I come by, but I don't want to start you worrying, so I don't say too much. . . . I thought I was doing something good for you by trying to stay out of your hair. . . . I get pretty screwed up sometimes, so I try to stay away when I might have a bad day. I know what it does to Mom, and I don't want to do that to her. I don't want to hurt her. It may not look like it, but I keep away because I thought that was best for you guys. I got my problems and I know they get to you, but you're all the family I have. (1990: 59)

In this example, the father's complaints convey an eroding sense of family; the son counters by showing how his suspect family feelings and commitments are actually intact. Challenge and response bring family into focus, producing an object to be claimed, contested, and interpretively reconstructed. Family ties are rhetorically constituted through the son's responsive "family project." As a meaningful entity, "family" is *continually* constructed and reconstructed; the project is ongoing, never complete.

Family may also be constructed to establish the caring side of relationships, even among non-kin, founding "family" as much on custodial as affectional grounds. This complicates the debate over the presumed essential nature of domestic order. Note, for example, the complex connections that produce a sense of family during involuntary commitment proceedings observed by one of the authors. At a hearing concerning the possible hospitalization of 27-year-old Conrad Moore, the presiding judge is uncustomarily impassioned as he tries to convince Moore that a "short vacation at the hospital" is in Moore's best interest. The judge argues that life will be less complicated in the hospital, something sure to aid Moore's recovery. The judge claims that the hospital is the most caring, compassionate environment that Moore can hope for:

They care about you at the hospital, Conrad. Those people really do. They can give you the kind of love and attention that you seem to be missing when you're living on your own. You don't have any family to love you, so it might be best to take what you can get. (Gubrium and Holstein, 1990: 59)

Multiple challenges reside in this plea, notably the assertions that Moore's life lacks "love and attention" and that he has no loving family around him. But Mr Moore responds:

You can't tell me they [hospital staff] care about me like my people. I got people at Briarwood [the board and care facility], man, they care. They're my family, man, my people. We're all in the same boat out there. We got each other, man, just like a family. Why can't you just let me stay? (1990: 59–60)

Questions regarding the existence of affectional bonds in Moore's life prompt Moore to invoke family imagery to characterize his relations with fellow residents of the board and care home. He casts his living arrangements in familial terms, directly responding to the affectional concerns; he calls his fellow boarders "family" to display their solicitude, warmth and devotion. Constituting his associates as family simultaneously instructs the judge about how to understand their meaning to him in these particular circumstances.

Family ties may also be discursively constructed to display the custodial capacity or rights one person has vis-à-vis another. In another involuntary commitment hearing, for example, James Robinson states that he will live with Sophia Mills – a woman identified by Robinson's public defender as Robinson's "common law wife" – if he is not hospitalized. Robinson proceeds to use family imagery to argue that there is adequate supervision in the household:

> I got a whole family there, and family takes care of its own. I got my old lady and her sister and some cousin or somethin'. Name's Esther. That kind of family ain't gonna let nothin' happen to me. Hell, they don't let me do nothin' period. (Gubrium and Holstein, 1990: 69)

In the process, Robinson descriptively consolidates the members of this household into a family unit that will unquestioningly care for "its own." In constructing the family here, he underscores their ability and willingness to take care of him, that is, family's custodial character.

Questions about the duration or durability of social relations also may prompt reference to family. How well or how long one person has known another are sometimes answered in terms of the familial, conveying a sense of stability and permanence. For example, when a community support worker in a mental health program is asked how long she has known one of her clients, she replies, "Long enough for me to be her mother." Family imagery signals caring and commitment extending beyond professional contact. The kinship reference capitalizes on the family bond to secure an appreciation of the relationship's history. Similarly, as Conrad Moore's commitment hearing progresses, the judge conveys his skepticism regarding Moore's relationships with his associates at the board-and-care home, asking "how long will it take for you to wear out your welcome with your buddies down at the board and care home?" Moore is adamant that the situation will remain cordial and supportive, reconstructing the judge's characterization of the co-residents as mere "buddies" into a claim to "family": "Why do you think they'll turn on me, man. We're tight. These are my brothers. You know what I mean? Brothers. They won't disappear on me. They can't. Family is *always* family, man" (Gubrium and Holstein, 1990: 61; emphasis in original).

Family's sheer presence or absence, then, is a practical discursive accomplishment. As the two senses of the word "project" suggest, family is both a constructive undertaking and an extending outward, a way of objectifying an aspect of experience.

Signs of Domesticity

As an abstract form, domestic order is not self-evident. Constructing family involves reading and conveying signs of the familial. Descriptive practice links abstract images with immediately available concrete signs. The practical semiotics of family raises questions about what signs are used to represent domestic life, and how they are organized in everyday interaction. Even seemingly insignificant aspects of material or interactional circumstances can be turned into telling evidence concerning the shape and condition of a family. Domestic order, for example, may be constructed from the mundane arrangement of family members in the chairs of a family therapist's waiting room or office (Gubrium, 1992). Therapists point to the existence of a well-organized, functioning family, for example, when the parents commandeer the more central, or "powerful," locations in the room, while family disorder is signaled when parents are seated at the periphery. In discussions of the family's structure and functioning, therapists refer to these and related signs, using them to construct the underlying order of the family.

The range of signs from which family is constructed is virtually limitless. Prominent, however, is the use of aspects of family's household location to signify the domestic order assumed to reside within. The assumption that houses are the natural sites of family life provides a framework for interpreting and describing what is going on within them. To note that a family "barely has a roof over its head" suggests more than inadequate shelter; it can convey a sense of familial instability, disorder, or irresponsibility as well. Interpretations of the appearances of physical aspects of the household provide the basis for discerning family patterns, themes, and tendencies – again, household signs taken and used to impart meaning to social life within.

Consider, for example, the use of household disarray and dilapidation as signs of domestic order. Members of support groups for caregivers of Alzheimer's disease patients routinely take the disarray of the victim's home as a sign that "things were coming apart." The messy apartment of an elderly husband who cares for his demented wife at home, for example, can be used to show that their relationship is "disintegrating." Similarly, a judge in involuntary commitment hearings might read family "breakdown" from a report that a candidate mental patient is living with her 21-year-old son and eleven cats in a two room apartment strewn with dirty litter and cat food cans.

Just as familial disintegration may be linked to the physical disarray of the household, a home's dilapidation can signal a lack of domestic stability or well-being. A social worker visiting an ex-mental patient, for example, encounters a small wooden frame house with a ramshackle exterior – peeling paint, rotting clapboards, cardboard covering broken windows. She takes these as signs of crumbling family life, explaining:

> Zandie [the client] has been raising her sons by herself for years but things seem to be getting away from her more and more lately. She's lost control of the boys; they're just hanging around waiting for trouble. Nobody's doing anything to keep the place up. Look at this dump. You can see it's no place to be bringing up kids. I mean it's only a matter of time before the roof falls in and we have to hospitalize her [in a psychiatric institution] and put the kids in foster homes. (Gubrium and Holstein, 1990: 83)

The social worker speaks both literally and figuratively as she envisions the "roof falling in" on this family whose disintegration she reads from the degenerating structure that houses it.

Residential permanence, too, is a common sign of a family's domestic order. Participants in a staff meeting at a residential treatment center for emotionally disturbed children, for example, make much of the discovery that one of their clients is living with her family in a trailer park. The trailer, one argues, is an undeniable sign of transiency, which in turn represents domestic instability.

> My God, now a trailer! What next? Do you think we might find them [the family] living under a viaduct the next time? . . . No wonder she [the client] blows up. Anyone would blow up if they never knew where they lived from one week to the next. . . . I'll bet that trailer is a real nightmare to the child . . . I mean what it tells her about her family and all. I think what it's telling us is that we've got to work on the bonding end of things. Marcia [the client] needs a secure home life. (Gubrium and Holstein, 1990: 88–9)

Family, then, like other social forms, is constructed from diverse signs that are taken to represent its underlying order. These signs, however, are not so much directly *read* as they are *practically interpreted*, taking their meaning from the way they are used. Taken out of context, their meaning is arbitrary; any particular sign might stand for any number of things, or nothing at all (Saussure, 1966). It is only through interpretive practice that signs of domestic order are "turned up" – noted, deciphered, and applied to the matter at hand in a constant interplay between sign and signified. In one context, household dilapidation might be interpreted as a sign of a degenerating family, but it might also be seen as unremarkable given the age of the neighborhood. A father's seat at the periphery of a therapy group session might be offered as a sign of his detachment from the familial unit, a sign of domestic disorganization. Or it might be taken as a mere artifact of the availability of seats as the family occupied the room. The point is that aspects of experience are offered as signs of family – descriptions and explanations of underlying order – within the overall descriptive work of figuring the domestic realities of the circumstances at hand. The meaning of signs is more a matter of how they are descriptively articulated with ongoing arguments pertaining to domestic order than it is an objective feature of the circumstances of concern.

Family Discourse in Organizational Perspective

While individuals construct and sustain family realities through "artful" (Garfinkel, 1967) descriptive practice, their interpretations are sensitive to social, cultural, and historical context. Envisioned domestic order is responsive to the interpretive demands, goals and contingencies of the situation at hand, and construed with reference to pre-existing, locally available images of family life. Family usage thus reflects commonly recognized spheres of understanding, local cultures born of shared, repeatedly communicated and routinized interpretive schemes (Gubrium, 1991). Accordingly, particular family realities emerge in response to the social distribution of signs and interpretive structures.

While signs may be arbitrarily related to the signified, context conditions the relationship. Family usage can thus be described as *organizationally embedded* (Gubrium, 1987; Gubrium and Holstein, 1990, 1991) – that is, grounded in, and shaped by, the social organization of the descriptive domains in which family is articulated. We use the term "organizational" here in its most general sense, referring to any socially structured circumstance. While our examples are drawn from formal organizations, the analysis would also apply to circumstances organized along different lines, say by reference to gender or race. The point is that alternate contexts serve to realize different domestic orders according to their varied descriptive options, constraints, and agendas.

Take, for instance, how contrasting organizational contexts lead to distinctly different ways of constructing family in two family therapy agencies (Gubrium, 1992). Westside House, an outpatient program, orients to domestic order as a system of authority. A functional family is one in which parents or other properly responsible adults are in control, making the consequential decisions of the home. The therapeutic aim is to re-establish traditional authority when it has eroded, that is, put the parents back in control, preferably with the father at the top of the hierarchy. In contrast, Fairview Hospital, an inpatient, psychiatric facility, orients to domestic order as a democracy of sentiments – that is, a relational complex where everyone's feelings are equally important. Domestic disorder results from the absence of a mutual communication of feelings between family members who are accorded equal status as members of the household. Clients who bring domestic troubles to these programs, such as drug or alcohol addictions, wife and child abuse, or truancy, encounter different understandings and languages for interpreting their domestic lives which are taken to be integral parts of the troubles.

Yet the concrete signs used to link these diverse orientations with the facts and elements of family life are remarkably similar. The seating arrangement and composure of family members in therapy, and members' styles of verbalization are used in both settings to assign order and disorder to households. In both programs, parents and children are scrutinized for their physical comportment and the way they present themselves and speak to one another. But these concrete signs, while similar, are organizationally embedded in that their meaning is related to local orientations to domestic order. For example, a father who at Westside House selects the so-called power seat (usually centrally located in the seating arrangement) and presents in a clear and commanding manner, tolerating no interruptions from other family members, is interpreted as showing that he is in charge of the home; the family is properly ordered, functional. Staff at Fairview Hospital, however, view a similarly presenting father as inappropriately using power to spoil what is considered to be a proper democracy of emotions in which every family member needs actively to share their own and others' feelings. In this instance, the father's behavior is viewed as a sign of family disorder.

Organizational embeddedness, then, helps explain how family might be differently constructed out of the same "objective" circumstance. Consider the contrasting interpretations of family in an exchange between a community mental health center psychiatrist, Dr Conrad, and the judge of an involuntary commitment hearing (Holstein, 1988). In arguing for the release of his patient, Tyrone Biggs, Conrad asserted that Mr Biggs's therapeutic program would be completely disrupted if Biggs were hospitalized. He claimed that Biggs was able to function adequately in a community setting and should not be committed. The judge was concerned about Biggs's living arrangements which led to the following exchange:

Doctor: Tyrone lives with his family. They have an apartment in Lawndale.
Judge: I thought Mr. Biggs was divorced last year?
Doctor: He was, your honor. But he's moved in with his girl friend and their two children. They share a place with her aunt. He really seems to be getting along fine.
Judge: Now who is it that takes care of him? You say these two ladies are going to be able to keep him out of trouble. How long has he lived with them? What happens when he gets delusional again?
Doctor: We're hoping that's under control. . . . I think it's important to understand that being close to his family is extremely important to Tyrone's [treatment] program. His family wants him there and they make him feel like he belongs. He needs that kind of security – the family environment – if he's ever going to learn to cope and he's not going to get it from anyone but his family.

Judge: That may be so, but you still haven't told me who will keep him under control. Who's going to make him take his medication? . . . I just don't see any family here to look out for him. You say this is his girlfriend and *her* aunt? How old is this woman [the aunt]? How are they going to handle him? I'm sorry, doctor, but this just isn't the kind of situation I can feel good about. I really don't see much of a family here. If I thought there were people there who could really be responsible for this man, it might be different. (Holstein, 1988: 272–3)

The judge and the psychiatrist view this case from different interpretive domains. Their contextually relevant conceptions of family are linked to, and shaped by, their professional and organizational backgrounds, orientations, and mandates. Dr Conrad uses the language of therapy, speaking of how he hopes to improve Biggs's mental health. He articulates family in terms of support for the psychiatric treatment regimen; from that perspective, people who provide a supportive environment are "family." The judge, however, is concerned with controlling the trouble that he anticipates from Mr Biggs, because he believes Biggs is mentally ill. The judge orients to managing trouble in order to avoid future problems. He sees no family in Biggs's life because no one is available to control him.

"Family" thus embodies the organizational outlooks and interests of the various parties involved in the scenario. The judge articulates his concerns in custodial terms; when family matters are raised, they are interpreted in terms of how "family" might help control and care for Biggs if he is released. "Family member" is used synonymously with "caretaker." Conversely, Dr Conrad reveals his profession's remedial concerns as he describes Tyrone Biggs's "family" in therapeutic terms. The same arrangement in which the judge finds no family to speak of becomes a "family environment" through the interpretive voice of the psychotherapeutic community. Embedded as it is in institutional interpretive procedures, family is constructed in the terms of local discursive conventions.

While circumstances supply interpretive resources for accomplishing domestic order, organizational embeddedness does not dictate family usage. A family therapy agency may have an explicit treatment orientation, but it may also employ therapists who hold different perspectives on individual and family well-being. Alternate perspectives, grounded in professional background, approach and mission, provide further resources for shaping the ways troubles and remedies are discerned, and the ways that domestic order may be formulated. Additional circumstances like gender, race, social class, or ethnic background may serve to specify particular interpretations of signs or to treat common signs as exceptional, in individual cases. Embeddedness, then, is "layered," various interpretive domains and concerns overlapping to provide diverse ways of constructing family meaning. In combination, descriptive resources ranging from widely promoted "family ideology" (Bernardes, 1985) to highly personal experience and interpretive orientations furnish distinctive local cultures of domesticity that convey family in their own terms.

In a sense, as Mary Douglas (1986) puts it, socially organized circumstances come to "think" and "talk" for their participants by providing conventional modes of discourse, practical agendas and shared interpretive perspectives. This helps account for the ways that organizationally embedded family usage produces and *re*produces particular and distinctive constructions of "family" that are relatively consistent from one occasion to the next. But we must also remember that practitioners of family construction are not "judgmental dopes" (Garfinkel, 1967) who merely react to circumstances and structural imperatives. Rather, they are constantly interpreting the recognizable features of everyday experience, sifting through cultural instructions, articulating available models with everyday occurrences to construct the coherent social realities they inhabit.

Constructionist Issues and Family Studies

Construing family in terms of descriptive practice raises several important issues for family studies, as well as for the constructionist approach generally. An initial set of questions focuses on just what the phenomenon under consideration – family – actually is, and where it may be found. The approach also raises issues regarding family usage and its practical objectives. Finally, our constructionist perspective on family invites questions regarding the social distribution of family discourse, particularly as it represents a source of family diversity and conflict over domestic meanings.

Studying "Family" as Social Process

Studying the social construction of family implies an analytic focus on interactional process. Family is constructed by practitioners of domestic order, "doing things with words" to assemble domestic reality (Gubrium and Lynott, 1985; Bernardes, 1987), *accomplishing* family in and through descriptive practice. Accordingly, the phenomenon of interest is family discourse *in use*. We attend not to any particular social unit that might be called a family, but to processes through which assignment of family status to that (or any) group or its members is made. Our interest is not in family as a "thing" per se, but rather in the process through which family is constituted as a thing, an object unto itself.

In order to describe and explicate family's social construction, we must seek our phenomenon in the diverse settings where family discourse is used, noting signs of domestic order wherever they are presented. Any and all situations where "family" is made topical – that is, where talk-in-interaction or other forms of discourse turn to family structure, characteristics, membership, and so forth – are occasions for constructionist family studies. Because family discourse flourishes both in and out of households, we are not tied to that location as a research site. The household is merely a locational *presumption* – the mundanely assumed site of domestic affairs. It is not the only place one finds "family." Similarly, there is no reason to believe that household members have privileged access to domestic meanings. Family discourse offered by any persons, under any circumstance may produce aspects of domestic order.

The Objectives of Family Usage
If family is construed as a way of characterizing social relations, we are less inclined to investigate the family-as-thing than to ask about how, and to what ends, family-as-a-category is put to use. As a form of social action, family discourse can be understood as a way that meanings are organized and manipulated, that is, controlled. The discourse is both expository and rhetorical. Like any discursive characterization, family usage promotes particular ways of understanding things and actions rather than merely representing them. As such, it assembles and shapes the social order it purports to merely describe (see Foucault, 1980). Yet, because family's constitutive practices are practically invisible, we are typically oblivious to the interpretive control they insinuate in everyday life.

Constructionist family studies, then, might examine the practical objectives of family usage. Family assignment practices, for example, may recommend particular social arrangements as "normal" or "acceptable" while proscribing others. Calling a single mother, her children and her live-in companion a "family" conveys a sense of responsibility, permanence, concern, and affection that may legitimate the cohabiting group in the eyes of the community. Conversely, withholding the term signals that they are merely living together, providing the interpretive possibility that they are, say, "shacking up," "sleeping together," or "cheating on welfare." At a broader level, "family ideology" is similarly used to constrain institutionalized domestic and gender roles to a narrow range of "conventional" alternatives (Bernardes, 1985; Smith, 1985). Family assignment practices implicitly sanction aspects of social life, advocating particular arrangements in ways that are profoundly influential, yet all but imperceptible.

Family rhetoric as a means of social influence is a topic of growing importance, both at the macropolitical and interactional levels.

Because "family" is laden with so many positive associations in most western societies, its rhetorical use is seemingly ubiquitous. Take, for example, how family is invoked by basketball star Michael Jordan in an attempt to ward off harsh criticism for failing to attend a team get-together with President Bush (*USA TODAY*: October 4, 1991). Teammates and the media accused Jordan of unbridled self-interest, a lack of respect and patriotism, and a failure to uphold civic responsibility. Among the tactics he used to defend himself, Jordan turned to family rhetoric: "How can I choose to be disrespectful to the president if I want to spend time with my family? I'm sure he'll understand. He has a family, too." Family accounts are used in situations like this, perhaps, because they are all but unassailable. On the strength of family's cultural capital, an appeal to "family obligation" reasonably supersedes nearly any other demand, including an audience with arguably the world's most important leader.

Family accounts are common in settings as varied as courts (Emerson, 1969), prisons Giallombardo, 1966), welfare agencies (Miller, 1991), and athletic venues (Gubrium and Holstein, 1990). Even Clint Eastwood, mayor of Carmel, California, and icon of unsentimental stoicism, cited family commitments as a reason for retiring from public office. The issue here is not whether users of family rhetoric actually do spend time with their families, or whether their sentiments are sincere. Rather, the selection and use of family as a rhetorical resource for managing everyday relations is analytically interesting. Part of the constructionist project, then, is to examine how, and under what circumstances, family is constructed and used to legitimate behavior, demands and interpretations, as well as to exert influence.

Domestic Diversity and the Politics of Description

Debate about family diversity abounds. Some argue for the legitimate diversification of familial experience (Thorne and Yalom, 1982; Bernardes, 1986, 1988), while others insist that non-traditional forms threaten the social fabric (see Melville, 1983). The controversy over the validity of alternate forms, however, presupposes a definition of family tied to concrete group structure. The dispute ultimately becomes a definitional contest over which groups can, and should, be assigned family status. From a constructionist perspective, the controversy is analytically fascinating because it reveals the situated accomplishment of "family diversity" in public forums, apart from, but not unconcerned with, domestic settings.

From a constructionist perspective, family diversity arises as a feature of the varied ways and occasions that the family image is applied. Family's diverse forms are as much connected with the circumstances of family usage as they are with diverse life-styles. But while various family depictions may be offered, they may also be contested, as the diversity controversy illustrates. In that regard, we might think of attempts to assign family status as instances of "claimsmaking" (Spector and Kitsuse, 1987) about the nature of social reality that involve a kind of "politics of description." Public contests or campaigns involving claims about the familial often materialize as "publicity" – that is, large-scale attempts (often involving mass media) to manipulate family imagery for explicitly rhetorical or political reasons. While much constructionist research has focused on mass movements, campaigns, or crusades in other public realms involving other social forms, we should not lose sight of the everyday inter-actional practices that underpin widespread public claims, linking images and interpretations to actual experience. Constructionist family studies cannot ignore the mundane circumstances of family usage. They must attend to locally distinct interpretive practices and cultures, examining the social distribution and organization of micro- and macropolitically charged claims and counterclaims about "what is family?"

References

Ariès, Phillippe (1962) *Centuries of Childhood: A Social History of Family Life*. New York: Random House.

Berger, Peter L. and Luckmann, Thomas (1966) *The Social Construction of Reality*. New York: Doubleday.

Bernardes, Jon (1985) "Family ideology": identification and exploration, *Sociological Review*, 33: 275–9.

Bernardes, Jon (1986) Multidimensional developmental pathways: a proposal to facilitate the conceptualization of "family diversity," *Sociological Review*, 34: 590–610.

Bernardes, Jon (1987) "Doing things with words": sociology and "family policy" debates, *Sociological Review*, 35: 679–702.

Bernardes, Jon (1988) Founding the new "family studies," *Sociological Review*, 36: 57–86.

Bilmes, Jack (1986) *Discourse and Behavior*. New York: Plenum.

Douglas, Mary (1986) *How Institutions Think*. Syracuse, NY: Syracuse University Press.

Durkheim, Emile (1961) *The Elementary Forms of Religious Life*. New York: Free Press.

Emerson, Robert M. (1969) *Judging Delinquents*. Chicago, IL: Aldine.

Foucault, Michel (1980) *Power/Knowledge*. New York: Pantheon.

Garfinkel, Harold (1967) *Studies in Ethnomethodology*. Englewood Cliffs, NJ: Prentice-Hall.

Giallombardo, Rose (1966) *Society of Women*. New York: Wiley.

Gubrium, Jaber F. (1987) Organizational embeddedness and family life, in T. Brubaker (ed.), *Aging, Health and Family: Long Term Care*. Newbury Park, CA: Sage.

Gubrium, Jaber F. (1988) The family as project, *Sociological Review*, 36: 273–96.

Gubrium, Jaber F. (1991) Recognizing and analyzing local cultures, in William B. Shaffir and Robert A. Stebbins (eds), *Experiencing Fieldwork*. Newbury Park, CA: Sage.

Gubrium, Jaber F. (1992) *Out of Control; Family Therapy and Domestic Disorder*. Newbury Park, CA: Sage.

Gubrium, Jaber F. and Holstein, James A. (1987) The private image: experiential location and method in family studies, *Journal of Marriage and the Family*, 49: 773–86.

Gubrium, Jaber F. and Holstein, James A. (1990) *What is Family?* Mountain View, CA: Mayfield.

Gubrium, Jaber F. and Holstein, James A. (1991) Studying family discourse in organizational perspctive, *Journal of Family Issues*, 14: 62–81.

Gubrium, Jaber F. and Holstein, James A. (1992) Phenomenology, ethnomethodology, and family discourse, in P. Boss, W. Doherty, R. LaRossa, W. Schum, and S. Steinmetz (eds), *Sourcebook of Family Theory and Methods*. New York: Plenum.

Gubrium, Jaber F. and Lynott, Robert J. (1985) Family rhetoric as social order, *Journal of Family Issues* 6: 129–52.

Heritage, John (1984) *Garfinkel and Ethnomethodology*. Cambridge: Polity Press.

Holstein, James A. (1988) Studying "family usage": family image and discourse in mental hospitalization decisions, *Journal of Contemporary Ethnography*, 17: 261–84.

Lasch, Christopher (1979) *Haven in a Heartless World*. New York: Basic Books.

McLain, Raymond and Weigert, Andrew (1979) Toward a phenomenological sociology of family: a programmatic essay, in W. Burr, R. Hill, I. Nye, and I. Reiss (eds), *Contemporary Theories About the Family, Vol. 2*. New York: Free Press.

Melville, Keith (1983) *Marriage and Family Today*. New York: Random House.

Miller, Gale (1991) Family as excuse and extenuating circumstance: social organization and use of family rhetoric in a work incentive program, *Journal of Marriage and the Family*, 53: 609–21.

Mitterauer, Michael and Seider, Reinhard (1982) *The European Family*. Chicago, IL: University of Chicago Press.

Nicholson, Linda (1988) The age of the family. Paper presented at the Symposium on Literature and Family, April 15, 1988. Milwaukee, WI: Marquette University.

Pollner, Melvin (1987) *Mundane Reason*. Cambridge: Cambridge University Press.

Saussure, Ferdinand de (1966) *Course in General Linguistics*. New York: McGraw-Hill.

Schutz, Alfred (1970) *On Phenomenology and Social Relations*. Chicago, IL: University of Chicago Press.

Shorter, Edward (1975) *The Making of the Modern Family*. New York: Basic Books.

Skolnick, Arlene S. (1983) *The Intimate Environment*. Boston: Little, Brown.

Smith, Dorothy E. (1985) Women, class and family, in V. Burstyn and D. Smith (eds), *Women, Class, Family and State*. Toronto: Garamond.

Spector, M. and Kitsuse, J.I. (1987) *Constructing Social Problems*, Hawthorne, NY: Aldine de Gruyter.

Stack, Carol (1974) *All our Kin*. New York: Harper and Row.

Thorne, Barrie and Yalom, Marilyn (eds) (1982) *Rethinking the Family*. New York: Longman.

Index